The Experience of God

American University Studies

Series VIII
Psychology

Vol. 4

PETER LANG
New York · Berne · Frankfurt am Main

David Terry Bradford

The Experience of God

Portraits in the Phenomenological Psychopathology of Schizophrenia

PETER LANG
New York · Berne · Frankfurt am Main

Library of Congress Cataloging in Publication Data

Bradford, David Terry, 1951–
The experience of God.

(American University Studies. Series VIII, Psychology; vol. 4)
Bibliography: p.
1. Schizophrenia – Religious aspects. 2. Phenomenological psychology. 3. Experience (Religion) 4. Psychology, Religious. I. Title. II. Series: American University Studies. Series VIII, Psychology; v. 4.
RC514.B66 1984 616.89'82 84-47697
ISBN 0-8204-0126-9
ISSN 0740-0454

CIP-Kurztitelaufnahme der Deutschen Bibliothek

Bradford, David Terry:
The experience of God: portraits in the phenomenolog. psychopathology of schizophrenia / David Terry Bradford. – New York; Berne; Frankfurt am Main: Lang, 1984.
(American University Studies: Ser. 8, Psychology; Vol. 4)
ISBN 0-8204-0126-9

NE: American University Studies / 08

Printed by Lang Druck, Inc., Liebefeld/Berne (Switzerland)

This book is dedicated to Nancy.

La blanca palomica
al arca con el ramo se ha tornado,
y ya la tortolica
al socio deseado
en las riberas verdes ha hallado.

Juan de la Cruz

ACKNOWLEDGMENTS

I have appreciated the attention given this work by Drs. David G. Edwards, Lelia Veaco, and H. Edward Tryk, and been especially grateful for the comments of Dr. Jack A. Pitt. The book's strengths are partially due to their involvement; its weaknesses are my own.

The contribution of M. J. Cavanaugh to the preparation of the manuscript has been invaluable. And the efforts of Inge Kauffman and her library staff have eased many of the problems of research.

TABLE OF CONTENTS

Chapter | Page

Chapter Page

The aim, first of all, of our research, here as everywhere else, is to reclaim the schizophrenic human being from the language, the conceptual apparatus, the theories and the habits of thought prevalent in clinical psychiatry. Our aim is to reinstate this human being in his full humanity, his existence, and his being-in-the-world.

Ludwig Binswanger

For the time being, the question remains open: why is schizophrenia in its initial stages so often a process of cosmic, religious, or metaphysical revelation? Such experience cannot be grasped simply in terms of the psychosis which is sweeping the victim out of his familiar world. Even if we speak of existence or the psyche as disintegrating, we are still only using analogies. We observe that a new world has come into being and so far that is the only fact we have.

Karl Jaspers

Chapter 1

INTRODUCTION

Numbers may be assigned the sadnesses of a disturbed person's life, but the quiet whirring of a computer is incapable of figuring the experience of living such sorrow. The present study shies from quiet whirring, glancing from the sharp angle of much empirically oriented psychopathological research, and focuses instead on the hallucinated sounds and imaginative vistas experienced by the psychotic person diagnosed schizophrenic. Karl Jaspers, whose massive textbook (1913/1963) established the field of phenomenological psychopathology, borrowed from the disciplinary divisions of Continental academia and spoke of verstehende psychology, contrasting it with other forms of psychological research which rely on the "hard" data of the pathologist, the technician, or the psychometrician. The one rests on understanding; it appeals to the common experience of human existence. The other kinds of investigation trace a different path, seeking explanation for phenomena which do not yield to understanding because they rest on biological deficits of an acquired or constitutional nature. The present study sets before itself the goal of understanding certain dimensions of the psychotic experience of persons diagnosed schizophrenic; in doing so, it acknowledges the value of alternative approaches which seek explanation, and utilizes their findings, but without sacrificing the goal specific to its phenomenological intent.

Names other than Jaspers figure prominently in the present study.

Ludwig Binswanger's case studies of schizophrenic existence have been influential. They established certain stylistic trends which receded from the forefront of phenomenological psychopathology and which the descriptive portraits of this study would revive. His framing the psychopathological findings in a broad anthropological network is central to the present undertaking, since both are grounded in the basic assumption that a life is never an isolated phenomenon, floating hazily on a detatched and objectively definable world, but is always the source and focus of a richly diversified and highly complex phenomenological world.

For the portraits of this study, the worlds of schizophrenic existence are often mythological, more so than Binswanger suggested. Other schools of psychology and psychopathology are implicated as a result. The mythological orientation of analytical and archetypal psychology, for example, has been important in shaping the methodology and the phenomenology of the present psychopathology.

Erwin Straus's phenomenology of sensory experience has been another significant influence. His role in phenomenological psychopathology is analogous to that of Merleau-Ponty's in phenomenological philosophy. Both sought to describe the primordial layer of immediate experience which clings to the lived body as a film of oil clings to a stone lifted from an oily bath.

To the patient's lived body, and the world which provides this body a home, is added a third point of orientation--the experience of God. Religious experience is not uncommon during schizophrenic psychosis. Data from the present study suggest that approximately one of three patients claims to experience God directly. This is not the kind of experience which provokes a sly grin from the patient, or sinks to a level of unimportance commensurate with other experiences indicative of chronic schizophrenia. Frequently patients are able to recall such an experience in exquisite detail years afterward and without it necessarily having become embedded in the convoluted fabric of a delusional system. The lived body and the experience of God may be viewed as two poles of an axis which spans the patient's world, organizing its other features.

The lived body, its world, and the experience of God for which this body and world provide an imaginative place and a temporal continuum--the exploration of these experiences requires a methodology. Its invention is a multifaceted task requiring the delineation of varieties of factual data, their organization in a hierarchy based on phenomenological criteria, an outline for the creation of phenomenological description, and a standard procedure for questioning psychotic patients. The method outlined in Chapter 3 is a two-edged sword, for a phenomenological approach adequate for investigating psychotic experience requires a transformation of the researcher's consciousness just as it focuses the researcher's and reader's attention on the transformed consciousness of the severely disturbed patient. An ethical dimension is implicated in such a project, since an alteration in the investigator's own psychology necessarily has an impact on his attitude and behavior toward the patient.

The present study moves along terrain not thoroughly explored. Some guidance is provided by the initial section of the second chapter, in which the bearing of psychiatry and the psychology of religion for the study of religious experience in schizophrenia is discussed. The following section outlines the phenomenological psychopathology of schizophrenia, with Jaspers, Binswanger, and Straus receiving foremost attention. The psychological intent of investigating the experience of God as a presence, rather than aligning oneself with one or another metaphysical stance with regard to the question of His existence, is considered initially in this section. Following the methodological reflection of the third chapter is the presentation of two levels of factual data and the descriptive portrait for four patients. The concluding chapter discusses the findings, questions, and conclusions born of the study.

Chapter 2

LITERATURE

The Bearing of the Psychology of Religion and of Psychiatry for the Study of Religious Experience in Schizophrenia

It is commonly known that religious experience is often a cardinal symptom of schizophrenic psychopathology (Buckley, 1981; Kaplan, 1964). The youthful schizophrenic bursts upon the scene of his fragmented and profoundly shy life with a wealth of religious experiences. Trees whisper messages, vague suspicions of messianic purpose arise, fleeting shadows portend religious truths. Finally, the pot of the psyche explodes with the rich affectivity and bizarre notions of the daemonically possessed schizophrenic. But the story may be more sedate, less dramatic, and take instead the form of the chronically deluded schizophrenic patient who remains entrenched in certain beliefs about his religious identity and cosmic purpose till the end of his days (Rokeach, 1964).

The Early Days of the Psychology of Religion

One would think the branch of psychology named for its involvement with religion would provide a texture of meaning and an array of insights bearing on the religious experience of psychotically disturbed schizophrenic patients. Not so. The psychology of religion is a wasteland populated by those who reify the religious experience of psychosis and transmute its native features into mere semblances of their former outline. The barrenness of the psychology of religion in this regard has not always been due to a materialistic, sociological, or positivistic disposition. True, there are scholars such as Leuba (1912), in many ways towering above those before and after, who rest their case for religious experience on the fundaments of a biologically based, quasi-libidinous energy, but there are others of the same generation who adopt a different perspective. Indeed, the functionalist interpretation of religious experience, of which Coe (1916) was the chief spokesman, would seem the most productive prior to the psychoanalytic revolution.

To discern the roots of the psychology of religion and to ascertain whether it provides significant guidance in examining religious experience in schizophrenia requires a step one generation further back. The past is rich. There is the exploration of a variety of methodologies, but without the foreshortened vision which narrowed the field upon the discovery of the Freudian unconscious. Hall (1904) linked conversion with adolescence at the turn of the century, doing so on a statistical basis. Several years later he completed a psychological study of Jesus Christ (Hall, 1917). His student, Starbuck (1899), probed further in similar areas related more closely to the immediate features of religious consciousness. A new constellation spun into view with James's typology of religious experience (James, 1902/1958). Decades later W. H. Clark (1968) remarked that *The Varieties of Religious Experience* is "certainly the most notable of all books in the field of the psychology of religion and probably destined to be the most influential book written on religion in the twentieth century" (p. 43). Such applause seems poorly grounded historically but well deserved on the basis of James's originality. Not until the massive turn toward introversion during the 1960s did academic psychology begin to mark its awareness of James's importance for the study of consciousness and spirituality. The title of Pope and Singer's (1978) anthology, The Stream of Consciousness, makes explicit the debt owed James.

For the phenomenological psychologist, the most important remark to be made about the prolific early days of the psychology of religion concerns its deeply interpretive, if not reductionistic, stance. The cultural background for this is sketched without difficulty. Comptian positivism held sway in the humanities. Its alliance with Social Darwinism was not an uncomfortable one. Missionary expansionism was a central concern in religious circles, thus shifting awareness from the intellectual and psychological subtleties of religious experience, just as the sociological and theologically conservative emphases of the social gospel movement veiled the intimate dramas of the individual's religion. Systematic work in the phenomenology and history of religion was in a germinal stage; few Eastern texts dealing with mysticism had been translated. The great machine of the Industrial Revolution was still wheeling along without interruption or disturbance. Its clatter rose above the volume of D. H. Lawrence and others who warned of its power to crush personal awareness. The climate of the entire era was materialistic and in this sense not unlike the cultural stage of the 1950s, pockmarked with bomb shelters and empty-handed in the face of flower children and hallucinogenic drugs. The basic point is apparent already: there was ample reason for ignoring the simple observation that religious experience, regardless of the population in which it occurs, might well be a phenomenon *sui generis*, and consequently merit being considered an object of study in its own right. However simple an observation, it was largely ignored during the early days of the psychology of religion.

Psychoanalysis and Analytical Psychology

With Freud a significant change occurs. The study of religious experience comes within the purview of psychiatry, which to this day has not relinquished its authoritative hold on the heuristic key promising to open the door to its ultimate meaning. That the meaning of religious experience is manifold and, in some cases, not only psychological, is hardly a secret. One has only to note the discrepancies between Freud's and Jung's understanding of religious experience to infer that a given psychiatric interpretation remains incomplete, if not untenable, in the sense of answering definitively the question of the meaning of religious experience.

This is certainly not to say one or another analytic interpretation of religious experience is without utility. Putting aside Freud's unusual story of the primal patricide and his Lamarckian explanation of its impact on subsequent generations (Freud, 1953/1975i), there remain areas other than the phylogenetic which bear ripe fruit of understanding when addressed from the analytic position. Freud demonstrated the interpretive power of his theory in brief case studies of religious experience (1961/1975h). His genetically based understanding of the link between obsessive behavior and religious ritual has immediate intellectual appeal (Freud, 1959/1975e). To my knowledge, his wonderfully descriptive notion of an oceanic religious experience has yet to receive its due in the phenomenology of religious experience (Freud, 1961/1975a). The link between the Brahmanic mysticism of the Upanishads (Hume, 1975) and the oceanic mystical experience seems especially apparent. To this day the analytical position with regard to religious experience retains its value as a cultural heuristic (Brown, 1959). And the same may be said for the value of the analytic position with regard to individual religious experience, although certain twists were initiated with neo-analytic theory which upset the basically psychopathological view of Freud. For example, Rizzuto (1979) has spoken of God as a transitional object, and a philosophical theologian well versed in depth psychology has critiqued the latter's work without finding it wanting (Howe, 1981).

A caveat similar to that registered with respect to Freud may also be applied to Jung's archetypal theory of religious experience. Its value as a cultural heuristic is without question. This was demonstrated by Erich Neumann (1954) and quite recently on a more popular level by Joseph Campbell (1968). Neumann broadened significantly, and in a mostly unnoticed way, the value of Jungian theory for understanding religious experience with his book Depth Psychology and a New Ethic (1973). Its ramifications for individual religious belief and society in general pose a burden conveniently overlooked by those who think depth psychology is a matter for psychology only. The value of archetypal theory for individual religious experience was demonstrated anecdotally as early as Jung's interpretation of the schizophrenic patient's vision of the sun's phallus in "Symbols of Transformation" (Jung, 1956/1974). What for many of Jung's readers is mere anecdotal verification of the validity of archetypal interpretation of religious experience becomes a routine experience for those who converse intimately with mad patients. I have talked with schizophrenic patients who reported spontaneously the Mithraic vision of the sun's phallus, the multiheaded green snake vision of Ignatius Loyola, and other, similarly archetypal images. But as with psychoanalysis, so with analytical psychology; each is to be faulted on the basis of claiming to provide the definitive explanation or understanding of the meaning of religious experience.

Certain elements of archetypal theory deserve special attention because Jung is often considered the chief spokesman for an understanding of religious experience which is not reductive and thus approximates a phenomenological stance more closely than possible for the mechanistic and explanatory approach of analytic theory. A detailed presentation of his psychology of religion, ranging from the psychiatric orientation of the early "Psychology and Religion" (1958/1969b) to the psychohistory of the later "Answer to Job" (1958/1969a), is unnecessary, since a brief historical sketch of archetypal theory provides an adequate background for the basic point that with the horizonal concept of the objective psyche, Jung advances beyond his psychiatric predecessors in establishing grounds for a nonreductive approach to religious experience. He advances toward the idea over a number of years, beginning with the association experiments which in their day were not the primitive sort of endeavor they now seem. They led directly to complex theory. Bypassing the attitudinal and functional typologies, there eventually appeared archetypal theory and the late conceptualization of the Self for which the latter was equivalent to the objective psyche. Often the clinic provided impetus for Jung's theory, and the theory was then utilized for elucidating clinical disturbance. This kind of circularity is not vicious: it is of the essence in developing a clinical psychology. Occasionally manifestations of schizophrenic psychosis were pivotal in Jung's grasp and presentation of theory. Such was the case with the Mithraic vision mentioned earlier and its bearing for his idea of archetype. All of this is to suggest that Jung's theory, especially its culminating idea of an objective psyche stocked with the perceptual and affective _potentia_ of archetypes, allows for a more accurate reproduction and serves as a finer interpretive heuristic for religious experience in schizophrenia than the systems of Freud and others. As an analyst once remarked, what hysteria was for Freud, schizophrenia was for Jung.

If Jung's theory is especially helpful in understanding religious experience in schizophrenia, what is responsible for its advantages? The answer has to do specifically with a certain dimension of religious experience which is reflected theoretically in the idea of an objective psyche replete with the natural, though transpersonal, conditioning factors of archetypes. This dimension may be characterized as the radical otherness of that which is known, or in which one participates, during religious experience. Sacred, holy, otherworldly, supernatural--these and other terms have been used from time immemorial to characterize this quality of otherness. Eliade (1968) is perhaps the chief scholarly spokesman for a view of religious experience which retains the distinction between the ordinariness or profanity of common experience and the sacredness of religious experience. But Otto (1917/1950) surpasses him in describing the central psychological marks of such experience. Jungian theory allows a deeper appreciation of this distinction and its experiential implications. Just as the collective seedbed of the archetype _an sich_ is not equivalent to the Freudian unconscious nor to Jung's early formulation of the personal unconscious, so the kind of experience which is essentially religious is of a wholly different order than that involving ordinary, worldly phenomena. Thus one may speak of religious experience in psychological terms which seem not to be reductionistic.

Classical Jungian theory approaches a phenomenology of religious experience, but not closely enough, since there remain dim layers of interpretation. Jaspers's (1913/1963; Kolle, 1957) biting critique of Kretschner is relevant: he is indicted for having disguised a _verstehende_, or understanding, psychology with an explanatory psychology. While the latter intends explanation, in the sense of confirming causal hypotheses with empirical research, understanding psychology appeals to empathy, intuition, shared human experience, and phenomenological description. Jaspers distinguished sharply between them, believing that advances in psychology and psychiatry demand a separation. Otherwise, there is self-deception and research of either kind becomes misguided. A serious handicap arising from the application of explanatory modes of thought to phenomenon for which they are inappropriate is the belief that a given phenomenon demanding understanding is fully explicable on the basis of mechanistically reductionistic principles. But this is not the only potential error; the matter is more complex. Phenomenological philosophers have distinguished a variety of ways language functions within understanding psychology alone (Delius, 1953; Kullman & Taylor, 1966; Munson, 1959); and phenomenological psychologists have discussed whether some explanatory psychology, with its reliance on the univocal, denotative function of most scientific language, is not finally reconcilable with interpretive understanding (Beshai, 1971, 1975). Without giving the reasoning adduced by Jaspers, I will simply state that religious experience comes within one or another psychological framework belonging to the broad class of understanding psychology. Consequently, one must retain a highly critical attitude toward interpretive systems which present themselves, even subtly, as explanatory. I think it is important to recognize that Jung was not without fault in this matter when he attributed the cause of religious experience to archetypal dominants and searched the world over for archetypal similarities of religious content, somewhat like a psychologist who relies on measures of central tendency to explain the features of a given individual's unique experience.

The Reappearance of a Psychology of Religion

A study of religious psychology arose once again in the wake of such expansive interpretive systems as those of Freud and Jung, but it was barely able to shake off the dazed, fragmented condition in which it was left after religious experience had been dealt with in so summarily and apparently so adequate a manner by earlier psychiatry. From this point, the variegated forms of psychology and psychiatry generally are reflected in studies of religious psychology. The array of topics and methodologies is too large even to list in its entirety. There are the journals dedicated to empirical investigation of religious experience--the fruits of which often recall Wieman and Westcott-Wieman's (1935) earlier disclaimer that the psychology of religion has nothing to do with psychopathology. Other kinds of empirical investigation are less stingy in allowing for a continuity between ordinary and pathological religious experience. Stark's (1965) taxonomy of religious experience, for example, includes a broad category of diabolical experiences which could be used fruitfully for investigation of schizophrenic persons' accounts of their religious experience. Outside the camps of the empirically inclined are others who work the field of religious experience without forming alliances with psychiatry. Allport (1950) would be an early example of this; Clark, Maloney, Daane, and Tippett (1973) a somewhat later example; and perhaps Greeley (1981), too, whose factor analytic studies of religious imagination escape, though just barely, the charge of a parochial Catholicism.

Traces of a Biology of Religious Experience

The psychiatric orientation comes directly to the fore with others during the past 30 years. Once again the topics and methodologies are too numerous even to list. A sampling gives a flavor for recent developments. An early spokesman for the scantily represented biological perspective would be Sargant (1957), whose Battle for the

Mind: A Physiology of Conversion and Brain-Washing is more valuable, partly for historical reasons, than the shrill note sounded by the title might lead one to believe. His appeal to Pavlovian learning theory and the physiology of the autonomic nervous system for explanation of mass conversion experiences sets a precedent which seems not to have been followed until quite recently. Surely the day is coming when a neuropsychologist will shift the area of biological investigation from the peripheral to the central nervous system. Magaro (1980, 1981) and Gruzelier (1981; Gruzelier & Hammond, 1976) have unintentionally laid the groundwork in their studies of functional brain asymmetry in schizophrenia. Once this shift is made, based on analogies between the neuropsychology of schizophrenia and the perceptual and cognitive features of some kinds of religious experience, a rich area of investigation will have appeared which links religious experience in ordinary and clinically disturbed populations alike. Ornstein (1972) treads this path without the scholarly conscientiousness of Sperry and others upon whom he relies for pairing religious consciousness with right hemisphere functioning. Perhaps the same could be said for Jaynes (1977) were it not for the sweep of history he offers and the consequent impact of his book.

Return to a Psychiatry of Religious Experience

Most of the recent psychiatric studies concerned specifically with religious experience in schizophrenia are of a theoretical and clinical nature rather than biologically inclined. Works here are numerous and of different orientations. Interesting examples of theoretical infighting appear. Macalpine and Hunter (1956), both psychoanalysts, take issue with Freud's interpretation of the Schreber case, doing so in a convincing manner which relies on a point-by-point handling of a case of schizophrenic religious experience similar in many respects to Schreber's. The libido model of schizophrenic religious experience should have been dealt a blow, but their book seems to have been little available and one rarely discovers references to it either in analytic work or in the psychology of religion. From the same decade comes a brief work of McCasland (1951) which could serve well as a model for psychohistorical case studies. He confesses relative ignorance of Biblical history and New Testament exegesis, yet forges ahead in a highly conscientious manner to discuss the psychopathology, or lack thereof, of four persons described in the Gospels. Relevant cultural factors are mentioned, and such questions as the differential diagnosis of schizophrenia or hysteria for the Caperneum demoniac described in Mark, Chapter 1, and its Lucan parallel are discussed.

A degree of variety comparable to the preceding decade characterizes psychiatrically oriented work within the past 20 years. A sample reflects its clinical emphasis. Studies such as R. A. Clark's (1980) concern themselves with correlations, often empirically determined, between denomination or religious tradition, on the one hand, and the delusional content of psychotic religious experience on the other. In a similar vein would be the study of Draper, Mayer, Parzen, and Samuelson (1965) investigating the diagnostic value of certain religious beliefs. There has also developed a trend of research which points toward a "discovery" long known within the major religious traditions and primitive religion--namely, that the kind of madness which manifests itself in religious experience often contains the germ of resolution and recovery. Bateson (1974) pointed out a madman's own recognition of this in his preface to Percival's narrative. Epstein (1979) spoke of the natural healing processes of acute schizophrenic disorganization. Sheikh-Dilthey (1976) mentioned the historical role of religious suffering in overcoming mental distress. And Horton (1973) professes the belief in his regretfully brief article that mystical experience has served as a suicide preventive in several cases of madness. The moderate success of some community-based, nonmedical treatment facilities for acute schizophrenia undergirds the trend represented by such authors (Gunderson, 1980; Matthews, Roper, Mosher, & Menn, 1979).

Some Recent Psychological Developments

John Perry (1974) and R. D. Laing (1967, 1969) are spokesmen for this trend. Their theoretical orientations differ, and Laing's early work in the area of schizophrenia and religious experience is rooted in the phenomenological tradition exemplified by Minkowski, and especially Sartre, in ways Perry's is not. Yet the two share certain ideas which foster the recognition of the curative power of religious experience in schizophrenia. Rarely is it recognized that Perry's historically rich and finely grained presentation of the sequence of psychotic religious experience has an historical precedent in the research and autobiographical account of a remarkable psychologist and minister, Anton Boisen (1960). His work might have formed the ground for a newly discovered psychology of religion, but it seems to have been largely neglected.

Laing, Boisen, and, to a lesser extent, Perry serve as transitional figures leading from a psychology or psychiatry of religion to a phenomenological psychology of religious experience. A tendency or clearly stated allegiance to phenomenology is evident in each case. Falling in the same category, and in some cases even more strongly committed to a phenomenology of religious experience in sane and mad alike, are Van Dusen, Hillman, and some other proponents of archetypal psychology.

Van Dusen's research is of four kinds. A beautiful, purely descriptive article entitled "The Phenomenology of a Schizophrenic Existence" (1961) establishes a class of its own. This is low order phenomenological psychopathology in the sense of a careful avoidance of explanation and little appeal to philosophical pointers for the formulation of methodology. The article's impact rests on this kind of purity. Works of comparable impact and of the same order of phenomenological psychopathology are scarce indeed. Henry's (1965) lengthy descriptions of families with schizophrenic children, the descriptive half of Sechehaye's (1951/1970) case study of a schizophrenic child, and Reed's (1977) biography of his wife's schizophrenic illness are the only others of which I am aware. A second aspect of Van Dusen's research is formed from three articles of a strictly clinical nature (Van Dusen, 1959a, 1959b; Van Dusen & Ansbacher, 1960). The remaining two classes differ from each other, and one wishes he had remained true to his earlier objectives. The research (Van Dusen, 1974) devoted to expounding the identity of Swedenborg's theosophy and religious experiences with the experiences and beliefs of hospitalized schizophrenic patients seems to have occupied most of his time, although in later works (Van Dusen, 1972) he turns, as do many phenomenological psychologists, to examine various means of transforming one's own consciousness.

With Hillman (1964, 1975) and the archetypalists, a highly sophisticated phenomenology which remains strictly psychological comes into view. But many presuppositions are turned upside-down with Hillman. For example, should his work not be called a phenomenological psychopathology because of his emphasis on "pathologizing," on pushing down through any given psychic phenomenon to arrive at its psychopathologically predisposed archetypal root? And what of the relationship between his psychology and the study of religious psychology? With Hillman's polytheism, the question is thrown wide open. Both Avens (1980) and Miller (1974) suggest that archetypal psychology is properly called, not a psychology of religious experience, but a religion of the psyche. And as for the relationship between Hillman and the archetypalists, on the one hand, and phenomenological philosophy on the other, the question is just as complex. A final answer may lie in what amounts to obviating the entire issue through tracing Hillman's idea of "root metaphor," not to a phenomenological stance which has discovered the constitutive activity of an intellect engaged in studying the psyche, but rather to a neo-Kantian analysis not dissimilar from Cassirer's (1955-1957) study of symbolic forms or from Jaspers's organization of psychological systems according to their methods rather than their content (Jaspers, 1913/1963; Lefebre, 1957).

Whatever the answer to these questions, archetypal psychology bears important implications for the present study. It has recovered an idea incipient in Jung's work and badly needed in clinical psychology. Corbin (1972) alludes to the idea's lengthy history when he refers to the *mundus imaginalis*, or what Avens (1980) calls, reminding one of Jung's label for the fruit of the transcendent function (Jung, 1960/1969d), the *tertium quid* of psychic existence. In both cases, the reference is to a zone of existence situated between the spirit of intellect and the hard world of *physis*. This middle zone is the psychic, known in many ways but most especially through imagery (Christou, 1976). That the corpuscular world of *soma* overlaps this zone, Hillman and others have shown, and from a different angle Merleau-Ponty (1942/1963) has made the same point with respect to an understanding of schizophrenic hallucinations. For my purpose, the middle zone is the landscape within which one is called to live when describing my patients and their religious experience. Since Jung, one of the finer means of transportation for moving about in this landscape has been imaginative amplification of the given focus of attention. The present study places emphasis on the link between corporeality and imagination, and so my presentation of imaginative analogies normally begins with the lived body of the patient. In this sense, my methodology is Jungian, archetypal, and grounded partly in Merleau-Ponty's phenomenology of hallucination.

A Concluding Evaluation

During its early days the psychology of religion demonstrated a continuity and a respect for the integrity of its subject matter. Subsequently, it was overshadowed by such encompassing interpretive systems as those of Freud and Jung. It seemed not to recover as a distinct discipline free of the psychopathological biases of psychiatry but rather was ramified into an array of different approaches to the psychology of religious experience, some of which may be regarded as transitional in the sense of leading from a psychology or psychiatry of religion to a phenomenology of religious experience. One can hunt avidly for findings and ideas significant specifically for a phenomenology of religious experience in schizophrenia. The hunt is mostly in vain, even more so when the focus is narrowed to include only the experience of God. From start to finish, the chief complaint is the reductionistic nature of the psychology of religion and of psychiatry when either has been concerned with the immediate features of religious experience in persons grouped or labeled in terms of psychopathological diagnosis. The degree and the kinds of reductionism vary. Psychologies intent on explaining religious experience are the least fit in terms of discerning a phenomenology. Psychologies intent on understanding are more suitable. Each has its place, but the confusion of the two, or the presentation of one under the guise of the other, poses special problems for the phenomenological psychopathologist who recognizes that religious experience belongs within an understanding psychology, and furthermore, that his particular interest pushes toward the removal of the interpretive layers of even an understanding psychology. How three of the most important spokesmen for phenomenological psychopathology have gone about this task will become apparent from an examination of Jaspers, Binswanger, and Straus.

The Phenomenological Psychopathology of Schizophrenia

To remove the interpretive layers which preform and constrict one's grasp of the experience of the schizophrenic patient, even when they belong to a psychology of understanding: such is the task which commenced with Jaspers's psychopathology and has continued at a varying pace in European phenomenological psychopathology. Psychology is perforce philosophical, said Straus, and this awareness characterizes not only the phenomenological psychopathologists to be mentioned, but other phenomenologists who have worked in laboratories and the field, with animals and mere tissue. Thines (1977) is exemplary in this respect; his epistemological critique of experimental psychology is an antidote to much American psychology. And not all schizophrenic patients have been fortunate enough to receive the kindness and quality of attention which the Dutch experimental phenomenologist, Buytendijk (1936), gave his dogs.

Karl Jaspers

Kolle (1957), Lefebre (1957), and Hoenig (1965) have questioned why the English-speaking world was long delayed in receiving Jaspers's *General Psychopathology* (Jaspers, 1913/1963) and, once received, why it seemed not to have the impact it deserved. The problems are more than linguistic; they may be of the same kind which distinguish European thinking from Anglo-American philosophy. A circumscribed history of ideas would provide answers, but the temptation to deviate from the psychopathological literature must be resisted. Spiegelberg's (1972, 1982) historical reviews remain the unrivaled source for a complete presentation of the historical precedents and philosophical currents operative in phenomenological psychology and psychopathology. Other books and bibliographies are helpful also (Hoenig, 1965; Keen, 1970; Kruger, 1981; Loewenberg, 1951; Lyons, 1959; Misiak & Sexton, 1973; Sonnemann, 1954; Tymieniecka, 1962; Valle & King, 1978).

Eventually Jaspers disavowed any connection with phenomenology, finding dehumanizing what he perceived as the idealistic and subjectivistic position of phenomenological philosophy. Yet he is deemed the father of phenomenological psychopathology due to his frequently expanded and revised General Psychopathology (Jaspers, 1913/1963). In the latter, he speaks of the phenomenology of psychic experience, referring to a systematic procedure for organizing, classifying, and naming psychopathological phenomena which are to be known initially through empathic involvement with the disturbed patient. He proceeds no further in outlining a methodology, although his later philosophical works concerned with existential communication press further in expounding means of securing phenomenological findings with respect to the other communicant.

In terms of concretely setting forth a methodology, Jaspers is not very helpful, and many later phenomenological psychopathologists would discern a weakness in his retaining rather stringently the subject-object dichotomy. The latter is reflected in his conclusion that schizophrenia is not amenable to understanding. Consequently, its investigation must resort to explanation. Schizophrenic experience, in this respect, is beyond the ken of human understanding and must finally be resolved by appealing to objectifying rather than phenomenological methods. Binswanger and others were in disagreement. The relative value of various techniques for participating in the experience of mental patients, and the more general matter of the limits of sharing vicariously in another person's experience, have been considered in a series of articles by Spiegelberg (1955, 1964, 1966). Jaspers's empathic involvement is mentioned; Spiegelberg would seem to have incorporated it in the formulation of his own technique of "imaginative self-transposal." Binswanger's "cooperative encounter" is not accorded the status it deserves, but I am in agreement with Spiegelberg in thinking favorably of Husserl's presentation of the passive constitution of the other person in the fifth of his _Cartesian Meditations_ (Husserl, 1950/1968). Surprisingly, Spiegelberg concludes pessimistically that none allows for a pure and direct phenomenological psychopathology. But the issue has not been laid to rest, as witnessed by Roos's (1974) article in the early 1970s.

If the relative simplicity and the circumscribed claims of Jaspers's phenomenological methodology are due partly to the natal condition of phenomenological psychopathology prior to the war, certain strengths of the text were continued in the tradition and have been retained to the present day. One of them is a fine attention to clinical detail and the organization of such detail on the basis of phenomenological rather than explanatory principles. For the most part, this tendency thrives still, and may be seen in such work as Casey's (1976). His comparative phenomenology of memory, hallucination, fantasy, and imagination has the potential of clarifying the confusion surrounding such simplistic and often inappropriately used terms of descriptive psychiatry as "hallucination" and "religious ideation." Howard's (1966) article, which appeals directly to Jaspers and Husserl while showing a conscientiousness about the historical precedents of phenomenological terms, could serve a similar purpose, as could Koehler's (1976), which notes in passing that a precedent for Schneider's first rank symptoms of schizophrenia was Jaspers's distinction between "thought insertion" and "made thoughts." Other phenomenological psychopathologists fall short, losing historical awareness and philosophical perspicacity. With such weaknesses, attention to clinical detail is not elevated to a level which illuminates the phenomenological significance of such detail. Holt (1971) on schizophrenia and Gudeman (1966) on schizophrenic delusions would be two examples. But by no means could this kind of criticism be directed at the works of Van den Berg (1952-1953, 1972, 1975, 1980).

Ludwig Binswanger

Lengthy delays attended the translation of Binswanger's work. To this day significant pieces are not available in English. May's 1958 anthology remains an indispensable initiation for one unfamiliar with phenomenological psychopathology. It is dedicated to Minkowski and Binswanger, the latter the most thoroughly represented of the book's contributors. Needleman's (1963) anthology is equally important. Predating both of these books are two articles of an importance which outweighs their relative brevity. In one, Binswanger (1960) outlines in an unusually lucid manner the basic discoveries of his research in schizophrenia. In the other (Binswanger, 1941-1942), he discusses Husserl, Heidegger, and his supplementation of the Heideggerian analytics with a dual or erotic mode of being.

Throughout these and other writings of Binswanger are clinical and theoretical matters of significance for the present study. Each will be considered, beginning with mention of the difference between _Daseinsanalyse_ and clinical psychopathology, moving to a critique of some traditional _Daseinsanalytisch_ terms, and ending with an outline of Binswanger's understanding of the development of schizophrenic existence. The intent is not always to offer a philosophically neutral critique or presentation, but rather to adopt a certain stance from which these matters are considered. This is especially so with the critique of the traditional terms. As a consequence, the theoretical orientation of the present study becomes more sharply defined, and certain findings born of description are anticipated.

A consideration of the question of God's existence has been interposed between the critique of _Daseinsanalytisch_ terms and the presentation of Binswanger's understanding of schizophrenia. This is a delicate matter because the behavioristic atmosphere of much current psychology has made it difficult to grasp the idea that the experience of God need not be a metaphysical concern. Certainly it is for theology and other areas of religious study, but not for the present research. To remove the experience from metaphysics involves articulating the meaning of "God" in such a way that the question of God's existence pales in importance beside the question of experiencing Him as present. Presence is necessarily a psychological matter, and though the metaphysical implications of God's presence extend beyond the strictly psychological, these implications need not be of central importance for a psychological study of the experience of God. This places the present study just inside the border separating psychology and psychopathology, on the one hand, from various theologically related disciplines on the other. The consideration of the question of God's existence is the one foray beyond this border--a programmatic foray having more the intent of a schematic outline and the setting forth of logically admissible answers to the question of God's presence than a substantative, philosophically attuned presentation. The intent is different, and strictly psychological, when the relationship between communication and the presence of God is considered in Chapter 3.

Daseinsanalyse and clinical psychopathology. To begin, _Daseinsanalyse_ is a phenomenological anthropology and only secondarily a system of psychopathology. The title of "anthropanalysis" has been suggested as a more fitting label for Binswanger's project (Cargnello, 1968). This is different from a psychopathology which begins and ends with clinical cases while appealing concurrently to supposed norms of psychological functioning. May's (1964) disclaimer aside, these remain distinct kinds of efforts, and the ramifications of the distinction are manifold. For example, the person who faults _Daseinsanalyse_ on the basis of its seeming irrelevance for psychotherapy has misunderstood, since it was not intended to provide a readily applicable basis for therapy. Cargnello (1968) has said Boss served as a transitional figure in this respect, moving from a Heideggerian anthropology to an existential therapeutic. How successfully and with what degree of conceptual congruence with Heidegger he did so, are two rather complicated questions. Whatever the case, the significance of the distinction between a phenomenological anthropology and an ordinary psychopathology is reflected on levels other than the strictly clinical, since with its appeal to be understood as anthropology *Daseinsanalyse* is involved instantly with tacit epistemological and ontological claims which warrant careful scrutiny (Blauner, 1957; Scott, 1973, 1975).

A critique of some Daseinsanalytisch terms. During his so-called "middle phase," when the lengthy studies of schizophrenic existence were composed, Binswanger was influenced strongly by Heidegger's fundamental ontology (Heidegger, 1927/1962; Spiegelberg, 1972). He seems to have thought the latter could be utilized in its original form for psychopathological investigation. Certain terms could be borrowed unaltered, certain claims comparable to those of Heidegger could be made without reservation, but on the basis of individual case studies rather than the Heideggerian thought of Being--so Binswanger assumed. The Heideggerian *existentialia*, for example, which have to do with *Dasein* in its openness to Being itself, were used by Binswanger with respect to *Dasein* as being-in-the-world. Such assumptions constituted what Binswanger admitted was a misunderstanding, but a fruitful one nonetheless. Among its fruit would be a stock of terms which have served phenomenological psychopathology well in its attempt to describe unusual forms of human existence. But the worm which has burrowed into some such fruit has occasionally been a terminological confusion and a vagueness unhelpful for phenomenological description. The fumigant of careful definition and relatively circumscribed usage is needed. The present study goes about this in the following ways.

First, the older terms are used sparingly. One is not to begin with them, forcing description to their mold. An implication of this is that description does not proceed according to categorically based analyses of symptoms and causation, spatiality and temporality, or the world of intersubjectivity. Though I refer indirectly to such matters, it is customarily when appealing to the reader with the invitation or challenge that he alter his own notion of these kinds of experience. In this sense, such categories have a phenomenological bearing for the reader himself, and are not used with ontological intent. The three modes of being which figure prominently in Binswanger's work--_Mitwelt_, _Umwelt_, and _Eigenwelt_--are also used with severe restriction. They serve basically as classifications or means of grouping certain kinds of phenomena. Aside from this formal restriction in usage, their specific content is rather sparse and is customarily to be discerned from the descriptive context. They are not considered as having to do essentially with human existence outside the special psychological conditions required for description of the portraits and for the reader's participation in the world of the portraits.

Dasein is an exception to this program of restricting and refining the traditional terms of phenomenological psychopathology. If some have plummeted from the sublime to the mundane, _Dasein_ is to retain its sublimity. Boss is to be preferred to Binswanger in this regard, and the present study recalls Boss's usage of the term on the few occasions it appears in the portraits. For Boss (1963), Dasein represents a concept totally inclusive of the modes and factical content of the openness which is human being in its concreteness. With this one stroke, the subject-object dichotomy is overcome, a feat which Binswanger's conceptualization of Dasein did not accomplish. Similarly, it becomes unnecessary and redundant, as Boss emphasizes, to speak in the plural of modes of being-in-the-world or modes of Dasein. In the same vein, to speak of a single patient as participating in several worlds, as Binswanger does, is to not recognize the inclusiveness of Dasein. Finally, with Boss's understanding of Dasein the very possibility of speaking of an existence as psychopathological is thrown into the question, because one is forced to consider first whether it makes sense to speak of either normal or abnormal Dasein. This is a dubious undertaking, since the distinction between normality and abnormality is erased with so inclusive a concept. Several authors (Scott, 1977) have noted that the theorizing and therapeutic interventions of Boss himself are not always consistent with his conceptualization of Dasein. Callanan (1976) would attain consistency by speaking of psychopathology in too general a manner as the forgetfulness of Being. In contrast to forgetfulness, he counterposes Heidegger's idea of Care. Such an arrangement would be to Boss's liking. Edwards (1981) goes further, however, and is generally an exception to this common incongruity between the meaning of Heideggerian and Bossian Dasein, on the one hand, and its theoretical and practical implications on the other.

The question of God's existence. The question of God's existence, and of the way it may be answered, is related to the theoretical stance on the basis of which the traditional terms of phenomenological psychopathology has been critiqued. To some degree, the present study is more closely affiliated with early phenomenological psychopathology *per se* than with its later existential variations. This is reflected in the ontically inclined understanding of most of the traditional terms, and in the emphasis given corporeality and perception during description. From this perspective, the question of God's existence is misconceived. But this is not only because of the circumscribed nature of the subject matter and the particular methodological principles which allow a delineated subject matter to come into view. It has to do more generally with a critique of an alternative perspective for which "God" refers to an object which may be known, or fail to be known, in ways analogous to those in which objects are known, whether they be concrete, as with an apple, or abstract, in the way of a mathematical formula. For this alternative perspective, the question of God's existence is viable and would seem straightforward; an answer would seem possible as well. But such a perspective is foreign to the present research, which allows one to pose the question, or seek an answer, only within the special interpersonal and psychological conditions of conversation, communication, and description. None of this is to imply that one should simply take for granted the existence of God. It is rather to say that the proper question is one of God as a presence during these three phases of research. Such matters must be pursued with the patient, and there is not a guarantee they are pertinent or able to be broached in every case.

There are three possible answers to the question of God's presence. Conversation may reveal that the patient simply misinterpreted his supposed experience of God, in which case his experience contributes little of significance to an answer. The pitiable, catatonic patient Sebastian is a case in point. His disturbed perception of time allowed a temporal transposition of an auditory hallucination and the speaking of the psychiatrist, such that he formed a logical, though erroneous, interpretation of the meaning of the voice he identified as God's. He recognized the error during conversation and was unable to correct or supplement his previous narrative. His experience was skewed in the sense that its interpretive or cognitive elements were incompatible with its remaining experiential features. Because of this incoherence and his inability to rectify it, the analytical and relatively objectifying mode characteristic of conversation could not evolve to the level of privileged interpersonal communion called communication. Only the latter serves as a possible basis for securing either a positive or a negative answer to the question of God's presence. The means of securing a negative answer within such a condition is unclear at this point in the investigation of the experience of God, since the theoretical outlines of such a possibility remain too vague to ascertain a method adequate to the task. The possibility of securing a positive answer is more readily apparent; its fulfillment is based on communication. Having secured a positive answer, one's experience would need to be adapted to a format such as this: God is present, insofar as He is known, and in the way He is known, by those who know Him during communication. The agonized manic-depressive patient Sarah is an instance of the fulfillment of this possibility, as is Mary, the patient diagnosed schizophrenic despite a complex medical history suggestive of cerebrovascular disease and a symptom pattern resembling an affective disorder more closely than a schizophrenic disorder of formal thinking.

Binswanger's understanding of schizophrenic existence. To my knowledge, it has not been noticed that Binswanger's eventual conclusions with regard to the development and structure of schizophrenic existence are analogous to the dramatic reversal of the individual's entire psychic constellation to which Jung gave the name enantiodromia (Jung, 1971). I feel sure this is not due to borrowing, conscious or otherwise, much less to thievery, despite the crossing of the two men's lives in intellectual and day-to-day matters. Heraclitus was influential for both, and Jung acknowledged his role in the formulation of the psychology of enantiodromia. A glance toward the historical context of Binswanger's (1957) schizophrenia studies shows that the period of their composition overlaps with that in which Heidegger gave his pre-Socratic lectures (Heidegger, 1943-1954/1975), at least two of which are concerned with Heraclitus. Additional investigation would uncover other coincidences, and not the least interesting would be a tendency toward formal dialectical thinking in the work of both Jung and Binswanger. For the present, the more important effort is to present Binswanger's findings and note in passing their likeness to Jung's.

Binswanger's conclusions regarding the development and structure of schizophrenic existence have added clarity when Husserl's idea of the constitutive role of time consciousness is given special emphasis. This is not entirely in keeping with Binswanger's own formulation during the course of his schizophrenia studies, but is congruent with his later reflections upon the earlier work, as found in the 1957 introduction to the collected schizophrenia studies. In summary, then, Binswanger comes to this: schizophrenic existence commences, or accumulates, like the blockage of some liquid which eventually forces past its borders, once the constitutive activity of time consciousness deteriorates. The temporal sequence of experience is no longer evident, and as a consequence the coherence of events spread out one after another is lost. Choice becomes an arbitrary matter, and the former pattern or design of existence is lost. The process of fragmentation is resolved, if the word be understood in a neutral manner, by the patterning of existence in accordance with rigid alternatives, with one side of these pairs of alternatives always being chosen over and against the other. Fatigue renders the process ineffective. Some of the florid manifestations of schizophrenic existence occur spontaneously as moves to bolster the flagging success of the entire shift of existence. For souls it is death to become water, said Heraclitus, and at this point schizophrenic existence runs to its opposite, drenching the disturbed person with one or another of the end-states which clinically identify the chronic schizophrenic patient. At this point also is the analogy between Binswanger's conclusions and Jung's idea of _enantiodromia_ most firmly based, since Jung, too, though not usually with reference to schizophrenia, spoke of the transformation and reversal of one's dominant attitude, function, and archetype coming about due to the exhaustion of possibilities linked with the previous attitude, function, and archetype. Among the historical cases of this turning, Jung spoke of St. Paul, whose flashing seizure-like experience on the road to Damascus led to a radical change of personality. Whereas Paul was blinded with a flashing light, the Paul of Chapter 4 was numbed and benighted during his most powerful experience of God. In each case, the experience coincided with a dramatic reversal of the person's usual mode of confronting the world.

Perhaps the most interesting coincidence is not that between Binswanger and Jung, but rather between Binswanger and Minkowski (Minkowski, 1926, 1933/1970; Laing, 1963; Zoila, 1976), an early phenomenological psychopathologist whose intensity and intimacy are much to be admired. Relying philosophically on Bergson, and clinically on the newfound goal of uncovering the "generating disorder" in any given psychopathological condition, Minkowski invariably discerned such a disorder in the patient's experience of lived time. Decades would pass before Melges (1982) demonstrated again, in a systematic and more comprehensive way than Minkowski, the theoretical utility of considering all psychopathological phenomena in terms of a basic disorder of temporal experience. For Minkowski and Binswanger, temporality was a matter of fundamental importance for understanding schizophrenic psychopathology. This gives one reason to wonder whether Husserl (1928/1964), in his analysis of internal time consciousness, was not vindicated in an important and mostly unnoticed way through Minkowski and especially Binswanger, despite the latter relying more heavily on Heidegger during the early stages of his schizophrenia research. For my reading, Binswanger's treatment of the initial stages of schizophrenic disorganization seems more reliant on Husserl's considerations of time consciousness than the temporality of Heideggerian *Dasein*. And the whole matter is not without more general implications, since the entire field of phenomenological psychopathology may be divided, as is done for phenomenological and existential philosophy, into the two broad classes of phenomenological and existential modes of psychopathological reflection.

Erwin Straus

With Straus, one breathes humid air rather than imbibing the spirit of existential abstractions. But mountain climbers know that descents are often more difficult than attaining the peak. The descent in question is to sensory experience; the path to be followed requires an amnesia for the objectifying perspective which splits off a benighted sensation from a knowing perception, renders sensation a mechanistic process reliant totally on the neural substructure, and discriminates radically the thinking and knowing being from its animalish mount. The grotesque fantasy which some modern psychology has made of sensory experience, and which is exemplified by these and related ideas, is critiqued with uncompromising rigor by Straus on a number of occasions. His intent is similar to Merleau-Ponty's in this respect. In longer works, Straus customarily begins with the Cartesian *cogito*, showing how the abortion which tore apart *res extensa* and *rex cogitans* has influenced and is still reflected in psychological theory and praxis (Straus, 1963, 1966, 1969). Pavlovian theory, Gestalt psychology, and the classical Behaviorism of Watson are brought under close scrutiny in this project. There is an eeriness associated with Straus's argument.

It has little to do with an impressionistic style, since he characteristically writes with aridity and precision, and more to do with the insight that much of modern psychology has convulsed human experience, tearing its roots from the lived body. Some psychology is eclamptic, and the loyal would hope it is not too late to rescue the fetus of human experience. Straus began the formulation of an antidote.

For the purpose of this study, a consideration of Straus's work may be sharply restricted in scope. Its implications for philosophical biology may be left aside (Grene, 1965), as may its ramifications for the study of disorders of memory, language, and perception (Dublin, 1972; Marsh, 1976; Straus, 1960, 1967, 1970, 1974). His studies of obsession, compulsion, and shame are also without direct bearing on the present study (Straus, 1948, 1963, 1966; Vallelonga, 1976). His explorations of schizophrenia (Straus, 1966) may be passed over as well, since his methods are mostly incongruent with the case-centered approach of the portraits and the narratives of the experience of God. But deserving of careful and substantive treatment is his psychology of sensory experience, which, in Straus's words, is the "physiognomic" dimension of the general "historiological" study of the "I-_Allon_" relationship (Straus, 1963, 1966, 1969). This requires the presentation of a new vocabulary; its initial obscurity fades upon realizing that Straus is struggling to recover the experience of sensation in its bare immediacy, and to show how sensation sets the mood of the surrounding world to which the lived body is attuned.

The psychology of sensory experience. An orientation to Straus's psychology of sensory experience requires a step upward to abstraction, followed by a step downward to reflection upon immediate experience. Proceeding with the former, one realizes human existence involves necessarily a tense, if not conflictual, arrangement of self and world. Straus believes the upright posture is the anthropological basis for this tension. Bachelard's (1968, 1969) term, "coefficient of adversity," later given critical significance in Sartre's (1943/1956) _Being and Nothingness_, is apropos here, with the difference that Sartre sets this coefficient in a wider philosophical frame than does Straus. The Other, or _Allon_, stands in a dialectical relationship with its "I." For that matter, the "I" becomes personalized, in a developmental as well as a cross-sectional phenomenological sense, concurrently with the differentiation of the Other. In the Other's responsiveness, one recognizes his own meaning and possibilities. But this is not to say the Other's identity is necessarily what is conceived ordinarily as a person, since personalization reigns at very basic levels of experience, beneath even those for which a human being exists in his corporeal unity and common sense knowability. It is at these more basic levels that one turns from general historiological concerns to an examination of the physiognomy of sensation. The immediate features of sensory experience come into view with this step. In stepping down, much could be said to amplify Straus's conceptualization of sensory experience. Merleau-Ponty (1945/1962, 1947/1964; Zaner, 1964) could be mentioned. Consideration could be given Husserl (1954/1970; Wild, 1964), whose writings on the life-world, or _Lebenswelt_, were published a number of years after Straus (1963) spoke of "the axioms of everyday life." There is recent work in the phenomenology of speech, olfaction, gustation, and kinesthesia resting on Straus's seminal study of the upright posture (Dublin, 1967, 1972). His conceptualization of physiognomic experience has also begun to receive critical attention (Hoeller, 1975-1976); its inconsistencies have become apparent as a result. But an outline of the meaning of physiognomic experience will suffice, since the latter delineates the landscape one is called to recognize, inhabit, and describe during portraiture (Eng, 1976; Fischer, 1976; Hoeller, 1975-1976; Straus, 1963, 1966, 1969; Titelman, 1976a).

Physiognomic experience is of two overlapping kinds: sensing and perceiving. For both, there is a second distinction: they may be either pathic or gnostic. Terminological vagueness is apparent, however, since it seems clear that Straus generally considers perceiving to be gnostic only, and sensing to be mostly pathic. With the perspective of several decades, it becomes clear also that Straus's pathic mode of sensing is closely related to what Husserl and, with certain reservations, Merleau-Ponty meant when speaking of the lived world. For all three, a fundamental and prepredicative dimension of human experience is in question, which is not at all to say that fully conscious, namable realities rest on the faulty support of a meaningless unconscious hollow. On the contrary, a richly variegated pattern of sensory texture and of incipient conceptualizations buoys up what otherwise would detach itself into a meaningless realm of vacuous abstractions. A history of Husserl's development of the *Lebenswelt* concept is beyond the needs of an introduction to Straus, but it is quite to the point that attention be drawn to the difference of focus in their investigation of the lived world. While Husserl reflects upon the perspectival and constitutive activity of a consciousness embedded in the lived world, Straus is concerned with what might be called, in keeping with Binswanger and later phenomenological psychopathology, the attunement or mood which is present for the lived body, and which pervades the entire surroundings, thus creating a landscape which is congruent emotionally with the body. Indeed, "landscape" is a technical term with Straus, as are "physiognomy," "pathic," "gnostic," and the rest. And it is the emotional bearing of the term which raises it to a degree of clinical significance which is relevant less often for Merleau-Ponty and not at all for Husserl.

A turn toward its clinical relevance brings Straus's idea of the physiognomy of experience into sharper focus. A preliminary observation is that Straus considered the examination of physiognomic experience and its landscapes to be a kind of categorical analysis, ranked alongside such other categories as space, time, and causation. For him, the entire effort of categorical analysis was as one lane of a wider road directed toward understanding psychopathology. Its other lanes were phenomenological description (which I think barely deserves this title because of its close similarity to ordinary case studies) and genetic-structural analysis (which I have no doubt is a novel and significant complement to the genetic and structural analyses of classical and neo-analytic psychoanalysis). But the particular brand of categorical analysis focusing on physiognomic experience is itself open to further divisions. These additional divisions are broken down neatly according to the traditional delineation of the modalities of sensory experience and their respective hylomorphic shapes. This allows one to speak of pain and its landscapes, of audition and its landscapes, of vision and the landscapes with which it is correlated whether before or after nightfall.

For example, one may ask where the hallucinating person lives. With disturbance of this degree, however, the better question might be whether the person is, in the sense of inhabiting any ordinary landscape. Consider the sensory features of such a person's world. Sound is experienced as distinct from its common sources. Mouths, bodies, and objects are no longer the sole sources of sound. Sound may not have an identifiable source; if it does, the source may be other than ordinary, or may project sound along oddly confusing trajectories. One's knee may talk, for example, or the tree speak words rather than cast its usual wheeze. The orderliness of the *Allon* is shattered, for its ordinary markers, which contribute to orientation in the common sense landscape of audition, are no longer present. Thus one is estranged from the earth. One may hover as a consequence, since the earth no longer provides reliable guidance in linking sound and sight, or sound and place. Every place becomes unreliable; there is no safety.

The profundity of the problem is more apparent when a categorical analysis of spatiality complements these remarks about the incongruity of the earth as commonly experienced and the personal landscape of the hallucinating patient. Space is the very ground of any landscape, regardless of personal idiosyncracies, and the earth itself is an assembly of personal landscapes which cohere on the basis of many persons' sensory experience. Our lives cross, we share the same vista, but only because of the consistency with which the longitudinal and latitudinal grid of sensory orientation reveals a coherent space within which we may create our respective personal histories. When this grid disintegrates, as it does for the hallucinating patient, space becomes diffuse and subject to momentary warps. There is no longer a common earth; even the possibility of another person existing is seriously attenuated. One's own existence is thrown into question also, since life history is grounded in historical time, and the latter, unlike chronological time, requires a coherent space within which movement may occur and a life be built. This is not to speak figuratively: movement is impossible under such conditions. The immobilization of some catatonic patients attests to this being sheer terror. Unusual bodily experiences are another consequence, as witnessed by two of my patients, Sebastian and especially Sarah, whose body was tortured and interred during a twilight state with catatonic features.

Chapter 3

METHODOLOGY

The Patients

Nine hospitalized psychiatric patients participated in the present study. Six would satisfy without question the criteria for a diagnosis of schizophrenia drawn from the _Diagnostic and Statistical Manual of Mental Disorders_ (American Psychiatric Association, 1980) and from the "five most frequently used systems for diagnosing schizophrenia" (Fenton, Mosher, & Matthews, 1981, p. 452) prior to 1981 (the New Haven Schizophrenic Index, the Flexible System, the Research Diagnostic Criteria, and the Feighner and Schneider criteria). Two others, John and Teresa, would do so as well, were it not for their failing to satisfy the Feighner criterion of the absence of a history of drug abuse within 1 year of hospitalization. Despite this, all eight have been given a schizophrenic diagnosis, typically chronic undifferentiated schizophrenia, over the course of many hospitalizations.

The exception to this group of patients diagnosed schizophrenic is Sarah, a woman who with similar assurance would be given a diagnosis of a cycling bipolar affective disorder. Her experience of God, which has occurred twice, and with nearly identical features, during the manic phases of her illness, serves as an affective counterpoint to the experience of the patients diagnosed schizophrenic. This provides some leverage with which the phenomenological features characteristic of the schizophrenic experience may be lifted out. The present study is not a comparative, diagnostically oriented investigation of the experience of God in schizophrenia and affective disorder, although such matters are of interest and will be considered in the concluding chapter.

Two other patients, who with equal assurance would satisfy the diagnostic criteria for schizophrenia from the six systems already mentioned, were possible participants for the study. One was invited and declined, the other was not invited. The first was a Caucasian woman in her late 30s with a history of many hospitalizations. Jesus was as near to her as He could possibly be, she said; He spoke to her frequently, and she was able to draw upon his power to cure illness. She prayed repeatedly that my nearsightedness be cured, but when I did not remove my glasses and proclaim deliverance after several incantations, she angrily refused to participate. The second possible participant was a hefty black man in his early 20s with a history of several hospitalizations. Jesus had appeared in the kitchen while the patient was cooking his breakfast eggs, and the resulting commotion and agitation led to the present hospitalization. This man was conversing with either God or Jesus while hospitalized; his words were drawn directly from scripture, with which he was exceptionally familiar, no doubt because his father is an evangelically oriented preacher. Upon engaging the patient, it was readily apparent he was unable and unwilling to speak in language other than scriptural. For every religious experience of his there was an explanatory scripture. This kind of patient is an unsuitable subject because the present study is not concerned with either scripture or a patient's scripturally based interpretation of religious experience generally. On the contrary, scripture and scripturally based interpretations of religious experience are inadmissible barriers to the gathering of information about a patient's experience of God. They are suspect not only because they may bias a patient's report of his actual experience or be substituted for his own interpretation of the meaning of his experience, but they may also attain the status of an actual, though inauthentic, experience of God. For these reasons, the second of these persons was rejected as a subject.

If the patient presented with religious experience of any kind, or had a history of such experience, I was alerted by ward staff of the 14-bed neuropsychiatric unit of the county hospital. This procedure was followed for the 8 months during which conversation was conducted and data collected. The invitation to participate was presented simply and straightforwardly. I would approach the patient as soon after admission as possible and before having engaged in any direct care of the patient. I would speak with the patient in private, remarking upon my interest in learning about the experience of God for persons who come to hospitals such as this one, and asking if he had had such an experience. If not, I would thank him for his time and assume *vis-á-vis* the patient the ordinary role of ward clinician. If so, I would clarify my intent by saying it is the experience itself which is of interest rather than his later interpretations, and adding that through learning more about his experience I would be better able to help staff members in such hospitals to understand what a patient means when he speaks of having experienced God. The only other prefatory remark concerned the frequency of the patient's experience of God: if he had experienced God only once, that single experience would be our chief concern; if he had experienced God more than once, his most powerful experience would be our chief concern. He was asked to sign an agreement form and assured of confidentiality. (None of the patients was under conservatorship; each was able legally to refuse or agree to participation.) We then scheduled a mutually convenient time for conversation. A single sitting was allowed for each conversation, regardless of the time needed for its completion. Some lasted 2 hours; most of them about 1 hour. Single-spaced transcripts of conversation range upward to nearly 50 pages. I did not engage in direct care of those who participated in the study, but assumed a cordial, clinically neutral role before and after conversation.

Four Levels of Factual Data

The factual data are of four levels for each subject: the audio recording of conversation, the narrative of the patient's experience of God, the case history, and the transcription of conversation. The recording was made during conversation. The transcript of conversation was simply a typed version of the tape recording. The narrative was written after conversation; it is composed largely of quotations drawn from the recording and organized in a manner allowing the sequential complexity and intrapsychic features of the experience to become more apparent. The case history is drawn from the medical records; it, too, is composed largely of quotations. The reliance on quotations from the medical records and conversation for the case history and narrative promotes an initial grasp of the different epistemological levels of these kinds of data. This would have been lost, or less apparent, had the information simply been summarized or presented with relatively few quotations.

In some cases, the history is rich and detailed; in others not. Medical considerations are given emphasis in some cases; in others not. These variations rest on the medical complexities of the case and on how well known the patient was in the county of hospitalization. For example, Paul was an indigent, not a resident in the county of hospitalization, and his stay was very short. Thus his history is brief. In comparison, Luke was well known and there is much history. Sebastian's history includes an amount of medical information regarding medication, since it had bearing on the diagnosis of catatonia.

A case history and a narrative have been included for each patient. A transcription of conversation with John is included also; it gives a sense for conversation with this man and shows select elements of the logic of questioning outlined in a later section of this chapter. The recordings are available under carefully monitored conditions, should the reader be interested. For those patients who have been portrayed, the history and narrative have been placed just before the portrait. The remaining histories and narratives are in Appendix B.

The four levels of factual data are not the same epistemologically. This is a matter of critical significance for the present study, which raises repeatedly the overarching criterion of experiential immediacy. For the factual data, this criterion centers on the actual conversation with its specific emotional, perceptual, conceptual, and neuro-psychological features. Those kinds of data more closely related to the actual conversation are given priority in the description of the patient's portrait; those more distant are of less importance. These matters require close consideration and belong properly to methodological reflection. Thus they reappear in a later section of this chapter, where the levels of factual data are spoken of in terms of an hierarchy of residue left from conversation and communication.

Criteria for Portraiture

Four of the eight schizophrenic patients have been portrayed. The criteria determinative for their being given this central place are several. First, gender variety was thought desirable. There should be at least one woman, despite the majority being male. Mary was selected: her experiences are more varied than the other woman's, and her vocabulary and the coherence of her cognitive state were better suited than Teresa's for reporting previous experience. There is the additional finding of Mary's complicated medical history suggestive of acute episodes of hypertensive encephalopathy, which raises interesting questions about the commonness of her kind of experience in a schizophrenic population.

Because of the frequent identification of a delusional patient with a renowned religious figure, it was thought desirable to have at least one patient with such a substitution of identity. Luke was chosen: he is Moses. Mark Thomas was the alternative, but his identity as God was determined on the basis of a technique so discrepant from that used by Luke or most other patients who identify with a religious figure that it was thought wise to exclude him. Mark Thomas's technique is given special attention in his narrative, however; thus one is able to understand the logic of this idiosyncratic means of delusional identification.

A third criterion called for portraying at least one case with a high degree of systematization to the patient's delusional beliefs and interpretation of the experience of God. John excels in this sense: his delusional system is conceptually rich and tightly structured; his interpretation of the experience is more complex than that of other patients. As might be expected, there is a correlation between the estimated intelligence of the patient and the degree of systematization to the delusional system and interpretation of the experience. Thus Sebastian, whose estimated level of intelligence is barely within the dull range, offered the most sparse and logically least coherent interpretation. His even having a delusional system apart from the experience's interpretation is questionable. But this is not to say there is a correlation between an estimated level of intelligence for these patients and the systematic quality of the experience itself. The interpretation and the delusional system are to be distinguished from the experience in its immediate perceptual, emotional, and conceptual details. While intelligence may correlate with the degree of systematization when the interpretation and the delusional system are in question, it may not with the experience itself. When applied to the experience, systematization could be assigned several meanings which need not be outlined fully. An example will suffice. Teresa and Sebastian are the most seriously disturbed patients in the series.

This is reflected in the simplicity of Sebastian's experience, his erroneous, though logical, interpretation of its meaning, and the probable absence of a delusional system. In contrast, Teresa's visions of God are ripe with interesting perceptual complexities. For example, a development in the perceptual structure of the two visions is evident: while the phenomenological landscape in which Jesus stood during the first vision was a black space hollowed from concrete of the nearby wall, Jesus stood in front of the wall during the second vision. In accordance with the greater perceptual oddity of the first vision, her fearfulness was more intense during the first than the second vision. Perceptually, then, the visions of this more disturbed patient illustrate a complexity, and a coherence of hallucinatory content over time, which might not be expected in a patient whose interpretation is relatively more confused and simplistic.

The final criterion for portraiture called for showing a variety in the way and the degree to which material similar to that of the Bible appeared in the experience of God. There is variety indeed; it has important bearing for questions of the function and role of scripture in psychosis which extend beyond the present study. A few examples will suffice. Paul is a Black Muslim; he employs relatively few images or ideas from the Bible in interpreting his experience. Yet his experience may be approached in terms of certain ideas of the apostle Paul and the apostle Paul's own experience of flashing light on the road to Damascus. John is somewhat familiar with scriptural ideas, but unlike Luke, who identifies with Moses and sides with God and the forces of good in the Bible, John feels he is the anti-Christ. Biblical ideas and imagery function differently for Mary than for the rest. She has adopted tacitly a Biblical cosmology without distorting it in the least. For her, the Bible is as a norm against which to judge the goodness or evil, the desirability or undesirability, of her experiences. In this sense, she might have been thought quite sane during certain historical periods.

The Prevalence of the Experience of God

A psychologist of religion interested in the relationship between religious experience in schizophrenia and in the normal population might find it remarkable that the percentage of hospitalized schizophrenic patients reporting experience of God in this study is about equal to the percentage of persons from the normal population of America and Great Britain reporting either an experience of God or a religious experience of a powerful spiritual force. When the eight schizophrenic patients of the present study are added to the two not interviewed, and these 10 weighted against the total number of schizophrenic admissions for the year (excluding both schizophreniform and schizoaffective diagnoses), the result is a figure of 30%. This includes actuarially based corrections for multiple admissions and for the projected admissions in the final annual quarter during which conversation was not conducted. For the normal population of America and Great Britain, the average percentage of persons reporting such experience is 33%. The latter figure has been determined on the basis of five extensive studies over the course of 20 years (Prince, 1979-1980).

To my knowledge, the only other empirical data even vaguely

pertinent for the question of the relative prevalence of the experience in normal and schizophrenic populations are from a study of Ruth's (1974). This was a two-group comparison of 50 unhospitalized, "healthy" Christians with an active church life, and 50 hospitalized, Christian, schizophrenic patients. They were matched on seven variables, including religious affiliation. Their responses to a set of symbols and photos of bodies or body parts, most of which were associated with the Christian tradition, were grouped according to kinds of social attribution. These ranged from communal responses of the "we" kind to those without social reference. The groups did not differ: the symbols and photos elicited a paucity of communal social references consistently across both groups. He concluded that religious experience is not dependent on one's psychological condition, and seems to have felt that his study struck at a psychologically reductionistic approach to religious experience. A methodologically sensitive critic would be imprudent to brag about this study, but it is not without interest. One would expect major differences between the two groups' responses to body imagery, especially when it is the body of bloodied, suffering, delirious, nude religious figures, precisely because the psychological dimension of body image is so often disturbed in schizophrenia. That such a difference was not found points to the phenomenological integrity of religious experience regardless of the population in which it occurs.

The consistency of the British and American studies mentioned earlier is remarkable; even more remarkable is their consistency with the prevalence figure from the present study. These findings point directly to the question of the possibility of distinguishing psychotic from normal experience of God. Facile answers are readily available. For example, one might hypothesize that the experience is abnormal, a definitive measure of psychopathology--in which case nearly a third of the population of Great Britain and America have been seriously disturbed. One would be forced to conclude also that 12% of the population of these countries has been this disturbed two or more times (Prince, 1979-1980). If one were to ignore the rule of thumb which forbids the formulation of causal hypotheses on the basis of correlational data, and rest one's case on the near equivalence of the schizophrenic and the normal figures, the conclusion would then be that an experience of God is symptomatic of a schizophrenic disorder. But this conclusion holds up poorly when set beside Torrey's (1980) careful compilation of prevalence figures for schizophrenia. In the United States, he said "prevalence rates of schizophrenia have varied from 1.1 to 4.7 per thousand" (p. 95). The line of thought which assumes that this kind of religious experience is symptomatic of a schizophrenic disorder is contradictory in that the largest estimate of schizophrenic prevalence--.47%--is highly discrepant from schizophrenic prevalence figures of either 12 or 33% predicated on the basis of this assumption.

The argument may be run very differently, however, by starting with the hypothesis that the experience is a phenomenon *sui generis*, which has the distinction of occurring without a significant mutilation of its basic features in normal and abnormal populations alike. Given this, one would anticipate equivalent percentages for the experience in both populations. The figures indicate this to be the case, and Ruth (1974) provides additional support. Parsimony receives its due as well.

Given the latter state of affairs, therapeutic matters press to the fore. As follows: if the experience of God is a phenomenon *sui generis*, it may serve as a touch point for the therapist who finds the schizophrenic patient otherwise quite impossible to reach. It may serve not only as a touch point in interpersonal encounter, but also as a means of social reintegration, in that the experience sweeps across the boundaries separating normal from abnormal and is found in nearly a third of all persons. The possible therapeutic value of religious ritual for schizophrenia is only one implication of this line of thought.

Terminological matters press to the fore as well. What is to be said for this phrase of psychiatric jargon, which is often given conceptual credence and attributed with diagnostic power: "religious ideation?" In some cases, it is overinclusive, if not simplistic, and may well betray a countertherapeutic sin of omission. And insofar as one draws near a patient in conversation about his experience of God, could it not be said that one has before himself, not a schizophrenic but simply another human being? From this point until the concluding chapter, I cease referring to "schizophrenia." In its place, I speak simply of the other person and his extraordinary experience.

Conversation

An Outline of the Experience of God

To draw near the other person requires a broad outline of the form of the experience of God. The outline is composed of several ideas, the most basic of which is that experience of God is a complex phenomenon in a sequential as well as an intrapsychic sense. To speak of the sequential complexity of the experience is to refer to its duration. One aspect of the experience follows another, and a sequence is built up which informs the parts and the whole. At a very basic level, then, the experience of God has coherence in that it occurs in a sequential manner, suspended between start and finish. These are simple, if not simplistic, assertions, but were the experience to be otherwise, there would be no sense in attempting conversation, since one would have concluded preemptively that the experience did not incur temporal duration and was therefore outside the reach of questioning based on the examination of its sequence. The experience would be an indivisible moment without beginning or end, and without being situated in the ongoing duration of life. Such a conception would remove the experience from psychological examination. The idea of sequential complexity serves as justification for asking the patient questions about the various aspects of his experience and their sequential alignment. These are simple questions of the "before" and "after" kind; they are imperative when speaking with someone detached radically from the ordinary world of experience. The idea of sequential complexity is also determinative for the sequential arrangement of the quotations and general presentation of the experience of God in the narratives and portraits. An atomistic notion of experience, which would delineate thematic units without regard for the specific moment of lived time to which they pertain, is thus obviated.

To speak of the intrapsychic complexity of the experience of God is to refer to its constitutive pattern, which comes about due to the coincidental layering of the various psychological forms operative during the experience at any one moment. The basic forms investigated are idea, emotion, and sensory experience. Regardless of how often their content changes, or how softly they occur to consciousness, each is to be investigated carefully.

The Logic of Questioning

Along with the ideas of sequential and intrapsychic complexity, three principles have been borrowed from formal logic to serve as guides in asking questions, and as a means to investigate the relationship between God and His manifestations (Ambrose & Lazerowitz, 1948). When demonstrated for the other person, they also provide a conceptual format with which he may formulate what would otherwise remain unclear. These principles are not always used in the manner for which they were created, or with the same intent. For example, the truth or falsity of the other person's statements has little bearing on securing a complete report of his experience. Similarly, I hold neither myself nor him to statements which could be framed adequately in the syllogistic format. Of interest, however, are such matters as the nature of God's presence and the kinds of identity relations which pertain to God and His manifestations. The first principle is the rule of the excluded middle, the remaining two have to do specifically with identity relations.

A definition of the rule of the excluded middle would run as follows: for every A, there are only two possible values, corresponding to A and not-A; "A or not-A" is thus accepted as necessarily true. An example will be seen in conversation with John about God's "talking in the thunder." Holding in mind the rule, one seeks to determine whether or not God is thunder. The question may be phrased "Was God thunder?" or "Was God other than thunder and simply speaking with thunder?" The weight of such questions guided by the rule is greater than one might suspect, since they partly allow a determination in such matters as the intrinsic pantheism, or lack thereof, in some experiences of God. Should a certain relationship be established between God and natural occurrences, one would have reason to suggest the other person experiences God as would a pantheist.

A prime property of identity relations is reflexivity, for which a definition would be: a relation is reflexive if an entity can bear the relation to itself; and since every entity is identical to itself, it may be said that identity is a reflexive relation. The significance of this principle is its providing instigation for questioning apparent inconsistencies among various manifestations of God either during a single experience or between several different experiences. Should God seem decidedly different from one moment to the next, or from one experience to the next, or should He suggest contradictory ideas to the other person, one has reason to bear in mind the property of reflexivity. Questions would be framed which sought to determine how the other person knew it was God only who was responsible for these differences or contradictions. He is thus confronted with the question of the meaningfulness of his experience, and the questioner has the opportunity to ascertain how the other person went about interpreting and giving coherence to his experience.

The other property of identity relations is symmetry, which is notated: If A = B, then B = A. It may serve as a logical scheme brought into play after application of the rule of the excluded middle, and in pursuit of the formal psychological features of the experience of God. Taking John's experience of God "talking in the thunder" as an example, the principle of symmetry would be utilized after establishing that God was not identical with the thunder. The range of possibilities remains large: the thunder may have been a kind of background noise within which God spoke with ordinary words, in which case the meaning of thunder might have little significance for either the words spoken by God or the content of his message. On the other hand, it might have been that God's very words were unusually modulated thunder, in which case it could be said that God's voice was worded thundering. In this instance, the property of symmetry holds for John's world: God spoke as thunder, the thunder spoke as God. Remaining questions would then be pursued on this basis. For example: "Is all thunder the voice of God?"; "Was thunder on this particular occasion different than thunder ordinarily?" In the former case, however, a different line of questioning would be required, perhaps beginning with a determination of whether thunder had any bearing on its having been God who spoke contemporaneously.

A New Attitude

Besides an outline of the form of the experience of God and the several ideas which constitute the logic of questioning, a new attitude is required for drawing near the other person. With this attitude, one is called to step outside the confines of narrow, conceptual schemes regardless of how adequate and subtle they seem. Certain dimensions of experience which are characteristically attributed to the heart and to intuition are in question when considering the full complement of factors present with the new attitude. Should it become pervasive, extending through each moment of awareness and questioning, the other elements of methodological theory become operative in praxis without one attending to them in a conscious manner. They cease functioning as mere theory, as something extra to be remembered and used like a tool which is carried and brought out when needed. This is a worthy goal, but since the other person always figures prominently in conversation, there is not a way to ensure its attainment. Despite this, the changed attitude deserves mention, not because it is new to psychology in an historical sense, but because much psychological research seems to have developed an amnesia for it. Strasser (1963), Van Kaam (1966), and especially Giorgi's (1970) platform for psychology as a human science point toward some aspects of this attitudinal change. A Duquesnean other than Giorgi has tapped certain of Levinas's (1969/1979) ideas regarding the meaning and depths of human encounter, constructing an outline for a Levinian theory of psychotherapy, but without enough attention to how radically these ideas would transform both therapy and phenomenological research (Halling, 1975). Along these lines one is led to think when considering what it means to draw near the other person with a heart informed in a manner Pascal would find reasonable.

First reflect upon the obstacles. Consider Sebastian, one of the nine persons who have contributed to this study: he exudes a foul odor; his pale body is encrusted with a waxy ooze of stale perspiration; his voice has sunk to a hollow squeak; his hands, arms, and legs are tremulous with fear. Should he be treated differently than someone clean, polite, and confident? The mouth responds "No" readily and without a twisted lip when the heart is informed with a changed attitude. But the obstacle may be of another kind. Consider Steven, another of the nine: he comes fresh from a bath with slicked blond hair, a beaming smile, pretty blue eyes, ruddy cheeks, and an almost endearing limp. Five minutes into conversation he tells of sexually molesting an infant and how afterwards he cleaned himself and her, all without blinking or any sign of regret. Moral indignation dictates that one malign the degradation of which he is the living symbol. But a changed attitude would promote detachment adequate to the task of grasping the impoverished existence which shapes such behavior. More subtle obstacles are posed by Teresa, who is only barely present cognitively, her mind skipping like a thin stone over the surface of ordinary reality, touching here and there with strange accounts of ghosts, banging garbage cans, jail cells, and Jesuses of many races and nationalities. When she does speak coherently, the problem of horrible grammar is compounded with the argot of black street people. Should Teresa be rejected, turned away from this research, because of these barriers to understanding, or is it preferable that one adopt an attitude for which the flights born of a disturbance of thought and language become the shimmering surface of another order of reality bubbling into the common awareness of her and her interlocutor? The latter alternative is to be chosen. Other kinds of obstacles are conceivable. Mark Thomas embodies one: he is a repulsive youth with a pitted complexion and coarse features, dressed in a poorly fitting, white hospital gown, leaning back in his chair scratching his genitals, and explaining in a nearly stuporous manner how he determined he is God. That he honors the questioner with his presence and contributes more than mere answers to questions will become apparent only when a changed attitude opens the heart to the gaping pit of need he camps beside every day of his life.

Odors, moral indignation, ugliness, and repulsiveness are not the only obstacles to drawing near the other person for the purpose of revivifying and participating in his memory of the experience of God. The gripping fear which tenses the chest, sends the heart galloping, and injects the tingling legs with additional doses of adrenaline is another obstacle. When God speaks of you, but not for your own ears, this can be a delicate matter, especially when the person who receives the secret message is reputed to be murderous and assaultive, as were John and Luke. The problem is compounded when one has yet to secure full clarity about some point of conversation and is reluctant to withdraw. The tensed body of fear is a significant obstacle to research; the threat of being struck galvanizes the realization that fear is justified.

Madness is another obstacle closely linked to fear. It intrudes in a tangible way when one has achieved a new attitude. Madness comprises moods and somatic states which have nothing to do with nosological classifications. The latter are as arid little abstractions without apotropaic power; they provide little safety or help when one would draw near the other person for conversation about his most treasured and disturbing experience. Madness is tangible: it is the chilled pulsing of mercury through the tubules of the sympathetic nervous system, a transparent sheet of dry ice encasing the body, a fire projecting one centrifugally from the common ground, a fog dulling the vision, numbing awareness, and bemusing the funny bone.

Phenomenological research directed toward the extraordinary experience of such persons as figure in the present study requires a gate, or rather a series of gates, through which one may pass safely, ever drawing nearer. Some elements of theory are helpful, since they provide an organized format for questioning. But an attitude other than the ordinary is an additional requirement. One prefers to remain seated emotionally regardless of how gusty become the emotional surroundings.

In speaking of a new attitude, the intent is to raise the discussion of methodology to another level than the strictly conceptual. Psychological factors other than those typically associated with methodology are thus implicated. In the classical sense of the word, an attitudinal change is most certainly a matter of theory, although much modern psychological research has neglected the meaning of *theoria* due to an overemphasis on praxis and the securing of factual data at the expense of consideration of the range of psychological changes which could potentially be called into play during research. An analogy would be to state-dependent learning: the learned associations are formed given certain changes of consciousness and physiology, otherwise the effect is too subtle to discover, if not absent altogether. Similarly, experiences which serve as subject matter for this study are unavailable for investigation without an alteration of one's ordinary state of consciousness. To speak of a new attitude is to refer to a multi-faceted concept; its various facets refer to a series of steps which extend the understanding of theory beyond the customary limit of conceptualization and include changes in the consciousness of the researcher. The necessity of this kind of change is apparent from the disturbed, and thus altered, state of consciousness of the subjects of this research.

The new attitude involves a series of steps which occur in an orderly sequence. In its entirety, the new attitude extends from conversation through communication to the final, descriptive stage of research. This is not to say, however, that each step is required for successful research. For example, a requisite step for communication--the suspension of disbelief in the factual existence of the phenomena experienced during conversation--is necessary for neither conversation nor description. The factual data may be collected and description completed without communication. The practice of mindfulness, which will be presented shortly, has a different and more fundamental status, however. Mindfulness is basic to the new attitude in several ways. It involves a transformation of consciousness which is required for conversation, serves as foundational for communication, and is demanded once again during the descriptive stage of research. Such words as "foundational," "requisite," and "fundamental" are used in a psychological sense, not with meanings pertinent for logic only. Methodological reflection is not the mere placing of one step after another without careful consideration of the psychological interrelation of the various steps, thus, when a step is said to be fundamental, as was mindfulness, this means that all subsequent steps may occur only under the condition that mindfulness is already in place. In this sense, the entire presentation of methodology involves description of psychological states which are mutually implicated. Rigorous methodological reflection is a double-edged sword: it requires careful consideration of the unique psychological demands presented by the subject matter, and the creation of a methodological project marked with a systematic presentation of the relationship between the various psychological factors which permit the subject matter to appear.

Double Entry Bookkeeping

The practices of double entry bookkeeping and of mindfulness are the two steps of the attitudinal change required for conversation. Double entry bookkeeping is a metaphor of Minkowski's (1933/1970). He gave the term little attention despite attributing it with clinical significance. The meaning is readily apparent: for the self-aware clinician's inner, mental ledger, there are two kinds of entries: those which pertain to his experience of reality, and those which are discrepant and pertain to the disturbed patient's own idiosyncratic experience of what is real. The practice has several purposes, but all revolve around the spontaneous, moment-by-moment tracing of the reality contact of the patient. The idea of reality contact and the discernment of discrepant senses of reality make apparent that for double entry bookkeeping the distinction between normal and abnormal remains. It is very much operative in one's questioning and perception of the other person during conversation.

The weighing and checking of entries during double entry bookkeeping occur automatically; one is figuring at every moment of conversation and on many different levels. Attention is drawn frequently to the unusual nature of the patient's experience. Ordinary categories of experience may hardly be present for his world. Auditory and visual hallucinations may contribute to conclusions which are otherwise rationally unobtainable. Magical thinking may replace causal thinking because of the peculiar associative features of the words linked in thought. This points to the importance of language for understanding the other person's experience and world.

Scholars have investigated language in psychosis (Kasanin, 1944; Laffal, 1979; Oxman, Rosenberg, & Tucker, 1982), but those focusing on content analysis and reductionistic explanations are less helpful for the present research, especially in its descriptive phase, than those who attend specifically to the phonetic and generally poetic features of the language of disturbed persons. The transcription of a remarkable conversation between a psychotic patient and the French psychoanalyst Jacque Lacan makes vividly apparent the importance of phonetics for understanding the patient's world and language usage (Schneiderman, 1980). A single homophonous association may reveal far more than its apparent superficiality might suggest. But Freud (1960/1975g) knew of the structuring power of poetics in verbal parapraxis; Downing (1977) believes he showed more subtlety in this regard than either Jung or Boss. More recently, Kugler (1978, 1982) has extended theoretically the results of Jung's verbal association experiments to show that depth psychological interpretation of language may be based firmly on the immediate perceptual features of spoken and heard language, not only on semantic associations. While the latter are of central concern in conversation, when the experiential referents for the patient's words must be traced with care and diligence, the poetic functions of language in psychosis receive their due in those portraits in which language is used to elicit the reader's participation in the patient's world and entice him into experiencing word usage as would a psychotic patient. Alliteration, assonance, onomatopeia, and prosody are some of the poetic principles prominent in the language of the portraits, though synedoche, metonymy, analogy, hyperbole, and other principles with genuine semantic bearing are of importance also.

Mindfulness

Mindfulness is the remaining step of the attitudinal change required for conversation. Its importance for communication and description has already been mentioned. The word is a technical term of antique origin which figures prominently in Buddhist psychology (Conze, 1962; Guenther, 1976; Johansson, 1969). It refers to a practice of importance for meditation--a one-pointedness of attention which retains focus without clinging or binding to any given content of awareness passing through consciousness. Its status in the Buddhist tradition is reflected in its being called the seventh step of the eightfold path leading to eventual enlightenment and the third of the five chief virtues. The meaning of mindfulness varies somewhat, depending on the school and historical era in question as well as the particular range of phenomena which are made subject matter for mindful attention. Despite this variety, the word retains conceptual integrity.

Some introductory remarks are in order before presentation of its significance for the present research. Certain parallel practices in Western psychotherapy and psychotherapeutic training will be mentioned along with passing reference to two scholars who have linked ideas from phenomenological psychology or philosophy, on the one hand, with Eastern ideas on the other. Several physiological studies of the past two decades which pertain to mindful meditation will then conclude the prefatory remarks.

The psychosynthesis training of Assagioli (1971) bears a similarity to mindfulness. He speaks of a technique for training intuition, thus removing this cognitive ability from the haunts of mystery, radical spontaneity, and other notions which are associated ordinarily with so elusive a faculty. He recognizes that a willed mental passivity is necessary for training intuition as well as for the proper function of a trained intuition. He recognizes also that for those so inclined, intuition may evolve, such that its modes of presentation and the patterning responsible for presentation of intuited information develop with greater training. These are valuable insights which advance the understanding of intuition beyond Jung's (1971) conclusion that it is basically nonrational and necessarily spontaneous.

The Gestalt notion of present-centeredness is perhaps more discrepant from Buddhist mindfulness than the intuition of psychosynthesis, but it is close indeed to the meaning of mindfulness as used in the present research. Naranjo (1970) has made explicit reference to Eastern mindfulness; on this basis, he permits himself to speak of the therapeutic encounter in Gestalt therapy as "verbalized meditation." In doing so, he sets the practice of mindfulness in an interpersonal context--exactly as does the present research when referring to the importance of mindfulness for conversation. Naranjo (1970) borrows the term "presentification" from phenomenological philosophy and speaks of the purpose of Gestalt mindfulness as the presentifying of reality and fantasy. Once again, this parallels closely the relativization of time past and time present during conversation and points toward the more radical transformation of time consciousness during communication.

Neither Mohanty (1972) nor Price-Williams (1957), the one an Indian philosopher writing in English and the other an English linguistic philosopher, have written on mindfulness specifically, but their work does demonstrate the closeness of certain Indian ideas to those found in phenomenological philosophy and psychology. Mohanty's review is more powerful and sweeping in this regard because it progresses purely on a philosophical level. But Price-Williams's is more pertinent psychologically. He refers to Buddhaghosa's Visuddhimagga--a meditation manual and veritable textbook of required reading for those who would practice mindfulness with the aim of eventually achieving enlightenment--and shows how its underlying assumption of the impermanence of the ego is coherent psychologically with the meaning of the words "I" and "me." Despite the seeming abstraction of discussion on a level so abstract as that of the linguistic philosopher, Price-Williams's argument rests on close analysis of the experience of motor activity and body schema. He concludes that the source of personal identity is to be sought within the organism, and thus lays the ground implicitly for linking Merleau-Ponty's phenomenology of the body and my emphasis on bodily focus during conversation and communication with the Indian idea of the impermanence of the ego.

For the present study, the significance of physiological investigation of mindful meditation is more restricted than one might first suppose. The point is not to demonstrate on the supposedly sound basis of empirical, physiological research that there exists a phenomenon called mindfulness. This is taken for granted. Hundreds of years of empirical phenomenological research into this technique has been conducted in the Eastern world: the provincialism of some Western psychology need not keep one from accepting the ingenuousness and rigor of work carried out in other areas of the world. Furthermore, the physiological research tends not to study the phenomenon while taking into account the purposes and religious teachings which are its context. Mindfulness and meditation generally are thus seen in a foreshortening, distorted lens. An apt analogy would be to the art historian who spends yeears studying square inch fragments of Monet's canvasses: the result would be a book as incomplete as the miniaturized perspective he allowed himself while facing the enormous swirls of pond water. In mentioning several physiological studies, then, the point is simply to provide a broader orientation toward some similarities between mindfulness, meditation, and certain concepts from Western psychology.

Working from the assumption that the Zen meditative practice of _zazen_ is a form of mindfulness, one could conclude that mindfulness is neither a hypnotic state nor the kind of suspended animation found in Indian yogic meditation (Kasamatsu & Hirai, 1966; Nowlis & Kamiya, 1973;

Wallace & Benson, 1972). Blood work, readings of oxygen consumption, and electroencephalograph (EEG) tracings do seem to indicate that yoga, in at least some of its forms, is a state of relative suspended animation. Mindfulness differs in several respects. It brings about a reduced metabolic rate, as do yoga and sleep, but one retains, even heightens, his sensitivity to perceptual stimuli. EEG tracings also show that one does not habituate to such stimuli as rapidly as during these other states. It is as if the mind were exceedingly alert, but without the physiological concomitants of anxiety. Such a conclusion squares nicely with Eastern writings about the phenomenal aspects of mindfulness as well as the subsequent presentation of the experiences occurring during conversation and communication.

Prefatory remarks aside, the way is clear for closer consideration of the meaning of mindfulness for Eastern psychology and the present research. The word which "mindfulness" translates (Skt.: smr-ti; Pali: sati) is built from the root "to remember." A special kind of memory is in question, somewhat similar psychologically, I would think, but without the metaphysical implications or historical context of Neo-platonic recollection. One recollects or remembers himself during mindfulness, not in the sense of recalling past events, but rather as a deer relaxes in a sunny grove and simply listens. Mindfulness prevents ideas from floating away and fights forgetfulness, mental carelessness, and distraction. It keeps attention from latching onto one or another mental content at the expense of concentration, freedom of attention, and consciousness of psychological ordering principles which fade instantly from awareness when mindfulness breaks down.

Of the original purposes of mindfulness, the most important for the present study is the protection of inward calm from the distractions arising from sensory stimulation, the passions, and discursive thinking. The last of these--discursive thinking--is an insidious barrier to mindfulness in that it orders the contents of awareness according to principles which are not necessarily intrinsic to those contents. Causality, in the strict sense of the word, is such a principle. The scientifically inclined consciousness is occupied frequently with establishing causal sequences based on material factors which supposedly order themselves chronologically. A tacit assumption of such a project is a kind of numerical, summative notion of time. Behind this is another which holds space to be the infinite, empty expanse of Newtonian physics. The life-world of Straus's landscapes is thus transformed into a vacant, cold stage across which one marches, checking his watch at each step. Mindfulness reveals this not to be the case: Chronos does not rule the passage of time during all kinds of experience, nor is space necessarily like the checkered page of a geometrical design. There are discontinuities in the experience of time and gradations of relative timelessnees, just as there are sudden shifts of experiential landscape, such that a consuming fear, for example, enhances experience of gravity and lets the body fall from an invisible cliff.

One's experience during conversation and communication could not help but change when protected mindfully from distractions born of sensory stimulation, the passions, and such principles of discursive thinking as causality. Some features of this changed experience are considered in the remainder of the chapter. The influence of mindfulness extends to description as well; its power is reflected in the portraits, especially those of Mary, John, and Luke, since these show the linguistic changes which come about when the ordering principles common for ordinary consciousness have begun to dissipate. Poesy reigns, or at least some variety of language reliant less on formal logic than on principles more immediately apparent for mindful consciousness.

The salience of mindfulness for conversation is its suspension of one's initial response to those qualities and features of the other person which were disgusting, ugly, immoral, or in some way repellent. One is not emotionally chilled, however; the felt response remains, though with less intensity and thus less potential for disturbing questioning or distorting double entry bookkeeping. In this sense, mindfulness may be spoken of as a condition of abstraction. But the word is not used in the restricted sense of a capacity for conceptually based generalization at the expense of emotionally toned responsiveness. On the contrary, the kind of abstraction in question heightens emotional responsiveness, breaking down and refining the gross contours of one's initial disgust or revulsion. The crudeness of the initial response becomes a faceted state of emotional awareness. With the deepening of mindfulness, emotional response of a visceral nature, or what is ordinarily called "affect," is altered as well. This is a subtle move with bearing for the potential dangerousness of conversation. Fear may be a prominent obstacle during certain moments; the fear is based in fact when the other person has a history of assault or intent to kill. Under such conditions, one's bodily integrity is at stake; the presence of quivering affect is a consequence. The prudent questioner would resort to an ordinary attitude, abort the entire endeavor, and leave the room--so it would seem. Yet fear for one's life is a conditioned element of consciousness; it too may pass with mindfulness. Not that one stupidly jeopardizes his safety: since double entry bookkeeping is operative during conversation, there is the concurrent weighing and testing of hypotheses about the other person's behavior, thus one has reason to feel assurance over finally emerging without being choked or struck.

A change of awareness concerned specifically with the repellent quality of the other person's features may occur during conversation. His nose, hair, or some other feature moves from outside the horizon of consciousness to a point of focal awareness. A chiaroscuro of vague outlines and shadowy feelings is thus transformed into sharply defined shapes and readily apparent meanings. This change involves a shift from emotionally toned perception to an aesthetic sensibility. The aesthetic sensibility is of an abstract nature in that perception of form becomes particularly acute. Not only visual form is in question: olfactory breezes, gustatory shadings, the textures of imagined touching, and the rapidly patterned geometry of motoric gestures are more highly differentiated. In this way, mindful conversation refines sensory experience as well as altering the experience of feeling and affect.

An implication of the turn toward an aesthetic sensibility is its dictating an initial and reoccurring focus on the lived body of the patient during the descriptive phase of research. There is a continuity between conversation and description in this regard. Both are mindful procedures; and just as the aesthetic turn of conversation brings the other person's physiognomy within the horizon of consciousness, so the mindful recollection of conversation during description prompts remembrance of these same features. This is more the case with Paul and Mary than John and Luke. The portraits of Paul and Mary focus upon and circle around their features and movement. The latter elicit imaginative analogues and function as standards against which to judge the symbolic congruence of the analogue with the lived body. For John's and Luke's portraits, the work of extending imaginatively the body's meaning is given more importance. New landscapes emerge; the patient is situated within geographies and under skies different from those of ordinary life. Occasionally the fulcrum which balances the lived body of conversation with the imaginative analogues of description shifts, such that the weight of a portrait falls purely on an imaginative landscape, its mythological inhabitants, and other elements which do not belong to the patient's ordinary life. This is world-building on a level more mythopoeic than physiognomic. A stylistic difference between the portraits of Paul and Mary, on the one hand, and those of John and Luke, on the other, follows from this shift in emphasis. The development of Paul's and Mary's portraits has more the design of one spiral upon another, with each spiral centered upon a feature or movement of the lived body. In comparison, the development of John's and Luke's portraits is freer in form, more expressionistic, and held together through the appearance and reappearance of *leitmotifs* which pertain more to mood and concept than perceptual elements of the patient's physiognomy.

The turn toward an aesthetic sensibility links this research with that of other phenomenologists who have recognized the importance of the lived body for interpersonal exchange and for understanding the meaning of embodied existence. Merleau-Ponty (1942/1963; 1945/1962), for example, has distinguished the lived body from the body which is studied anatomically. While the latter is a physical organism with mechanistic properties not unlike those of machines and parahuman organisms, the former is an ambiguous reality, neither matter nor spirit, which is responsible for the dissemination of all meaning, regardless of its epistemological level. In this sense, the lived body is not only the historically conditioned and concretely situated reference point for experience of the external world, but is also the self-transcending force which ever and again breaks its tegumentary confinement and extends forward in time and space to what is other than itself. The present research shares certain aspects of this conceptualization of the lived body and outlines a method for their realization during conversation and communication. For example, the body which is conceptualized as the generative core of meaning may be experienced during conversation, and especially communication, in this way: as questioning uncovers the intrapsychic complexity of the experience of God through probing for the specific content of its ideational, emotional, and sensory forms, one experiences the lived body of the other person as perfectly congruent with this content. A quivering of Mary's shoulders is known to be of the same essence as her flirtatiousness toward God; John's strange, angular gait is of the same essence as his rigid, unbending attitude upon hearing God talking with thunder; the constricted, wheezing breath of Luke is of the same essence as the crushing guilt he expresses when God commands him to stop talking. To speak metaphorically, the forms of intrapsychic complexity which pertain to the experience of God are experienced as nestling snugly around the patient's lived body; they reciprocate and at times are the consequence of his embodied presence.

Research may proceed, and portraits be composed, on the basis of conversation alone. Holding in mind the general outline of the experience of God, the logical principles, and exercising the ability to formulate questions on their basis during mindfulness, one may secure all the information needed for later description. Memories are retained and recalled with unusual facility; mindfulness contributes to this clarity. When memory falters or draws a blank, these lacunae may be filled or recognized by reference to the audio recordings, the narratives, case histories, and the transcriptions. But research may proceed past conversation to communication. Double entry bookkeeping is then put away, questions of normalcy and abnormality are replaced with questions of the ordinary and extraordinary, and even the latter dissipate as matters of concern.

Communication

The transition from conversation to communication is precipitated by a suspension of disbelief in the factual existence of the phenomena experienced during conversation. The change may be the intended result of a decision; or it may be unwitting, in which case the change occurs without preplanning. In neither case, however, is it the inevitable consequence of one's own behavior and psychological condition. For another person is involved, necessarily so, and this second party is as integral a contributor to communication as oneself. The means of stepping from conversation to communication is analogous to Husserl's "psychological reduction" though more restricted in the scope of its application. A presentation of the Husserlian procedents for the suspension of disbelief may be restricted as well, since an historical review directed toward Husserl's understanding of the epoche' and the various reductions would lead too far afield and not prove particularly helpful in setting out what is meant when referring to a suspension of disbelief. Some secondary references, not necessarily in their order of reliability, would be: Lauer (1958/1965), who discerns six forms of reduction in Husserl's work; Brand (1967), who has set the reductions in the broader context of a consideration of intentional analysis; Kockelmans (1967), whose article is relatively more comprehensive in terms of situating the reductions within the entire Husserlian project; and Spiegelberg (1982), whose revised history of phenomenological philosophy includes a section which attempts to delineate the elements common to several authors' understanding of the reductions. For distinguishing the psychological from the transcendental reduction, and determining the assertions legitimate for each, Scanlon's (1972) article is particularly helpful.

A second and less important source for the idea of a suspension of disbelief is Husserl's own source for the term epoche'--the Greek Sceptic Pyrrho (Patrick, 1929). Husserl's concern was not to revitalize antique Greek ideas but to choose a term suggestive of the purposeful withholding of judgment regarding the truthfulness of philosophical and common sense assertions about the nature of reality. The goal was not utterly discrepant from Pyrrho, who described a general psychological condition marked not only by a suspension of judgment as to the adequacy of any truth claim based upon sensory perception, but with the additional marks of *adiaphoria* and *ataraxia*. The latter refers to a state of emotional tranquility while *adiaphoria* ("it means the same to me") has to do more with an intellectual neutrality. The neutrality in question is a special kind: as with Pyrrho's *epoché*, or suspension of judgment, *adiaphoria* refers to an indifference toward the relative veracity of sensory perceptions in representing the nature of reality. Given certain emendations, *adiaphoria* describes nicely the attitude born of the suspension of disbelief in the factual existence of the phenomena experienced during conversation. The emendations may be summarized in this fashion: rather than sensory perception only, the suspension of disbelief involves both sensory perception and imaginative experience. In general, the idea of a suspension of disbelief is situated midway between the Sceptic position and the Husserlian: it attempts to recover the broad psychological bearing of the former position while retaining the intellectual significance of the latter.

When disbelief is suspended, double entry bookkeeping dissipates, since the determinative influence of linearly oriented perception and causal thinking grows weak. The latter are means of situating oneself in the ordinary world. When their influence weakens, the horizon which circumscribes the world as ordinarily known shifts and grows wider. The border demarcating ordinary from extraordinary experience all but disappears. Double entry bookkeeping becomes an uncertain procedure with even a little movement in this direction.

Conclusions based on its application are not absolute.

This is not to say chaos reigns once the determinative influence of causal thinking and linearly oriented perception is weakened. In its place is substituted another principle of organization associated with the intrapsychic complexity of experience. Complexity of this nature is experienced during conversation as a clustering of psychic contents, each of which pertains to one of the psychological forms of idea, emotion, or sensation. This clustering is not fundamentally a sequential process, though it would seem so because the analysis of intrapsychic complexity requires the uncovering of conscious contents in a sequential manner. In this sense, the sequential appearance of clustering is an artifact of the analysis of intrapsychic complexity rather than an essential feature of experience. With the suspension of disbelief, however, the analytic process is inactive, a more passive condition of consciousness having taken its place. As a consequence the contemporaneous clustering of conscious material extends beyond the cross-sectional analysis of clustering for specific experiences: it extends throughout the temporal continuum. The result is a disruption in the stability and undirectional nature of the temporal continuum. Events narrated by the other communicant, as well as the events occurring in the immediate present, are not ordered according to a chronological sequence as with the ordinary experience of duration. There is instead a concatenation of various events--an unfolding organized in terms of emotional salience, the vividness of sensing, or some other magnetic core of experience. The possibility opens of becoming conscious of the assembling, the dissipation, and the reassembling of an array of events reported by the other communicant. A metaphor borrowed from Sartre's Nausea (1938/1964) is apropos: the objects of consciousness may be experienced as drifting into existence, and exiting on winds as uncertain as those which carried them initially. An analogy more pertinent for psychological research would be from the Abhidharma psychology of Hinayana Buddhism, for which a given object of consciousness lacks both permanent substance and an integral structure. Upon realizing this, an object is experienced as a temporary concatenation of elementary conscious contents, each contributed by one of the several forms of consciousness.

The broadened range of experience precipitated by the suspension of disbelief encompasses other changes. Experience becomes more variegated in terms of the kinds of objects to which consciousness attends and the modes of awareness available to consciousness. For example, imagined objects have more potency than ordinarily, whether proffered by the other communicant during his verbal report or arising spontaneously for the one who has suspended disbelief. Regardless of the degree of the other communicant's disturbance, his reported experience is more accessible in that one has enhanced capacity to imagine the sensory features of what he describes. One may also indulge in an unusual form of hypothesis testing, inquiring in such a way as to determine the congruence of one's own imaginative imagery with that of the other communicant.

Another implication of the suspension of disbelief has direct bearing on the question of God's presence during communication. To see this requires more extended reflection upon the impact of the suspension for the experience of temporal duration. The stability and the unidirectional nature of the temporal continuum fail with the suspension of disbelief. Consequently, the experience of time past, as opposed to experience of the present, is barely apparent. Past events reported by the other person hover in the present. His gestures, the tone of his speaking, and other features of his corporeal existence are present concurrently with the events he narrates--events which would be experienced as belonging to the past under ordinary circumstances. But these events are now experienced as present. This opens the possibility for one to experience, in the present and with the other person, those events which previously seemed to belong to a private and irrecoverable past. Experience of that to which the other person refers when speaking of God is not excluded. It remains a vivid possibility, the most powerful and esoteric of the many which present themselves with the attainment of communication.

Description

The descriptive process is composed of six steps and may be likened to ascending a spiral staircase. Step by step one mounts to the fourth. A rearward glance reveals the preceding three; they remain in view. A leap is required to arrive at the fifth, and by this time one will have turned the final spiral and thus left behind the possibility of viewing the first and second. One comes to the platform of the sixth step without effort, the chief difficulty having been to step initially onto the fifth.

The analogy may be extended with the addition of an interpersonal context. Pretend an exceptional conversation has taken place; it glimmers in one's memory yet remains distant. One remembers more of the conversation and of the other person upon stepping from the first to the second, and from the second to the third step. The very words of conversation are vividly present upon arriving at the fourth step; the aura of distant memory born of earlier steps fades. A desire to recover the experience of this other person and his experience of God is present. With one's feet upon the fifth step, this desire is no longer simply a desire: the other person is present again; he is re-presented in the imaginative context of a world built from his lived body and his religious experience. One all but glides from the fifth to the sixth step. There upon the top platform of the sixth step awaits the other person. He has been calling all along; one's desire to recover an earlier conversation was his drawing, his pulling, his informing one's effort to recover his presence.

The actual steps of the descriptive process may now be linked with those of the analogy. The first four steps of description include the factual data and the psychological activities responsible for gathering, generating, and organizing these data. These data and their respective psychological dispositions are ranked in value depending upon their psychological proximity to the earlier conversation with the patient. A hierarchy of factual data is apparent as a consequence; it ranges from the case history, the transcription of conversation, and the narrative of the experience of God to the audio recording of conversation. Ranked above this hierarchy are the two remaining steps of description: the recollection of conversation and communication and the wording of recollection during the creation of the patient's portrait. The remainder of the chapter is organized in accordance with these three divisions. The first gives detailed consideration to the hierarchy of factual data; the second presents the technique of recollection entitled "imaginative analogy"; and the third concludes the chapter with a poetic reflection upon the practice of creating portraiture.

A Hierarchy of Factual Data

The factual data may be considered as residue of one's previous contact with the patient. To extend the analogy, let the residue be receding pools of dross formed from the refining process which was one's actual conversation with the patient. The further circles have cooled and retain little of the original experience, the nearer pools remain warm and thus provide more accurate information about the special intersubjective event entitled "conversation."

The case history. The range of one's contact with the patient extends beyond sitting face-to-face and conversing: it includes perusal of the medical record and the construction of a case history on the basis of information gathered from the record. The patient is not required for this lowest step of the factual hierarchy, and the general psychological disposition necessary for reading the medical record and constructing the history is different from that required for activities conducted on higher levels. For example, to understand the record requires knowledge of psychodiagnosis, of the customary format of the medical record, perhaps something of the legal ramifications of brief hospitalization, and a little of psychopharmacology and proper dosage ranges. Such knowledge is conceptual, highly verbal, systematic in the manner it was learned and cognitively stored; more importantly, it is born of a fundamentally objectifying view of the patient, and draws its validity and persuasiveness from a massive social network reaching far beyond the psychiatric ward and infiltrating the federal courthouse. Szasz (1970) has developed the latter point with erudition and unsettling effect; the former point, that the psychological activity belonging to this lowest level of factual data is restricted to relatively abstract verbal-conceptual knowing, is meant to supplement Szasz's and thus further accentuate the difference between the activities and data of the lowest step and those of higher steps. True, the elements drawn from the medical record are basic: they provide a history, albeit constructed from chronological rather than lived time, and as viewed by others rather than the patient. But regardless of their quantity, these elements are insufficient and provide inadequate leverage for developing a picture of the patient's experience on the basis of factual data.

The value of the case history is considerable, however. It serves as a kind of reality-based counterpoint for information ascertained through other means. For example, Luke's case history remarks upon his standing motionless in a hallway at home for days before his first admission. Seemingly this was a catatonic episode, and so it remains for the history. But the narrative of his experience of God discloses the actual intent of his rooting himself in the dimly lit hallway: he was awaiting Jesus' wink from the painting hanging on the wall opposite the living room door. Even this might seem a mere trifle--

another psychotic oddity. But Luke's portrait enables one to step beyond the levels of factual data altogether and see that this wink signalled the explosion of his madness--the complete and final initiation into the world of hallucinated religiosity.

Another value of the case history is its providing a wealth of clinical information able to serve as a data base for additional research. This is the minimal legitimate goal for phenomenological research--to simply gather and assemble information on the basis of fresh categories. Once the data are assembled, interesting discrepancies become apparent that might not have otherwise. For example, Mary's history shows that her case is unique in the series due to the probable medical complications of recurrent episodes of hypertensive encephalopathy secondary to a stenosis of the right renal artery. The narrative allows one to see that Mary's experiences of God are also unique because of the strong affective component of her most powerful experience. The only other patient with a comparable affective experience is Sarah, whose history gives evidence supportive of an affective diagnosis. The neuropsychologist who recalls that non-dominant hemisphere dysfunction has been associated with affectively disordered psychotic patients and dominant hemisphere dysfunction with patients diagnosed as Mary (Flor-Henry, 1979; Gruzelier, 1979; Gruzelier & Hammond, 1976; Magaro, 1981; Newlin, Carpenter, & Golden, 1981) would then have reason to hypothesize that there are at least two basic neuropsychological patterns of God-experience--one, right dominant, the other, left dominant. With such a hypothesis based on comparison of Sarah, Mary, and the remaining patients of Mary's series, the speculative groundwork is laid for a new branch of the psychology of religion: the neuropsychology of the experience of God.

Ordinarily the tendency would be to determine the neuropsychological specificity of one or another kind of God-experience on the basis of psychopathological diagnosis. The development of the preceding paragraph is guided largely by such a tendency. But this may reflect a clinical bias marked by insufficient emphasis on the phenomenological integrity of the experience of God. That such a bias may, in fact, be a bias is reflected in the only empirical data of which I am aware having to do with God-experience, neuropsychology, and psychopathological diagnosis (Goldstein, 1979). The evidence is drawn from an electroencephalographic (EEG) study with a chronic mental patient given the same diagnosis as Mary. While attached to the EEG, this patient's record showed a sudden right hemisphere power shift above the right-left baseline mean. When questioned as to her thoughts, she said she had begun thinking of God at just that moment. Here, then, is a patient diagnosed as Mary, but without the medical complications which seemingly conduce to right dominant God-experience in patients of this diagnosis; yet this patient shows a right dominant shift, as Mary and Sarah are supposed to have undergone. A working assumption would be that Mary's experience of God is like Sarah's not because of a missed diagnosis for Mary due to underemphasizing the affective component of her psychiatric disorder, but simply because Mary's medical complications predisposed toward the kind of God-experience which happens to be found more often with affectively disordered persons than those diagnosed as Mary. Such an assumption preserves the phenomenological integrity of the experience of God and would protect research from a clinical bias which might prove uninstructive. That such a bias is unwarranted in this case is supported by Goldstein's (1979) conclusion that hemispheric EEG power shifts do not arise only from stimuli differences (verbal versus non-verbal), and more importantly, by Gruzelier's (1979) conclusion that neither of the major forms of psychosis can be associated with simple hemispheric differences in arousal.

The transcript of conversation. The transcript of conversation occupies the next level of the hierarchy of factual data. One might suppose it belongs higher since it seems to approximate more closely the actual conversation. Yet its proximity rests only on the conceptual uniformity of the semantic value of the typed words of the transcript and the semantic value of the words spoken during conversation. An array of psychological and neuropsychological factors remain absent (Hecaen & Albert, 1978). The transcript is not heard, nor does it speak: its perception relies upon patterns of cortical dominance and their respective cognitive modes which differ from those required for listening to another person while attending to his lips and studying his face. The emotional undertones of conversation are also absent from the transcripts; if they become present, it is as an addendum added after conversation and by someone different, or at least in a different mood, than the one who originally conversed with the patient. And whether it be a new reader or the one who originally conversed with the patient, in neither case are there vocal intonations and gradations of volume required for an ongoing check and correction of the accuracy of one's interpretation of the original emotional tone. For that matter, the conceptual uniformity of the transcript and the actual conversation may itself become problematic because both the creation and the reading of a portrait require adopting a psychological disposition marked more strongly by intuition and emotion than by intellect.

The methodological formulations and praxis of much American phenomenological psychology remains saddled with the problems inherent to this level of factual data. The platform represented by Giorgi (1970, 1975), exemplified in the early days of Duquesnean research by Colaizzi (1948/1973, 1978) and Van Kaam (1966), and promoted more recently by the South African Kruger (1981), is a case in point. Ordinarily this approach relies on transcripts of discussion between the investigator and the research subject; the discussion may be guided by a preestablished protocol, although in some cases the need for actually talking with the subject is obviated by having him write answers to a standardized questionnaire. A so-called thematic analysis is then applied to the transcript or questionnaire. Needless to say, the data of this approach are heavily conceptual and their utilization is likewise based on a psychological disposition marked predominantly by verbal-conceptual knowing. Indirect evidence for this is found in how neatly Koestenbaum (1971, pp. 460 ff.) was able to outline the logic of an inductive, thematic-type phenomenological approach while complementing it with imaginative introspection in a psychological research method more comprehensive than that of the Duquesnean school.

For this approach, the choice of themes is not arbitrary, but neither does it grow from a preliminary phenomenological investigation, as would be expected for an analysis which intends to retain the suspiciously atomistic notion of themes while remaining phenomenological. Once selected, the themes are said to be used in an inductive fashion, the more generally applicable ones being constructed on the basis of those more concrete. The sequential complexity of the experience serving as subject matter is lost easily under these conditions, although its recovery is often attempted in the conclusive descriptions offered as the final product of this kind of research.

Perhaps the major oversight of this approach involves the frequent claim to have investigated the original experience of its subjects. The philosophical and psychological implications of such a claim are not treated with the rigor they deserve. A convoluted chain, difficult to unravel, ties the original experience of the subject to the written protocol; its links belong to different times, different kinds of times, to different moods and spaces, to different neuropsychological patterning. Not all such places and times are amenable to thematic analysis. Titelman (1976b) has tried to circumvent indirectly such problems with his suggestion that the written transcript be considered a "text" demanding a hermeneutical reading _à la_ Ricoeur. The original experience of the subject may indeed be approached in this manner, but considerable distance remains. Sardello (1975) has spoken of hermeneutical reading, too, but on grounds more legitimate in that he appeals for reading the "classic texts" of psychology in this manner and does not imply that the author's original experience is thus made available.

The spectre of German Structuralism, maligned by Behaviorists and said by some to hover over Pittsburgh, is far distant from a new development in American phenomenological psychology. It makes for strange bedfellows when some of this newer work is published alongside the older in the several volumes devoted to Duquesnean phenomenological psychology. Jager (1971, 1976) is an important spokesman for this new trend; his essay on Dionysos is an archetypal *tour de force*; his study of the meaning of horizontality and verticality is an exploration of lived space ranking beside those of Straus. Lingis's (1976) study of the experience of anxiety is of a similarly high quality, though more existentially oriented, and something similar may be said for Arcaya's (1979) study of fear and Keen's (1975) brief introduction to phenomenological psychology. The present reseach claims an American kinship with work of this nature and would also appeal to a methodological rigorousness displayed in an exemplary manner in the phenomenological psychology of another American--Don Ihde (1976, 1979).

The narrative of the experience of God. The narrative and its construction constitute the data and the psychological activity of the penultimate level of the factual heirarchy. The intent of the narrative is to show in detail the sequential and intrapsychic complexity of the experience of God while retaining as much as possible the patient's own words. The narrative's clarity is not a measure of the patient's nor is its exactitude indicative of the coherence of conversation. These patients are mad, sometimes incoherent, at times hallucinating, as was John toward the end of conversation. Consequently, the construction of the narrative requires diligent concentration on the audio recording as well as having conducted successful conversation.

Having committed to memory salient portions of the recording, one is able to assemble them in print, always prepared to verify one's supposition as to intrapsychic and sequential complexity by returning to the recording. The result is a reference from which to draw quotations for the portrait and a reliable record of sequential complexity from which the portrait is not allowed to deviate. The narrative may also be used as a data base for later research focusing on features of the God-experience not of central concern for the present study.

The kind of description which Jaspers (1913/1963) and Straus (1948) called phenomenological psychopathology belongs to this level of the factual hierarchy; Van Dusen's (1961) case study would, too, although his work rests somewhat higher because it has fewer marks of what Laing (1963) called "clinicism" and displays more attention to the intersubjective dimension of description. But for the present research, the data of this level are not phenomenological and their arrangement in the narrative is not the doing of phenomenology. This is simply careful detective work guided by the basic principles of sequential and intrapsychic complexity. Just as the detective relies on the dispassionate collection of clues for piecing together the events of a crime antedating his careful hunt, so the construction of the narrative progresses dispassionately and with as little imaginative and emotional involvement as possible on the part of the one conducting research.

<u>The audio recording of conversation</u>. The audio recording is the epitome of factual data because it approximates the actual conversation

more closely than the data of other levels. To say "it approximates the conversation" is not to establish an analogy between conversation and the experience of the recording, as if the two were distinct and clearly differentiated experiences, nor is it to suggest a similarity without extensive psychological and neuropsychological likenesses. The experience of the recording taps the same neuropsychological patterns as those dominant for conversation and establishes the same data base utilized for questioning during conversation. For these reasons, it is prerequisite for recollection and the wording of the portrait. The food upon which recollection feeds, the stimuli upon which it relies--its being galvanized into action--all depend on the experience of the recording. Recollection supplements the process of revivifying the patient's presence begun with the experience of the recording, and it re-situates his renewed presence in a dimension of intersubjectivity which is in continuity with the earlier intersubjective experience of conversation. But the revivification of the patient's presence is impossible without the establishment of a data base and the piquing of neuropsychological activity congruent with the original conversation. Living with the recording, coming to know it, and through it, the patient, are thus prerequisite for recollection and portraiture.

Consider the proximity of conversation to the experience of the recording. Originally one listened to the patient; now one listens to the recording. One questioned the patient and heard his words; now one hears himself question the patient and has opportunity to re-question him. One saw the patient while speaking and listening; one may now imagine the patient while listening and re-questioning. One felt a certain way upon conversing and noticed the patient's emotional response to this feeling; the same is apparent again, but amplified by newer feelings. A mood was set originally by the banging and rustling sounds of the hospital ward; the mood re-asserts itself because the same sounds are present. Even the odor of smoke becomes apparent when one hears a cigarette snuffed out in a cheap, tin ashtray. Silences were ominous or fraught with meaning originally; they are known a second time because the steady tempo of the recording allows an emotional re-creation of such features of lived time. Gradations of volume, subtle defects of articulation, nuances of intonation--all are apparent again. The texture and hardness of one's chair is not an exception: one shifted in his seat--it is heard--and thus the chair is known as yet another feature of an event lingering in memory but drawing closer moment by moment.

Recollection of Conversation and Communication

The fifth step of description is the recollection of conversation and communication. The depth or frequency of one's previous communication is not particularly important for recollection, since it presses for renewed communication and sustains this intent with varying degrees of success regardless of the nature of one's previous communication. Recollection is the first step of description which may be called phenomenological in that none of the preceding transcend the objective stance required for collecting and understanding the factual data. The word "recollection" is meant to carry a significance which extends beyond commonly held notions of memory and the measurement of its accuracy in terms of objectivity. The first section of the presentation of recollection critiques such notions on neuropsychological and physiopsychological grounds, then offers a phenomenological understanding of memory which more closely approximates the meaning of recollection for the present research. The second section introduces the technique of recollection entitled "imaginative analogy" and mentions several other techniques which bear some resemblance: psychoanalytic free association and the techniques of amplification and active imagination from the analytical psychology of C. G. Jung. The final section of the presentation of recollection is lengthier and tied more closely to phenomenological concerns *per se*. This section compares and contrasts imaginative analogy with the technique of Husserlian transcendental phenomenology entitled "fancy." The conclusion of this final section introduces one of the most important elements of the entire methodological reflection: the experience of the ambivalent or "bi-vocal" nature of intersubjective involvement guided by imaginative analogy.

Recollection and memory. For the common sense perspective, objectivity is customarily considered a chief mark of sound memory and accurate recall. The associative-behavioristic view of memory is allied with this perspective, much less so the Gestalt and information-processing views (Ellis & Hunt, 1977). The veracity of such an assumption is questionable, however, and may be critiqued on neuropsychological and physiopsychological grounds as well as phenomenological. From the peripheral sensory receptors to Luria's primary zones of the central nervous system for receptive processing (Luria, 1973), memory is characterized by selectivity. The same is true *a fortiori* for the secondary and tertiary zones of all sensory modalities. A possible exception would be for echoic and iconic memory; perhaps also for a tactile trace memory, should such a mechanism be discovered (Russell, 1981). These first memory registers for sensory information are extraordinarily brief; their material is almost completely unprocessed by the brain. Only with short-term memory is such material organized in a fashion accessible to consciousness and congruent with consciously attainable schemes. But my opinion is that even these trace memories are highly selective. Ratliff and Hartline's (Ratliff & Hartline, 1959; Ratliff, Miller, & Hartline, 1958; Schneider & Torshis, 1975) discovery of image-sharpening mechanisms at the retinal level of the horseshoe crab points in this direction, as does Kuffler's (1952, 1953) and Lettvin's (Lettvin, Maturana, McCulloch, & Pitts, 1959, 1961) discovery of stimulus-specific coding mechanisms in the optic nerve of the frog. Given the presence of selectivity at so fundamental a level, the question of objectivity looms with special force.

The meaning of "objectivity" and its serving as an unquestionable criterion for the accuracy of memory may be a matter of "begging the question," as the logician says, since both are felt to be beyond rational reproach when in fact they are unverifiable presuppositions. The philosophical ground upon which they rest is ascertained without difficulty: the bifurcation of experience born of Cartesian dualism and the *tabula rasa* conception of subjectivity promoted with British empiricism form the base without which the commonly understood notion of an objective memory would collapse. But this is not to say anything new: what is interesting and novel is that such a critique is suggested and, to some degree, supported by data born of the scientific approach which holds to the veracity of the idea of objectivity. This gives an eery feeling, as if one were chopping down a tree without recognizing that his seat is a branch suspended high in the air.

The recollection of conversation and communication does not appeal to commonly held notions of memory and the marks of its objectivity. To do so would embed recollection in the very problems which the neuropsychological and physiopsychological critique of memory have uncovered. Recollection has little to do with recovering exact sensory images of conversation; consequently, its accuracy is unable to be measured in terms of varying degrees of objectivity. Recollection is not to search in a dusty drawer for a photograph or a recording of a casual get-together. Remote memory has only the faintest relevance. But most important for establishing the difference between recollection and commonly held notions of objectivity and memory is that the recollected material eluded, and continues to elude, the objective stance for which conversation or communication would be simply another item set alongside an apple, a number, a body, or some other kind of object. Conversation and communication are intersubjective events: they are not objects. The human mind could be a *tabula rasa*--a pure sheet awaiting the pristine imprint of unadulterated sensory stimuli; and human nature could be a bifurcated reality, its thinking and extensible substances running parallel without the twain meeting: but neither conception, nor the two together, would provide adequate grounds for an understanding of these kinds of experience and their recollection.

To what kind of memory, then, and to what standards, does recollection appeal? Straus (1960, 1964, 1970; Marsh, 1976) provides guidance initially with his suggestion that a past memory is in fact present--present to consciousness. This insight promotes awareness of how the experience of memory as the remembering-of-the-past is better described as the awareness of a present reality which refers to a past one. But the past event, whatever it might have been, was and remains irretrievable in an objective sense; and even that which one is supposed to have known, and to which one now refers in speaking of the past, is also irretrievable--irretrievable in the sense of recovering the past-as-past and situating it in just this sense within present awareness. What could "memory" mean given this state of affairs? Memory, so it would seem, is simply one of several temporal categories which describe the immediate experience of conscious awareness. Memory is a feature of present-consciousness, in other words; or, since consciousness is necessarily a present reality, the same may be said like so: memory is a consciousness of presence.

Such a conception of memory allows one to conceive of recollection as the re-presentation or "re-presencing" of conversation and communication, or as the resumption of a conversation which was adjourned temporarily due to practical considerations. The factual basis of the newer conversation and communication is the same as with the original experience in that the hierarchy of factual data provides the stimuli and the format of sequential and intrapsychic complexity upon which to concentrate. Such a conception also allows for using a standard other than objectivity for the determination of the accuracy of recollection. One may speak of gradations of memory ranging from less to greater intensity of presence: the remembered item of the original conversation which retains its distance from the hot core of lucid presence, as if it were spied at the other end of a dim tunnel, is remembered more poorly than the item which gorges consciousness with its immediacy. On the other hand, the remembered item which is raised to the level of lucid presence is well remembered; and furthermore, it may provide the stimulus which confronts one with the possibility of communication for the first time. In this manner, recollection is not only the resumption of conversation, but the opportunity for raising conversation to the level of communication.

Methodological coherence demands that recollection progress under the same psychological conditions as did conversation and communication. Were it otherwise, recollection could not evoke the patient's presence or re-present conversation and communication. Mindfulness is thus prerequisite for recollection, as it was for conversation and communication; and by the same token, those emotional and perceptual conditions precipitated by mindfulness during one's earlier contact with the patient are operative again during recollection. What was said much earlier of mindfulness could be reiterated now.

The widened horizon of consciousness attainable for mindful recollection shimmers with possibilities; the present research directs its attention toward one of them: the presentation and sharing of another person's experience of God, and the creation of a possible world with which this experience is congruent.

Imaginative analogy. Imagination may awaken to the patient, and the vaguely outlined presence of his world be brought to fruition, through the application of imaginative analogy to the factual data. The technique bears resemblance to psychoanalytic free association--a procedure mentioned first, though without this title, in "Interpretation of Dreams" (Freud, 1953/1975c). It next appears and comes within its own in the essay "On Beginning the Treatment" (Freud, 1958/1975f). It is accorded the status of "the fundamental rule of psycho-analysis" in the latter essay (Freud, 1958/1975f, p. 134). The importance of the analyst himself enacting free association is implied, for Freud speaks of "giving himself over to the current of his unconscious thoughts" as well as advising the patient to become as "a traveller sitting next to the window of a railway carriage and describing . . . the changing views you see outside. . . . [without forgetting] to be absolutely honest, and never to leave anything out because . . . it is unpleasant to tell" (Freud, 1958/1975f, pp. 134 f.). The "rule" appears in "The Dynamics of the Transference" (Freud, 1958/1975b) and elsewhere, and is later given the title of "free association."

The experience of imaginative analogy may bear a resemblance to that of free association, but this is not to say the theoretical underpinnings and the purposes of the two techniques are similar. Imaginative analogy progresses without the steamer trunks of psychoanalytic doctrine normally carried when one practices free association as an analytically oriented psychotherapist or during moments of analytically inclined self-analysis. The interpretive stance of the classical psychoanalytic orientation toward genetic etiology is anathema for the practice of imaginative analogy. There is hardly a better way to truncate recollection.

Imaginative analogy is more closely related to the techniques of analytical psychology entitled "active imagination" (Jung, 1960/1969b, pars. 166-175; Jung, 1963/1970, pars. 752-5) and "amplification" (Jung, 1960/1969d, pars. 403 f.; 1953/1966, par. 122 & nt.; 1953/1968b, par. 403; 1975, pars. 173f.). While free association grazes the psychopathological complex, embodying it partially with personal historical imagery, some of which may bear the marks of such defensive measures as displacement, active imagination is directional. It is a funneling downward toward the more impersonal archetypal structures responsible for patterning the psychopathological contents. It not only guides consciousness in an autonomous manner, but tends toward a goal which is intrinsic to one's engagement with the imagery. In this sense, it is not mere observation, as if one were "sitting next to the window of a railway carriage and describing . . . the changing views" (Freud, 1958/1975f, pp. 134 f.). Active imagination may cross over to the process of amplification, though the latter is customarily utilized in isolation. In comparison with active imagination, amplification is more nearly an intentional procedure; one draws purposely on a wide scope of erudition with the aim of seeking parallels for a given image from the domains of mythology, legend, *belle lettres*, and the arts. The general purpose of amplification is to ascertain the archetypal influence responsible for patterning both the image and its amplification.

Just as one's voyage is slowed and monotonous when burdened with trunks of psychoanalytic doctrine, the baggage incurred when travelling the orthodox Jungian route may also become heavy. But much is to be retained--for example: the special epistemological status accorded imagination; the emphasis given mythology and assorted material from the humanities which might otherwise be viewed as merely the result of sublimation; the nonreductionistic stance toward symbolic presence; the correlation between <u>psyche</u> and <u>physis</u> in synchronistic phenomena; the relative a-temporality of a collective psyche; and the theoretical bridges between a collective psyche and religious experience. And yet the press for immediacy and presence at every stage of this research restricts the use made of an interpretive system. Techniques borrowed from such a system may be used--this being the case with active imagination and amplification; but certain other aspects of the system may not--this being the case with the Jungian effort to ascertain and define archetypal structures or reduce psychological phenomena to archetypal factors in a causal manner. Coining the term "imaginative analogy" serves two functions in this respect: it distinguishes the technique from the theoretical underpinnings and the interpretive function of the procedures of active imagination and amplification, yet shows, with the word "imaginative" specifically, the close similarity between the actual experience of these procedures and imaginative analogy.

<u>Eidetic intuition and the "bi-vocal" nature of portraiture</u>. The purpose and experience of imaginative analogy attain greater clarity when compared with the technique of transcendental phenomenology entitled "fancy." For that matter, imaginative analogy may be considered a species of a more general class bearing this name. Their

purposes vary, however, and in certain respects are at odds. For comparing and contrasting their respective purposes, it is unnecessary to trace the history of Husserl's use of the term fancy or examine the different shades of meaning given the related, if not identical, operations of "ideation" and "variation." Nor is it necessary to examine closely the differences between fancy and sensory perception or the modes of presentation pertinent for each. The English translation of Husserl's *Ideas* (1913/1975) is the chief source for the understanding of fancy drawn upon for this penultimate section of the presentation of description.

Fancy holds a privileged position in transcendental phenomenology. In this respect, it is somewhat analogous to the *via regia* of dream interpretation for early psychoanalysis. For those unfamiliar with Husserl's overall project during this stage of his research, certain sayings about fancy are rather dark. Not the least provocative of them asserts the special status of fancies for eidetic intuition in the following manner:

> There are reasons why, in phenomenology as in all eidetic sciences, representations, or, to speak more accurately, free fancies, assume a privileged position over against perceptions, and that even in the phenomenology of perception itself, excepting of course that of the sensory data. (Husserl, 1913/1975, p. 182)

Fancy is utilized after one or more of the reductions is in place. Should it be the transcendental reduction, fancy provides the varying phenomena on the basis of which essential patterning is intuited. The latter is spoken of as "eidetic intuition" or "essential insight." For the purpose of distinguishing imaginative analogy from the role of fancy in transcendental phenomenology, the point to be made is that the former technique does not have as one of its goals the achievement of eidetic intuition. It could not, since it is conducted under the condition of mindfulness, just as were conversation and communication, and is thus concerned with a region of investigation more akin to that revealed with the psychological reduction than the transcendental.

But there is a more important aspect to the distinction between imaginative analogy and the role of fancy in transcendental phenomenology. Eidetic intuition and imaginative analogy are not mutually exclusive psychologically; to say that eidetic intuition is anathema for imaginative analogy would be to establish false psychological boundaries. The intuition of essences does occur spontaneously, as if the practice of imaginative analogy tended naturally to reveal essential insight. There is a gradient, in this sense, with the accumulation of imaginative analogues for the other person's features leading directly to intuition of an essential quality of his existence. Determination of the precise nature of this experience is of critical importance and provides guidance for further investigation of the relationship between imaginative analogy and fancy.

The word "ambivalence" and the newly coined term "bi-vocal" may be used to characterize the experience which occurs at the moment imaginative analogy yields essential insight. The customary psychological understanding of "ambivalence" is not in question: the word is used in a more neutral, etymologically based sense to mean the influence of two symmetrically balanced strengths or values. "Bi-vocal" refers to a specific and more concrete instance of ambivalence: a literary composition may be bi-vocal, or a particular word, if either elicit an experience of ambivalence. These are formal definitions; there experiential content is what matters, and to this reflection now turns.

The ambivalence of the moment when imaginative analogy yields essential insight may be characterized in the following manner. On the one hand, recollection comes to an abrupt halt. It seems terminated; its ebb and flow settle instantly. A feeling of relief is present. Tension is dissipated. Hovering before the eye, present in the print of the portrait, is certain knowledge of a comprehensive meaning pertaining to the other person. On the other hand, there is the simultaneous experience of doubt, if not skepticism, as to the comprehensiveness of the insight and the adequacy of its wording. The subtle awakening of ordinary consciousness from the pacific range of mindful attention further accentuates the doubt. The very sense of certainty and adequacy seems the springboard from which rises the doubt.

To pursue the meaning and practical ramifications of this ambivalence requires a guiding question: Granting the presence of essential insight just prior to the juncture of ambivalence, how could it be possible for ambivalence to arise? One would think the transcendental status of essential intuition would rule against the occurrence of such ambivalence. To simply say the other person is contradictory, or that his life is riddled with ambiguities, is to argue on other psychological levels than those for which mindfulness and essential intuition are relevant. Likewise, to say the doubt over comprehensiveness and adequacy is basically a matter of excessive scrupulousness on the part of the portraitist would be to deny the genuinely ambivalent nature of the experience. At least two paths open at this point: either one foregoes the possibility of essential intuition, at least in its original sense within the context of transcendental phenomenology, and instead assigns intuition to another region of investigation, of which the psychological would be most likely; or one discards altogether the idea of essential intuition, substituting perhaps a mode of transcendental experience for which any form of objectification is irrelevant. These alternatives bring into view certain foundational problems of existential-phenomenological philosophy. The latter alternative recalls Heidegger, perhaps also Jaspers's philosophy of *Existenz*. The former alternative recalls Merleau-Ponty, if the work published posthumously is excluded. But another thinker more pertinent than these is Levinas, whose phenomenological research revolves around the fundamental structures of human encounter. For this reason, his work promises guidance, since the entire presentation of methodology, in all its aspects and phases, may be understood as an essay upon the bearing of human encounter for psychological research.

For recollection, and for the mumbled and imprinted wording of recollection during portraiture, the most salient of Levinas's ideas is "the infinite" (Levinas, 1969/1979; Strasser, 1982). It substitutes for intentionality as the fundamental structure of human existence and is discerned, not through transcendental analysis of the co-constitution of the intersubjective world, but within concrete encounter with another person. Transcendental consciousness collapses, or rather is fused with the kind of knowing present for persons during encounter and born of their unique historical circumstances. For encounter, the horizon of ordinary experience is altered: no longer delineated in terms of the structure of intentionality, it opens onto an infinite range of possibilities and realizations, each of which points beyond itself, and finally, altogether beyond the knowable. The puzzling experience of ambivalence may be clarified with the idea of the infinite serving as reference point; the significance of eidetic intuition for imaginative analogy also becomes clearer, as do certain practical ramifications of the idea for the wording of recollection during portraiture.

Reflection begins with the experience of ambivalence, which heralds in a puzzling way intuitive certainty as to the meaning of the other person. Recalling Levinas, it may be said that ambivalence is of the essence of recollection insofar as the latter is genuinely an encounter of this person. Since encounter is characterized as the opening of the infinite, it must be the case that an intuition granting certainty, and thus pertaining to transcendental reality, would be paired with doubt as to its comprehensiveness and the adequacy of its wording. Odd, indeed: one's certainty in knowing the other person is matched necessarily with doubt over the meaning of the other. Odd again: doubt over the meaning of the other, when paired with intuitive certainty as to his meaning, is a mark of one's intuition having genuinely been certain. Ambivalence, then, is not the enemy of recollection: it is of the essence of recollection.

A ramification of the essentially ambivalent nature of recollection for its wording is obvious: the wording must not let slip moments of ambivalence in either their certainty or their doubtfulness. Similarly, the portrayal of the wording of recollection must also reflect this ambivalence. The portrait which neatly summarizes the meaning of the other person is truncated and false; the portrait which widens the horizon of the other's meaning is true to encounter. Inherent to the experience of composing the portrait during worded recollection, inherent to the development of the written portrait, and inherent to the reader's experience of the portrait: to each must inhere one or more experiences of the ambivalence of the patient's meaning. This is the measure of encounter--the portraitist's with the patient, and through the portrait, the reader's with the patient. The portrait which elicits this experience from its creator may be called bi-vocal, just as it may for the reader who encounters the patient through experiencing portraiture .

Bi-vocality is an important value of the present research, not merely of its goals: it is the portraitist sharing with the reader an experience of the limitless meaning of a person who might otherwise be known as simply a sick pariah.

The Wording of Recollection

Words accumulate as recollection flows, and as recollections accumulate, words flow. Words transform recollections; recollections inform words, even push them from the mouth. What could be more fluid than the mutual mirroring of wording and recollection?

Watson's (1924) was not the last word when he spoke of subvocal talking, saying it was the basis of thought, going so far as to identify it with thinking. What he did not mention is the wording of recollection in the quiet mumbling of mindful reflection. This does not take place in the pristine self-enclosure of a silent, mental auditorium, nor is it an intellectual calisthenic which flushes platysma, orbicular oris, and buccinator with blood. It is talking, as may be heard with the ear, though which ear--whether inner or outer--is unheard. Or is it unseen, since the wording of recollection is also a seeing, though with which eye--inner or outer--is unclear? Husserl's words: "Here as a challenge to spontaneity there opens a chasm which may be crossed only in the essentially new form of realizing action and creation, wherein the power to hallucinate at will must be taken into account" (Husserl, 1913/1975, p. 288).

Odd that the wording of recollection, more concrete than any aspect of description, is so elusive, yet without escaping its concreteness. The words imprinted on the pages of the portrait are in question; they are the _telos_ of description: the black forms on the white page--the _telos_ for what otherwise is mostly unknown, or if not unknown, then easily forgotten, even by the one who conversed. This research is literary in the most concrete sense of the term.

If the phenomenon to be portrayed encompasses the entirety of one's experience of the other person, then the wording of recollection must be one of its features. But is this to disturb the self-absorption of recollection and interrupt its flow? Why words, if recollection proceeds smoothly? Because recollection _is_ a wording, a wording which constitutes the other's presence, brings it before the eye and ear, though which eye and which ear--whether inner or outer--is unclear and unsaid. Description is not foreshortened by recollection taking the form of words: it is made whole.

To embody recollection with words is to reconvene conversation, but with a difference which radiates with significance for another person than either oneself or the person with whom one conversed originally.

This other person is the reader. For the wording of recollection bears the face of Janus: it is a backward glance toward the person with whom one was conjoined originally and a gazing forward toward the reader. The wording of recollection restores the other's presence to eye and ear, transforms that presence to print, thus setting it before the reader, who is then invited to again restore presence to the person with whom one conversed originally. This is the circle of description: a widening, arcing circle which incorporates facts and images, images and words, words and reader. Ample data are available to the reader who would advance description through the worded recollection of those patients who have not yet been portrayed.

As an occasional wave cuts deeper rivulets on the shore than others, so the relationship of recollection and its wording elicits closer attention. Recollection is *a* wording, but recollection and its wording are not identical. A kind of wording evokes recollection, other kinds do not. The kind which does has been called the *telos* of recollection. Aside from the black imprints of the portrait, how may such a wording be defined? Or rather, how may it be described? It is the quiet mumbling of internally worded reflection, an envisioning mumbling which satisfies eye and ear. Since inclusive of recollection, it too must be a mindful procedure. Mindful mumbling. An incantation, a spell to entice the reader, a sorcery which entraps both magician and bystander. An incantation, an ensorcelling, a web spun by a black spider. Indeed, the persons recollected are mad, poisoned with madness, tightly surrounded with a web of madness. They spin webs of madness, ejecting a pale white substance into their surroundings. It falls and clings, binding the mind with undetectable subtlety. The firm and narrow walk away; their white jackets are of the same shade as the web trailing from their finely parted hair. The strong and delicate pause, draw near, and ask to endure safely the flash of pain disguised as a web of madness. The other person is a conflagration of pain. But the fire is pale for those who draw near, because there is safety in the other's pain for those skilled in suffering. A worthy method teaches such skill.

Chapter 4

RESULTS

Paul, Mary, John, and Luke are the central figures of this chapter. The sequence of their portraits preserves the order in which they were created originally. A case history, a narrative of the experience of God, and a portrait are given for each. Together with the audio recording and the transcript of conversation, this material forms the mosaic of results pertaining to these four patients. A transcript of conversation with John is given in the appendices along with case histories and narratives for the five patients not portrayed. An extensive glossary is also included in the appendices; it may prove helpful in elucidating certain names, places, and references evoked during portraiture and appearing in the portraits of Paul and the others.

Paul

History

Paul is a handsome, fit, 32-year-old black man. He had been living as an indigent for several years, hitchhiking across the country, his journey interrupted on several occasions with psychiatric hospitalizations. History is minimal. He was treated briefly and released within 2 days. His previous medication of Fluphenazine, last given a week before, was continued. The evening before our conversation he was alongside the highway and approached a security guard to request an ambulance be called because of his "fear of hurting himself." He was "depressed" and "sad" at admission because "God took the earth away from him." Additional admission notes remark that his "speech was coherent and relevant" with some "looseness of association." He "denied suicidal or homicidal ideation." There was "no significant evidence of organicity," nor was a history of drug abuse elicited. The admitting diagnosis was chronic undifferentiated schizophrenia with acute exacerbation; my impression was of chronic paranoid schizophrenia. I would estimate his level of intelligence to be within the bright normal range at minimum.

Our conversation took place the evening following his admission. He was exceptionally articulate, speaking with ease and a rich vocabulary. His explanation of the somatic hallucination which was the center of his most powerful experience of God was punctuated with his making sound effects designed to convey the sucking, tense sensation about his skull during the experience. He had been a Sunni Black Muslim for 10 years. He referred to the _Koran_ several times and once broke into glossolalia, explaining that his words were Arabic, although he had never learned the language and is unable to translate his sounds. He recounted two very different experiences of God, of which the following is the most powerful. He has entitled it "The Experience of Supreme Justice," a name given him during the experience itself. His memory for its details was remarkable, considering it occurred 5 years prior. But Paul is accustomed to reviewing his life "24 hours a day so he can try to do better." This enables him to remember the past in exquisite detail.

Narrative

Having nearly walked across a park in Berkeley, California, Paul sat on the grass at some distance from an attractive black couple. They were "lovers," and being a "lover himself," he enjoyed their company. Without actually hearing their words, "he mentally heard them talking about America, the future, and the revolution." He figured prominently in their conversation since they, as had others before them, wanted him as "their leader in the revolution." He is the "field marshall," the "leader" of a revolution which is "nation-wide." Paul lay back upon the grass and shut his eyes. He envisioned "on the inside of his forehead" a scene in which he was "dying of thirst in the middle of the desert" when "Adam, the first man, appeared in the sky as a black man's head." Adam "looked down from the sky and spit," thereby "creating an oasis." The lovers nearby were aware of Paul's "vision." He stood up, feeling as if he were "radiating J.C." He described this as a "state of understanding"; it was "not fearful," but "peaceful," and reminded him of the Biblical expression "let not your heart be troubled." It was "like he <u>was</u> J.C."

When Paul reached the sidewalk he was confronted suddenly with a thought worded in exactly this manner: "This is supreme justice, my friend! If you pass, you have it made!" Such was God's preparatory statement announcing the coming test. A "split second" afterwards, Paul experienced a "suction of some kind" in which the "skin" of his head was "sucked to the bone." Were it not for the "conditioning of his mind" and his "physical state of being," he would be "dead" as a result. During this experience Paul was not aware of his surroundings, nor was he conscious of his body below the level of his head, although he was convinced that the remainder of his body was "sucked empty" as well. The demarcation of bodily awareness is not peculiar to this experience: Paul considers it a Muslim teaching that one should attend to the "upper part," not the "lower." As he said, "I live up here," gesturing toward his head. He has "trained" himself "to step," to walk with a rapid, steady gait, not allowing attention to move beyond the rhythmic motion of his body. This constitutes part of the "conditioning" without which he might have experienced the suction reaching below the level of his head, "moving to the rest of his body." This would have "destroyed" him.

Paul described the suction about his head and the clinging of the flesh with numerous metaphors. It was like a "plastic bag filled with air"; the bag collapses once the "air is taken out." Or it was like "two plugs were removed from his ears" and the content of his head was drained. He "felt the absence of air in his head." It was as if his head were "empty." Walking under these conditions was like "walking in a dark cave"; "you can't see anything, but you know you can step." It was as if "his face caved in, as tight as it could, to his skull." His "jaws and teeth were closed." "It was like gasping for air and there is none." He felt "warm." It was more a "sharp" sensation than a "dull" one. The sensation "didn't have a direction"; it simply enveloped him. The experience ended instantly. He was fully oriented, without confusion or a residue of unusual bodily sensations.

A series of thoughts, forming a spontaneous interpretation of the experience, occurred immediately afterwards. The thought, "they took

J.C. through the same changes," was partly responsible for his concluding that the experience was of God. It also kept him from hurting the couple: "If I hadn't thought of J.C., which makes me more merciful than I really am, I might have hurt them." After all, the couple was indirectly responsible for his having to endure the horrendous "experience of supreme justice." They "saw his qualifications and requested he have the experience" for the purpose of disciplining him and ensuring that "his future wouldn't be so dim." They "needed someone to take authority" and this was an important means of training him to do so. The experience was not an exception because of the couple's involvement since "most of his experiences from God come because of other people." Finally, "Allah" is involved with all experience--"there is a purpose for every moment"; consequently, his must have been purposeful. Paul concluded that his self-emptying was brought about so that he might be filled with "divine nature." How, then, could he "challenge God when He does something to him?"

Paul is prepared to sacrifice certain wishes due to his mission. Were it possible, he would prefer to have "a house by the ocean in L.A. and be an architect or a psychiatrist."

The Portrait

Paul's body. For one fearful of his electric body, feline tension, and the rapidity and precision of his speech, Paul is approached with difficulty. But fear is unnecessary, for the cooly modulated tension which arises naturally for one inadequately prepared for conversation is a fading glimmer of mood for the mindful conversant. Thus Paul may be approached in the manner which is most fitting, which allows him to provide guidance rather than subserve the fearful aims of those inadequately prepared. The proper question is how Paul approaches others, given this freshness of eye and ear, this fearless stance which serves as the ground from which one may be swept away, pulled in the gust of Paul's smooth furor.

A young black man approaches, remarkably fit, but without the protrusion of muscles and gangly tautness of weightlifters. He is spry, a sprite, a quickening light which pulses through the air and illuminates corners and surfaces of walls. There is not the feigned calm and rhythmic walk of some blacks who thrive on the street. His walk makes known a music different from pounding drums and synthesized quivering. He touches down, he soars. His rhythm is noticeable from the absence of a correlation between drummed sound and bodily movement. A rhythm known from the absence of audible expression! Yes, Paul lives his body differently than the ordinary person. Consequently, his body and its movements must be understood in ways different than those useful for others. For what could "body language" mean when one's embodiment is more akin to a space station from which is launched warfare and further explorations than to the weighty corporeality of a life oriented toward the pulls and tugs of the flesh?

Conversation compels one to examine fragments of Paul's movements more closely than can be done when first glancing him move through the patterned light of the otherwise dim hospital corridor. Look closely--at his hands, his face and eyes, his legs and feet, his mouth. This is more akin to watching a movie than studying a photograph. Consider the discrepancy between a photograph of his outstretched arm, rigidly straightened fingers, and bent wrist--consider the discrepancy between these pictorial fragments and the fluidity with which the arm assumes this position, the snap with which the fingers align themselves, and the nearly undetectable moment when the wrist becomes cocked at an angle which accentuates perfectly his slim fingers. A photograph could hardly convey this gestural happening; an accuracy of greater value is inherent to a description shaped by the very moment when his movement is experienced. Trust is placed in experience, in the immediacy of seeing and hearing the gesturing, moving presence named Paul.

The fineness of Paul's fingers may be emphasized, but this would be an error if the impression were given of them being disjoined from the remainder of the body. This is not the broad-beamed pianist whose facility is limited to the roving dexterity of fingers pressing black and white levers. This is the electric body Whitman sang, the body of one who lives every muscular fiber of its tegumentary surface. The fingers speak for the body, they converse in the same language. Certain words block reception of Paul's body; to speak of appendages and digits, of central and cephalic anatomical coordinates, is to not know the continuity of trunk and arm or trunk and fingers. The fingers and body are one.

Paul's mode of embodiment is taut coherence. Is it necessary to proceed to his face and eye, his mouth and what remains lower down? Indeed. The lived body may be known already, its meaning glimpsed fleetingly from a hastily drawn portrait, yet many details will have escaped should description halt with the gesture of Paul's arm. The question is how this mode of embodiment is articulated in other gestures. How is it incarnate in other dimensions of the bodily mass? Description resumes with the head because Paul values this pole of the bodily axis more highly. "I live up here," he said, pointing to his head. Such an evaluative hierarchy is not his creation: he claims it is a tenet of the Sunni Muslim faith to which he adheres, and which would have one distinguish between "the upper part" and the "lower part" while prizing the former most highly.

Goethe mentioned those eyes. His words were not the last about the sympathetic correspondence between the eye and the visual qualities of objects which the eye apprehends. For this perspective, the eye emits light; the eye is of light itself since its very substance extends to caress envisioned objects, proffering them before the organ without which they would be invisible, if not nonexistent as visual realities. Paul's eyes are of light; they are lit; and what is seen is similarly lit--is enlightened in accordance with his knowledge of the world's purpose and made coherent with the organ which composes his net of visual presence. More is to be said of this pervasive, tightly woven net. Straus's elucidation of the upright posture provides guidance.

Upon assuming the upright posture, man struggles anew with the tugging force of gravity. One must not totter, leaning to the side or bending too far forward, otherwise he collapses. Ambulation becomes a delicate matter. But how much further one sees! The clean sweep of the horizon is present where the world's edge had been ruffled with trees or creased with hillocks. The eye assumes a different position; it allows orientation in terms of greater distance. One may fix his sites upon more distant targets. So Straus, who proceeds to accentuate the cultural advantages which accrue from the upright posture. But for those able to see further than ordinary persons, the upright posture is a dangerous stance. Imagine the precariousness of the posture which allows the eye to roam at will, randomly and without interruption. Pilots behave strangely in a dense fog or an amorphous snowstorm. The spiraling tubules of the inner ear turn hypnotically. The world is without visual pattern; direction is without goal; the way is lost. The danger of the upright posture is more significant for understanding Paul than is the cultural boons accrued from standing.

The upright man tends to bypass the close. The at-hand may be too close; it goes unnoticed. This is the case with the person who becomes used to his glasses. But more important is that the at-hand is now lower, nearer the feet, the legs, the thighs. The earth was once an immediate support and the root of things which blocked the way. Now it is more distant, thus one may stumble, the at-hand having shriveled toward an earth which finally shrinks to the importance of a nicked platform or a chipped stage rather than maintain itself as a rocky, moist support. Posture and value go hand in hand--this is the point. A mere step, quick and hazardous, separates a distant earth and the lower part of the body from the devaluing of both the earth and the corresponding range of embodied experience.

With this step, an experiential hierarchy of embodiment is tacitly established. The world becomes different. The body is then characterized as a polar arrangement having two distinct ends, just as the person so incarnate is said to have two sides to his personality.

The upper, lit end is the positive pole, the distant, dark end, the negative. The upper, lit end is to the eye and head as the lower, dark end is to the trunk, the legs, and feet. Similarly, vision and its vista are to the light end as the proprioceptive and earthy are to the dark. The analogy may be extended with frightening accuracy. Just as the existence of a magnetic field requires a seemingly incontrovertible difference between the forces generated by the atomic structure of the distantly situated magnetic poles, so the preservation of the experiential hierarchy of embodiment requires rigid demarcation of the meanings and forces present for the existence structured in a polar manner. Relax and consider what might happen otherwise. The earth is known to have reversed its poles such that what is now north, the point of attraction for a compass, was once a magnetic lacuna, a mere spot of tectonic impotence. Imagine the experiential analogue for one whose embodiment is structured with a polar hierarchy. Paul knows; his experience of God is formed accordingly.

For the polar body, vision and its eye assume a highly placed position, literally and figuratively. They are valued more highly than other organs with their respective perceptual modes. One would expect these other organs to shrink in importance, to atrophy or become diseased from lack of use. The theme is echoed time and again in mythology. Odin, the one-eyed Teuton, god of war and wisdom, hung upside down for 9 days, earning the power of prophecy and extending his range of vision to the earth's entire surface. This god dragged an injured foot. Maugham's hero, the young physician consumed with desire for life's meaning, was born clubfooted. Corrective surgery further crippled his step. For one who prizes vision and its eye exclusively, there awaits a turning, a reversal of poles, a collapse of the hierarchy, a shattering experience of darkness. One would expect a dimming of light reflected in a loss of vision, or perhaps some more general atrophy of the phenomenological-anatomical seat of awareness known as the head. This was the fate of the cyclops, and he is still present in the bestial, earthy dimension of existence situated in the trunk and legs of the man who lives only for "the upper part."

Bright-eyed Paul!--the eyes shaped more like almonds than would be expected for a black man; almond eyes set in a handsome face with aquiline nose and fine, tense lips. Dark-skinned Paul!--the flesh radiant with molten blackness. Is there limit to his vision? Certainly not. He sees everywhere, all about himself. He tells of seeing in back of his head, every tiny crevice of the wall immediately behind his chair. So speaks a man deeply forgetful of the other pole of the bodily axis, a man whose lived body is hardly more than a globe of awareness, a single eye roving where it wills.

Noses usually deserve special attention. A person may smell, thereby prompting consideration of the meaning of odor for him and those who smell him. Or his nose may run, the excretion mixing with tears, thus drawing attention to the liquidity of other aspects of his existence. Not so with Paul: his nose is a nonentity, an insubstantial outline, as with an ink sketch when certain features of the physiognomy are merely hinted with a deftly placed line. But often with phenomenological investigation, presence is known through absence and absence through presence. The absence of Paul's nose during conversation is itself communicative. What is veiled by absent-mindedness of Paul's nose during conversation? He did not smell, nor did he sniff or sneeze. But the sound of his voice is recalled clearly, the swishing of air through his mouth, the jetting propulsion of breath passing between the lips. He created sound effects by forcing air through compressed, puckered lips, intending to convey the sensation occurring during his experience of God. Once he broke into a strange, hissing glossolalia--the spitting language of an angry cat--explaining this was Arabic, a language he had never learned but which came to him spontaneously, enabling him to pray the Koran in its original tongue.

There is no place for a nose on Paul's face. Its value has declined drastically, its functions usurped by the mouth. One had only to recall the tantalizing sensuality and perfumed air of Baudelaire's poetry to realize the nose and the olfactory dimension of embodied existence would pose intractible problems for one who lives only for "the upper part" and with only the eye and mouth. Paul's nose was understandably absent from our togetherness: its absence is indicative of its devalued status and the sign of the presence of alternative, more highly valued modes of sensory experience. Quite naturally one is drawn to Paul's eye and mouth, failing to attend to his nose.

Paul's mouth creates uneasiness in the listener. To stand within the visual aura of a sphere of awareness is one thing, but listening to words formed on the basis of such awareness is something different and inescapable. This is not to say the eye and mouth are separable: the objectifying stance which measures distance with a ruler and distinguishes mouth from eye with an explanation based on retinal anatomy and atmospheric patterning is misleading. A human is present--he compels attention, eliciting witness to the rapidly changing appearances of his and his confidant's togetherness. Analogies flicker, evoking words; mutual attunement is guarded from the sparseness of ordinary consciousness. For one disposed in this manner, the eye and mouth are not distant; they may be the same. But one must also guard against precipitous conclusions--the sparseness of ordinary consciousness is not the only pitfall; to do so requires closer consideration of Paul's mouth. Attention is a butterfly hovering above an orifice of unknown proportions and suspiciously uncertain force.

These are electric words. They saturate the air and are barely associated with the formation of lips, cheeks, and jaw. Paul does not speak to the listener: he gives voice to meanings so transparent they seem not to require auditory reception or spoken conveyance. One does not listen to Paul: one knows in advance of the meaning he sounds. The hovering delicacy of attention would be blown aside should one resist, attempting to maintain a recalcitrant hold on reality and the lack thereof in what Paul says. This is an alert sibyl, his mouth an oracular orifice. He speaks of "a nation-wide revolution" for which he is "the field marshall." His ears are attuned to messages from distant accomplices. Words spoken under his breath or within the cephalic globe of silent awareness reach far beyond the location of his body.

Words blend with other kinds of sounds, Straus has shown. Speech is not restricted to sounds articulated on the basis of learned meanings. It is only with the gnostic moment of perception that the object of awareness becomes nameable. But this is the termination of a lengthier sequence. Patterns of relationship on which worded knowledge rests, and which the latter may misrepresent when language strays too far from its rooted sensuousness, are present in earlier moments of sensory experience. For with the gnostic moment of sensation patterns of relationship are established already. They may be isolated and understood to be sensible. To do so requires a guiding question: What is the speaking which is the mouth's participation in the gnostic moment of sensory experience? What is sounded when the mouth acknowledges the confrontation of person and thing? A remark of Straus's prepares an answer: "Sensing is to knowing as a cry is to words." Thus one must look to the cry, the grunt, the wheeze, the laugh--to those mouthed sounds which are analogous to the spontaneous gestures of the silent body. This is done easily with Paul; the task was begun when reflecting upon his nose and its absence.

Remember the swishing of air through Paul's mouth, the jetting propulsion of breath passing between compressed lips, the feline spitting of his Arabic glossolalia. All of them odorless, windy sounds, like the crisp Autumn breeze passing through the dried leaves of a tree with retreating sap. As the tree is easily set ablaze in its dryness, and as the sound of wind heralded the presence of the Spirit's fire above the apostles' heads, so Paul's sounds signal the vigilant passivity of a head set ablaze with the hallucinated presence of messages from beyond the confines of an ordinary body. An emphysemic cough would be out of character for this man, sinuses bloated with mucous would be some sort of atavism. Nietzsche said he belonged in the thin, cold air of mountaintops. So Paul. The Taoist forest haunted by the valley spirit, the misty glade populated with Debussy's faun--Paul would never be found in such places. More likely is the possibility of imagining him aboard a camel in the Arabian desert, the sail of a white burnoose unfurled behind him.

Consider the camel, envision its gait: steady, monotonous, as regular as the sinusoidal wave of a pure tone. Paul calls his most important form of spiritual discipline "stepping." He has "trained himself to step," to walk rapidly with a steady, even gait, not allowing attention to move beyond the rhythmic motion of the body. This "conditioning" is of considerable importance. It allows Paul to concentrate on "the upper part," hypnotically laying to rest the "lower." God's touch would have enveloped his entire body and "destroyed him" had he not known how "to step."

With mention of God's touch, the moment is present to turn from description of Paul's body to his experience of God. Reflection upon the upright posture has anticipated certain features of the experience. The world which God will darken has been glimpsed. Rilke conveys the boggling effect of His appearance:

> And then all alone in space, in lightness, in cold.
> But deep in the shape he has made to stand erect
> he takes a breath. . .
>
> Then God explodes from his hiding place.

The vision of Adam. Paul wandered to Berkeley, California, during the summer of 1976. An indigent eye, he could not help but be a voyeur, his attention roving to the benighted dimension of experience linked with the "lower part." Indeed, his account of the experience of God begins with his describing a pair of black "lovers" seated together on the emerald grass of a park across which he was stepping when they were targeted.

The lovers caressed, enjoying each other's company. Paul enjoyed their enjoyment as well as his enjoyment of their enjoyment. This is not the verbal turning of a specious convolution. Paul's eye roves where the ordinary eye is unable to penetrate; his ear hears what is inaudible for ordinary bodies. The couples were conversing about "America, the future, and the revolution." This he "mentally heard." He was with the couple without being present to them in body. Thus he would be able to determine their mood without having to rely solely on sifting it from his own feelings in their presence. Conceivably Paul could enjoy their enjoyment without thereby enjoying his enjoyment of their enjoyment. He is that close, present with that degree of closeness to their togetherness. The globe of awareness may become transparent, lacking substance of its own.

Imagine the tingling sensuality present with the lovers; set beside it the evaluative hierarchy of embodiment. It is hardly surprising Paul would find the experience bordering on the disturbing. Is a voyeur not secretly jealous and equally intent on isolating his arousal to a glassy linen-white place? Sartre's furtive voyeur stands upright, blanching and dehumanized, upon suspecting he is watched. Laing has spoken of the danger of embodiment for "a self which wishes to be wed to and embedded in the body, yet is constantly afraid to lodge in the body for fear of being subject to attacks which it cannot escape." The anonymous face which transfixes the voyeur, startling and transforming him, may be expected to appear. Its presence is hinted already with Paul's conviction that the experience of God was directed to him by the couple's desire that he be "disciplined." It was by their request, and with the hope Paul would thereby become fit for his missionary role as "leader of the revolution," that God touched him with painful consequence.

A world is not easily toppled or disrupted. However truncated its existential possibilities, Dasein is too fundamental for a crimp in the modes of existence it undergirds and unifies to go uncorrected. Boss identifies psychopathology with such crimps; their swelling and correction he identifies with the essence of Dasein. Paul's vision is the smoothing of the crimp accentuated by his enjoying the tingling sensuality of the lovers. He sits within sight of the couple; laying back, he shuts his eyes. "On the inside of his forehead" he sees himself "dying of thirst in the middle of the desert when Adam, the first man, appears in the sky as a black man's head. Adam looks down from the sky and spits, creating an oasis." Paul then rises in a "state of understanding," feeling "peaceful" and with "an untroubled heart." His feeling is of "radiating J.C." He feels "like he is J.C."

Consider Adam's face, a replica of the angelic faces swarming over the ceilings and in the corners of some Baroque churches. These anatomically abbreviated beings typically have glistening, staring, black eyes in the colonial churches of Latin America. They are divine presences, bits of supernal knowledge--they are God's thoughts. Thus speaks Medieval angelology. Such understanding was not without hagiographic and scriptural precedent. God's appearance to Francis was a fiery seraphim; its carbuncular marks were the body's engram of Christ's suffering. Isaiah knew the same: the seraphim of his vision burns the tongue, raising it to the status of a prophetic mouthpiece for the Lord's thoughts.

The equation which identifies divine thought with angelic head is recognizable in the many statues and pictures of Our Lady of Guadalupe, the dark-skinned mother at whose feet is placed an angelic head with smiling face. Our Lady is held dear in God's thoughts: how else could she be impregnated if not in a way different than that linked with the "lower part." Also in view is Athena, another virgin goddess held dear in another god's thoughts: she sprung from Zeus' head, his own daughter, when Hephaestus, the smithy god of the underworld, cleft his skull with an ax.

Nodal points of meaning are readily apparent: the cephalic globe of omni-awareness, which before was Paul's incarnation, is now envisioned as the sky-high facing of godly omniscience toward a different Paul--a destitute, earth-bound, dried Paul. The evaluative axis of the body has assumed cosmic proportion, and Paul had slid down that axis to the dried emotional texture of desperate need. Paul has fallen from grace; he has lost his head. The seduction of the eroticism and emotional closeness of the lovers has grounded him. As with lightening, a grounding is required before the bolts are thrown. The storm is brewing already, moving from the horizon of Paul's world toward its center, his neglected, parched body.

Parsimony is crippling unless the wealth embedded in an experience has been grasped through the mindful application of careful imaginative activity. What has been neglected? Adam's spitting, the bonding of sky and earth. It seems nearly to reverse the cosmic axis, restoring Paul to a state of radiant, peaceful understanding. It brings him to his feet literally, restoring the upright posture, since just afterwards he stands and steps away. Our Lady has been neglected also, as has her more interesting sister Athena. More interesting because she allows discernment of what Our Lady veils: she shows the goddess to be the fruition of God's thought. Athena springs directly from Zeus' head; the angelic intermediary is unnecessary. The angel may be the presence of God's thought, but the goddess is that thought embodied. The discovery was announced at Ephesus when Mary was proclaimed _Theotokos_.

A skein of meaning is apparent; it must be untangled. Paul has fallen from his vigilant celestial outpost. He has been grounded due to the threat posed by the lovers on behalf of "the lower part." Consequently, the hierarchical axis established in accordance with the upright posture has assumed cosmic proportion, stretching itself between the heavenly seat of God, present in the angelic face, and the parched earth upon which lies the downcast Paul. The penultimate thread is woven by Our Lady and Athena. Both are the virginal recipient of a god's wish for materialization, the mirror of his angelic thought. Both are the transformation of recalcitrant matter into the encompassing embodiment of a celestial wish. They are the collapse of the polarity of the anatomical-cosmic axis.

For the tradition providing Mary a home, this collapse is equivalent to the person of Jesus Christ, who enacts his graceful intent through a sacrificial expiation of human sin. Ricoeur traces the idea of blood-letting expiation far back of Jesus Christ to dim Old Testament days. The word used frequently then to speak of this kind of forgiveness is borrowed from the sacrificial rite of sprinkling. Sprinkling--the letting fall of a moist substance, often blood. Forgiveness of this kind, brought about through this means, is linked with a critical moment in the developing experience of guilt--the moment when God becomes an omniscient viewer capable of destroying human existence. Through sprinkling one may escape this threat. But what of the man whose head is swollen to the impersonal proportion of the empryrean? His Icarian flight brought low, he, too, may be absolved of attempting approximation to godly omniscience. It would be through sprinkling that the breach in his world between the "higher part" and "the lower" could be healed. The desert of Paul's vision became an oasis; he sprung to his feet and stepped across the emerald grass when the angel sprinkled his earth with saliva. It could not be otherwise.

God's touch. Rumbling often precedes the showing of lightning during an electrical storm. The flash which bonds earth and sky happens momentarily once the preliminary warning is sounded. The analogy with Paul's experience of God is exact. His vision is a rumbling.

Stepping along the sidewalk after leaving the park, a clearly worded thought commands Paul's attention: "This is supreme justice, my friend! If you pass, you have it made!" Thus God announces the coming test. Instantly "a suction of some kind" envelopes Paul's head. Simultaneously "the lower part" ceases to exist, as if he is "walking in a dark cave unable to see anything." "The skin of his head is sucked to the bone"; his "face caves in as tight as it could, clinging to his skull." It is as if "two plugs were removed from his ears" and the content of his head drained. It is implosive, as when "a plastic bag filled with air" is made to collapse. He feels "an absence of air in his head, like it is empty."

Paul "came to himself." He was fully aware of his surroundings; he saw clearly, knew where he was and what he was about. A series of thoughts became apparent. "They took J.C. through the same changes" was one, leading Paul to conclude that the experience was of God. A fortunate thought, indeed, since "if he hadn't thought of J.C., which makes him more merciful than he really is, he might have hurt the couple." They were indirectly responsible for him having had to endure the horrendous "experience of supreme justice"; "they saw his qualifications and requested of God that he have the experience" for the purpose of disciplining him and "insuring that his future wouldn't be so dim." The "revolution" was in need of someone "to take authority"; the experience was a means of preparing him to do so. Given Paul's belief that "there is a purpose for every moment," Allah must finally be accountable for an event even as terrible as this one. Echoing the feeling of another Paul, who said "God makes all things work together for the good of those who have called according to His decree," Paul concluded that it was inadmissible "to challenge God when He does something to him."

Paul is a thoughtful man who "tries to do better" by reviewing the events of his life "twenty-four hours a day." He has concluded that the ultimate purpose of his divinely initiated self-emptying was for him to be "filled with divine nature."

A series of questions elicits understanding of Paul's implosive experience of God. To begin: Does the content of a vacuum apply pressure or adhere to its containing surface? A nonsensical question; there is not substance which might provide force. But if the force were applied from outside? With enough turbulence, and given a degree of fragility of the containing surface, there would be a collapse, an implosion. Would this implosive force disturb the content of the vacuum? A nonsensical question; there is nothing to disturb. Then what is implosion? The grating and abrasive mixing under great pressure of the containing surface, its intact form now fragmented and blown about by the incoming force. Implosion is the surface adopting an altogether different form once its perfection has been fragmented and its pieces forced to commingle in a less orderly and pure way.

Abstraction proceeds this far, but imagination remains discontent. It would have the vacuum become human, the implosion, anthropomorphic. What may be said of implosion under these conditions? It is the external world's violent entry into a pure space hollowed from a neglected surface. Yet more is demanded. Then let implosion be the virgin hermaphrodite's self-rape--the seemingly perfect creature falling prey in the most sensuous way imaginable to its heedless isolation from the touch of other humans. And would not the same be expected for the man who lives entirely for "the upper part," wholly within the vacuous globe of awareness which hears and sees at a distance without benefit of the body? How might the world rebound from such perfection if not by simply hugging the flesh of Paul's scalp, forcing acknowledgment of the tegumentary surface which is the means and point of contact between one person and another? This is judgment, a somatic analogue for the prostration Allah demands of his followers five times each day.

Consider the Muslim standing to pray in front of the Kaaba, the *sanctum sanctorum* of the holiest of cities, and the site of the volcanic boulder which Abraham set in the temple wall. His burnoose rests in folds after fleeing successfully from earthly trials; his head is covered in protection from Allah's glory. His knees bend, touching the worn texture of the woven jewels of the prayer rug. He leans forward, the arms and hands bent inward toward the chest. The head is drawn downward conscientiously and with due respect for religious propriety until the forehead is pressed to the earth in submission. Nothing less is acceptable; Allah demands complete submission of his followers. Those who resist--those with heads too swollen to press painlessly and willingly against the earth, receive their due on judgment day. Faces will then be blackened, says the *Koran*. Spectres with charred physiognomy will hover near the pock-marked face of the Kaaba's stone.

Paul refuses to submit. His world's center is an exalted globe of awareness focused like the enormous dish antennae of the New Mexican desert receiving microwaves from blackened stars. Messages from a legion of invisible followers pulse into awareness. They would have Paul direct the revolution. Rather than Paul submit, the world submits to Paul. For one who reverses the axis of the divinely decreed world, setting his throne in place of God's, Allah bears a grimy palm.

God's touch is linked to judgment and Paul's experience set within the eschatology of his own religious world, but without exhausting its meaning. Recall Paul's understanding of God's touch: it came about that he might "be filled with divine nature." The incongruity is apparent: the experience of God's touch is punishment, on the one hand, while on the other it is the means of Paul's diluted embodiment becoming concentrated with divinity. Paul provides guidance; his words cue recollection.

Consider the letter of another Paul, a leader and missionary himself, when he recounts the means whereby Jesus Christ assumed divine status. "Though he was in the form of God, he did not deem equality with God something to be grasped. Rather he emptied himself and took the form of a slave, being born in the likeness of men." Thus sang the early Church, basking in the holiness of Christ's adapting himself willingly to the form of a person for the purpose of identifying in the closest way with the embodied status of human beings. The theme is incarnation. John sings the same with greater sophistication: "The Word became flesh and dwelt among us." His amazement at the hallowing of human flesh is apparent elsewhere when he proclaims "what he has heard . . . seen with his eyes . . . looked upon . . . and his hands have touched." But what is the consequence of Christ's embodiment? His punishment. And the consequence of his punishment? The magnification of fully embodied human being. Our Paul has not lied. God's touch is the means of Paul's punishment; his punishment a means of embodying divinity. Paul speaks as did his namesake centuries before. Both recount instances of judgment and incarnation.

Mary

History

Mary is an overweight, 37-year-old Caucasian with dark hair, dark eyes, and rounded cheeks. The first of nine psychiatric hospitalizations occurred in 1977, when she was 31. Preceding this and overlapping some of the later psychiatric hospitalizations have been others for significant medical problems. The psychiatric history is complete; little social history is available. Since the medical problems may have had a significant, though unexamined, influence on the psychiatric difficulties, they will be reported along with information from the psychiatric admissions.

In 1971, Mary was hospitalized for a "stenosis of the right renal artery"; "secondary to this was severe hypertension with a systolic blood pressure of 240." Surgery was performed later in the year--a "resection of the right renal artery and re-anastomosis to the aorta." Hyptertension (220/130 mm Hg) was mentioned 6 years later on the first psychiatric admission. She "was brought to the hospital by her husband," who reported that she had been acting strangely "for about a year." The initial evaluation mentioned "paranoid thoughts and delusions." She claimed to be "the woman from Revelation clothed in the sun and possessed by the devil," who was also "taking over other people." A year later she was readmitted, having been "incoherent and disoriented for a day." She had "apparently had a fainting spell" as well. Prior to admission she had been "stacking Bibles around an open furnace" and had been failing to "go to work as a teacher's aide." She had been "sleepless for several nights" and seemed to be "talking to people who weren't present." Of particular interest is the note remarking upon her having "a waxing and waning disorder of consciousness" and "sometimes a clear sensorium." Between this admission and the next in 1980, she injured her left eye--apparently from a self-inflicted wound--and underwent a "left corneal transplant." She was found to be hypertensive and was also treated for "left lower lobe pneumonia."

The tenor of the remaining admissions is different from the preceding ones. The overall symptom picture changes and diagnoses are consistently paranoid schizophrenia. There is frequent mention of her "striking out at board-and-care operators" and "shouting 'Jehovah' and 'I love you'" for no apparent reason.

Mary has paid dearly for her life with "God," "Jesus," and "the angels." She has been unable or unwilling to allow another person to participate in this world. That she allowed me was an honor, and, to her, "enjoyable." Recounting the cost, she said:

> I know it sounds too far out, unbelievable, but it's all the truth. It was the cause of--I was married, had three lovely children, I had a beautiful home. I started hearing voices and my husband divorced me. I told him and he didn't believe me, so he sent me to a psychiatrist. He talked to my pastor, and he didn't believe me. And _I_ was the one going to Church--not him! No one believes me. Some men were put in prison for believing and preaching about Jesus. I got put in a mental institution. That's terrible!

Narrative

Mary's experience of God began "about 6 years ago" and has continued uninterrupted, save for those occasions, often as long as "3 or 4 months" in length, when "He goes away." Her world turns around God, who is Himself the most prominent of the other divine and angelic figures with whom she communicates. Consequently, it makes little sense to isolate one or two more important or powerful experiences of God. Rather, it is a matter of describing a way of life and the world predicated by this way of life. This is a more painstaking task than conscientiously describing a single, most powerful experience. I will go about it in as simple a manner as possible, namely, by grouping together parts of our conversation according to certain similarities. These similarities are of different kinds, not all of them pertaining to conceptual content. I will begin with lengthy description of the inhabitants of Mary's world. These spiritual demographics will be followed by a presentation of the forms of communication in Mary's world. This creates an opportunity to see how reciprocal communication takes place between a person and her voices. Afterward will be a description of the emotional dimension of Mary's world--her feelings and confusion in living the way she has for at least 6 years--and the behavioral consequences of having exchanged this world for the ordinary one. A final description will encompass a presentation of her religious mission and of the quasi-Biblical cosmology informing her world. These last two parts of the account are relatively abstract; they are somewhat removed from the elements of direct experience. And yet they are based upon them, having been deliberately pieced together over the years in a coherent, if mythopoeic, manner.

The occupants of Mary's world are God and Jesus; the archangel Michael and the accompanying angels of God; Satan and his angels, who are identical to "Hell's angels"; another peculiar feminine angel named "Silvania"; and the "spirits" of those who have died. Each of these figures--if the word may be used in so exhaustive a sense--is a voice. There would seem to have been a single "vision" during the entire 6 years, that of an angel whose message had bearing on a previous experience of God which was "the most beautiful" she had ever had.

Silvania is the most difficult of the bunch. She is the only female, and besides those of "Hell's angels," hers is the only voice which becomes "loud." The others are "soft" with great consistency. Silvania identified herself by name, as has been the case with Jesus and most of the angels. In contrast, God has not identified himself by name and the angels have identified Michael. Silvania curses Mary, calling her "an 'M.F.,'" and "bothers her all the time." In contrast to her confessed "love" for God, Jesus, and the angels, Mary described Silvania as a "bitch" whom "she doesn't care for at all." One might think that "Hell's angels" would be the object of a similar sentiment, especially since they have been "mean" and have threatened "to hurt Mary, her children, and her family," but this is not so. Initially they were "mean," but "after Mary and the angels got to know each other, they weren't like that." She introduced them to the ways of "the earth." "The truth changed them," she said. What truth? "She told them about different things, about the things she does and what she likes, without putting them on or anything." They "began to follow her around." They "would listen to music" with her and she "would sing to them before she had a radio--children's songs, rock-and-roll, country western--all the music she likes." Satan's angels were quite taken with this and would say, "Sing it again, sing it over, sing it over." Satan and his angels become "amused" at the wrangling between Silvania and Mary. Rather than come to Mary's defense, Satan will comment, "Those two are going at it again," when Silvania begins cursing at her.

God and Jesus have different voices and this is a cause of theological puzzlement for Mary. After all, "Jesus is God and Jehovah is God, but I believe Jesus is the sole God--that's what I was taught to believe." This is a rather fine point, however, in contrast to the "awe" and "wonder" of talking with God. With a tone of endearment, Mary said, "I love to talk to God." During the time when He is "gone for 3 or 4 months," she "wants Him to come back, and stay with her and talk with her."

In the early days of their relationship, it pained Mary for God to leave. "At first she missed Him, but not now; she just has to accept it--that's the way He does things." His departures and "playing" with her in this manner have elicited sore feelings. Recalling an instance of His "tricking" or "playing" with her in the past, which led to her feeling "mad," Mary said:

> He disappeared once and I thought he was going to come back. He told me He was on a certain day--in 2 years. I waited and waited, marked the calendar, counted the days until that day came. But He never did come. Another time He told me 5 more years and I waited.

Did she miss Him on that occasion? "No, I was kept busy. I had the angels talking to me. That's how I keep from getting so bored." Speaking of the angels, she continued:

> I take them to the Chinese Restaurant and say, "Taste this for me, or taste this with me." I'd say, "Eat with me." It would fill them up. They'd taste it and say, "No more! I'm full!" I just wanted them to try different things and share it with them. We cry together and laugh together, have a lot of joy together.

And are they like a family? "They _are_ my family! And they'll be yours, too, when God comes and we'll all be together. There won't be no more death then."

Mary and God began their relationship with the curiosity and trepidation of lovers. Recalling their early days, she said:

> He set me at ease. He can do that where I can just talk to Him. And one time He told me, "Tell me!, Tell me!," because He didn't know how to talk to me either! And so I did, in my own way, and He understood it, and we understand each other now.

Mary's relationship with Satan's angels had a similar beginning. She "just started asking questions because she was curious. At first they wouldn't talk back. I knew they were there. I would just talk to them. Pretty soon they started opening up and before long we were just talking back and forth."

Mary's world would seem to have a rather stable population, but this has not allowed her to know the number of its inhabitants or to determine refined means for distinguishing one figure from another. She once asked, "How many of you are there?" but "they wouldn't tell her and never have." When asked how many kinds of voices there had been during the past week, she said: "There's no way I can tell you, there's been so many. All mixed up and all that. There was Satan's angels and God's angels--I don't know the difference between their voices except Satan's have real soft voices."

The forms of communication between Mary and God, and between Mary and the angels, vary. In order to "talk" to God, she "sends thoughts to Him by thinking a thought back to Him after He speaks." She "sometimes talks out loud" to Him. When He responds, "it's like He's talking with His mouth." He is able to answer because He "heard the thoughts or words." When asked about the language she uses and the ease with which God understands, Mary said: "I talk real simply with short, simple sentences, and He knows, He understands. I talk with the same kind of words and language as you talk to anyone else. That's the only way I know how to talk." In general, the voices also use "short" sentences "where Mary can understand them." When asked how "smart" Satan's angels seemed to be, she first said they were "not smart," then changed her mind, saying, "They're intelligent, but didn't know better. Their way of life is so different from heaven and than it is on earth." And how many figures might be present at once? "Two or three angels and another voice." But does this mean that many voices talk at the very same time? "No, no. Uusally I just hear one, but it's like two people are saying the same thing at one time." Like if you and I were reading the same page of a book out loud--different voices but saying the same thing? "Yes." As if your thought and the voice copied one another?

> Yes--it's terrible! They try to say the same thing I do at the same time I do. They play the game "Jinx--you owe me a Coke," like we used to do when we were teenagers. You're just talking and it so happens you say the same thing at the same time as the other person, and you say, "Jinx--you owe me a Coke!" They throw my thoughts down and put their words in my thoughts at the same time. Then they say, "Jinx!"

A most taxing game, which leads Mary to feel that "her mind gets all full." "It just blows my mind. I tell them to stop when it gets too much for me." And how does she organize the voices, what with this kind of experience being so complex? "I don't, I just let it come, just let it happen. That's the only way I can."

Several aspects of the emotional dimension of Mary's world have been mentioned already--the "awe" and "wonder," the "love," the frustration and fear. Other aspects become apparent upon describing the behavioral consequences of living as she does. The most obvious and disturbing consequence, both to her and others, results from what is commonly called "command hallucinations." These may be set in their proper emotional context given what Mary tells of her world. For example, God "just tells her to shout Jehovah." What exactly is said, and how is it said? In a "low, steady voice, He says, 'Scream my name,'" --an order which she "does not like to do," not "wanting to bother anyone." She has "refused," and those times she has "thought something terrible was going to happen--not because God said something was going to happen. I just thought that was the way it would be." And did something happen? "Nothing would happen. I had to live with it--the guilt feeling." The specific nature of the feeling assoicated with these commands and the way in which she places it in a broader, even cosmic, perspective is apparent from these remarks: "Yesterday they told me, 'Shout Jesus,' and I thought, 'Not this all over again.' I don't want to scream and holler, but I don't want to let them down because they trust me. I might fail them in some way--in what they're fighting for, trying to save everybody." A feeling of resignation surrounds these incidents: "Maybe it had to be that way. I don't know why."

But the problem is not only an oppressive feeling. When voices give orders, they might not cease harping when she declines: "They just tell you, and I do it. If I say, 'No, I won't,' they keep on and keep on, telling me over and over. That's all they do--just blows my mind.

They like to play." There is also the fear that "Satan's angels might do something." For example, Satan once "had her children" and she "didn't want anything to happen to anyone." With surprise and indignation, Mary recounted having to strike another patient when she was at the state hospital. "I assault people that God tells me to, even one that was pregnant! A girl was pregnant! She was laying in bed not doing a single thing, and God said, 'Fight her.' I said, 'God!?,' and He said, 'That's how they do it.' So I went over there and hit her." Mary has yet to fully understand the rationale for such a command, but supposes it has to do with "evil spirits."

The behavioral consequences of Mary's participation in the other world are not limited to her striking others or shouting at the instigation of God and the angels. An apparent happenstance may be the effect of an angel. For example, Michael "made her mad" when Mary was "locked up at the state hospital." As she said: "He bothers me. Little things he does over and over. I'd have my purse on my shoulder and he'd make it slip off. I'd put it back on, it would slip off. He makes my purse strap slip off." She did not know how he brought this about, and he did not identify himself as the agent. But the "spirits, they told her it was Michael doing that."

Mary's tacitly held conception of the divine economy may be glimpsed without difficulty in the light of her religious mission. She wants to be a "fighter like Michael" and identifies herself as a "fighter for God." How she goes about this is apparent already: she "assaults people that God tells her to." She, God, and Michael are always "battling and fighting." Together they have "saved the people who are not controlled by God." Her "responsibility" is great. "If she doesn't do it, no one else will." "I'm not a preacher, evangelist or missionary," she said, "and I've really never accomplished anything in my life, never amounted to anything, just a housewife and mother. Had a nice job and lost that. I haven't much confidence in myself. I feel good about myself now--battling, fighting and screaming."

Given her special religious stance, Mary would understandably have reservations about others who claim to have a similar mission. For that matter, the only time during our conversation when Mary raised her voice and made plain her anger was when talking about such persons:

> It amazes me to hear someone talk about God or Jesus. They don't know a damn fucking thing about them. I went through it. They don't believe--or they do believe, but it's so phony. It makes me sick. Like Billy Graham. He's filth! He doesn't know what he's talking about. He's just in it for the money. And Oral Roberts especially. I've been there where they haven't.

Satan's place in the cosmic scheme would seem somewhat ambiguous. Mary remarked that without her "fighting" for God, "something would happen out of the angels' control, because Satan wants everything too." I asked whether Satan might get the "upper-hand," to which she replied: "I don't know. I know he can't, but I don't know." Indeed, she claimed with certainty earlier that Satan's threat was ultimately of no importance. When asked then how God showed His love for her, she responded: "He saved Satan. I heard it. God never said it, but He did. I know He did." Surely these remarks have an implicit and important bearing on her immediately preceding answer to the same question: "I was so filthy and wicked and dirty, and He cleaned me up and made me clean. I was damned, I wasn't even saved. God saved me. I couldn't do that by myself."

Though most of the evidence so far would point in this direction, it would be an error to assume that Mary's world is rigidly bifurcated with God, the angels, and the rest abiding always in their own realm, contacting Mary purely through word and never through some form of physical or at least visual presence. There are two exceptions to this. The first became apparent when Mary was asked if she missed other people--the kind of persons who have bodies--to which she replied: "No, they look just alike, like human beings. The person you pass on the street may be an angel. Angels come to earth a lot of times."

The second exception to Mary's holding a rigidly bifurcated conception of the cosmos was not a matter of a declaration, as was the first, but rather concerned a specific experience of God in which an angel figured importantly. It occurred "3 years ago" and was "the most beautiful experience of God she had ever had--like nothing she had felt in her entire life." She had been "praying" when "God showed her His feelings for her." "Oh, my God, it was so beautiful!" she said;

> they were just feelings, not my own--they could only come from Him. His feelings for me were good and beautiful, perfect, clean and good. Just like when you hold a baby, like when you take your son and hold him on your lap and squeeze him and love him and kiss him and he does it back to you. Then he feels your love for him, knows you love him. When God did that to me, it was His feelings towards me. I can't describe them. I didn't know what to do. I said out loud to Him, "I give it all back!" I went on and a couple of days later an angel came. A man was suddenly standing there--it was an angel--and he said, "You gave it all back." Then he disappeared.

The angel was wearing a suit.

The Portrait

Her cheeks are bulbs, iris if not narcissus, crinkled and yet luxurious rounds of flesh. She was seen before, and now her cheeks have bloomed, are rosy, and her heart luxuriates in a depth of feeling for God, Jesus, and the angels of Heaven and of Hell, all of whom communicate with her and each other according to unpredictable timetables of their own creation. But how account for this change, this transformation: the taciturn, wizened woman who 3 months before and for no apparent reason struck me on the arm with all her force, then stood and walked away without explanation, is now the open face with rosy cheeks which absorbs the attention bestowed as we talk of her experience of God? Change of this kind and of this degree must be accounted for. An answer requires she be carefully described and thus better understood.

Mary, handmaiden with a leaping heart, a heart not unlike Elizabeth's unborn John, who leapt with happiness in the doubly hidden presence of his Lord. But Mary has no need for someone else's baptism. She is her own baptism. Her tumultuous heart is the source of tears which renew her time and again in the struggle to hold fast and with loyalty to a world populated with demonic and angelic voices--a frequently darkened world, rent with persecutions launched under the aegis of sanity and the lavender flag of solicitude.

Faith grows, say the popular religious tracts, and certainly this is true of Mary, whose extraordinary religious experiences began 7 years ago. Consequently, the soil of her faith must be worked. But worked not only in retrospect and solely on the basis of Mary's report of her religious experience. Not at all. Rather, it must be worked in the present and by both of us. Here, now, with only the two of us present. An impossibility? Only for those who restrict presence to bodies positioned on operating tables and restrict time to the chronological tic of clocks which measure irrecoverable past moments. Such bodies are not relevant. The lived body holds attention. The meaning of clock time must be forfeited as well, and the strange circularity of chronometry substituted with the various kinds and intensities of lived time. And so Mary is to be recalled relying only partially on her exact words and even less on her case history. Her presence is to be revivified, saturated with an attention which approximates the passion of her own faithful adherence to that extraordinary world of voices and visions.

Many children should be so fortunate to bask in this face, to absorb the natural rouge of the double sun of her cheeks. A face rubefacient, it gives warmth and equally receives warmth. Is there a single feature which juts or abbreviates the roundness? Neither the high forehead nor the rounded chin. But to list the features of her physiognomy is to slant contrariwise to the impression of receptive wholeness which seems the essence of her face. How, then, draw near the face in its wholeness, in its limpidness, without resorting to discourse which has lost touch with the immediacy of experience?

Already is the moment for retreat, for a recovery of balance. This quickly was Mary known; this quickly was it written that the essence of her face is receptive wholeness. This is too quickly. A precipitously drawn conclusion without the precedent of carefully wrought description is as inimical as the kind of abstract discourse which has lost touch with the immediacy of sensory experience. But even this instance of "jumping the gun" may be revelatory. Perhaps Mary herself is one to "jump the gun," to explode emotionally without the prerequisite of careful reasoning and planning? Is she finally an impulsive child, the polar opposite of the wizened, silent woman who wordlessly struck me? The possibility must be kept in mind, tucked away, perhaps awaiting to emerge at a later moment during description. Its appearance is anticipated, for imaginative insight born of sudden immersion in the other rarely proves completely erroneous.

Having recovered balance, Mary is present again but more quietly. The uroborus of imagination feeds on the fantasied metabolites of sensory details. And so details will be brought to the fore, brought before the senses, and of necessity, the heart. Of her cheeks, something is known already. Their natural redness, their roundness, their buoyancy against which little deflected but much absorbed. These are the cheeks of a Raggedy Ann doll. Is the rest of her physiognomy as floppy and indiscriminately placed as the stylized features of a doll? Consider her chin, or rather double chin, even triple chin. There is a protrusion; something there is discernible, is pointed. Her chin is the slightest bit cleft, and this is a relief since passage is now provided past the inoffensiveness of her initial appearance. A faceted diamond may be turned in the palm, but without special instruments one is at a loss to segment its parts and examine its internal structure. Mary's chin is such an instrument: the flawless innocence of the face is penetrable now that the barely discernible jutting of the chin is apparent.

And the cheeks are not so perfect after all; the corners of the eyes are wrinkled as well. Yes, these are lines: she does age. She has said she is 37 years old. Even the complacent muscular tone of the high forehead is occasionally creased, lined with worry over unrequited love for Jesus. But is it worry only? There is a pungency about this woman without any odor being present. Pungency, as if measured by poignance and especially moistness. This is a delicate moment, an attempt to step from the forehead to a pervasive quality of existence, and so the method of choice is to ensure the validity of the move by anchoring awareness in bare details of immediate experience. With this done, the transition from forehead to existence is made more easily.

The mutuality of our experience was detached from the mooring of immediate experience upon mentioning the wrinkling of the forehead. To this we must return. Consider her response when asked what it is like for Jesus to speak. The forehead wrinkles and becomes moist; the cheeks balloon or bubble and redden ever so slightly in doing so; the lips draw in, puckering; the shoulders rise and are then subdued with a sigh; the mouth says, "He just slips in"; and the entire body then gives a wobbly shiver disguised with a strange, abbreviated chuckle reminiscent of a child's delight in satisfying some devious curiosity. She has given herself away and done so in more ways than one. For a moment this is the body of a pubescent girl delighted with the finicky eroticism of immature sexual play--a seeming Raggedy Ann doll who for reasons yet unknown has failed to match the stature of the lived body of a woman.

The spongy vagueness of the pungency which provided the hint for these explorations is now clarified, and, finally, vitiated. It was the experience of womanly fullness, manifest in the physiological flowering of perspiration and the diapedetic rushing of blood to the surface of the flesh. In its place, there is simply poignance--the poignance of the mismatch between the lived body and the normal expectations for the working of a body of this chronological age. With Mary, there is something out of joint, the generative source of selfhood known as Eigenwelt not having been matched piece for piece but rather lagging behind the bodily form of Umwelt. In this sense, she is the reverse of Binswanger's Ellen West, whose existential aging far exceeded the biological pacing of the body. Mary is a conglomerate: A Rubens in appearance, but floridly alive like a Madonna of Tintoretto only wishfully. She could never have posed for the masons who hammered and chiseled the heraldic seated Madonna on the forehead of the portico at Chartres. This other woman is a "real" Mary: firm, legs splayed yet utterly dignified, the linen draped in folds which obey set rules, and the child, too, firmly and squarely seated on her lap, arm raised in blessing. Where is that wizened, taciturn Mary who struck me 3 months ago? In her absence, is this what remains: the pubertal adolescent caught in giggles and childish eros? Recollection of the rest of her face provides guidance in answering these questions, unsettling if not unwelcome guidance.

Dare to consider her eyes: stelliferous pools of black lava. Her depth is within her eyes, even around them in the form of black eyelashes which echo the sinuous melody of the wavy black hair careening from the scalp and banking off the neck. The cheeks and chin have lied! The eyes and hair are of the truth! Or is the fault a tunneled and tunneling vision which pretends to discern difference and incongruity where there is simply the interplay of harmonic elements? Are Vivaldi's concerti imbalanced because of the dully present continuo, or do their very sway and momentum result precisely from the interchange of base line and melody? I have been fooled! Or rather, I have deceived myself. I have been too much the casual visitor who tours the landscape of Mary's physiognomy, seeing only the cheeks and chin, glimpsing the hint provided by the wrinkles and moist forehead, but failing altogether to account for these eyes and this hair. But does this mean that earlier discoveries need be relinquished? Not at all. Every relationship requires a spell of "getting acquainted." An Italian pieta may lurk in the folds of Ruben's buxom Madonna.

It has taken this long to "catch on," to experience as if by some unusual form of interoception the passionate gust which burns this woman and carries her heart to the vociferous heights of Heaven and the equally talkative depths of Hell. Such a gust recalls the simoon wind whipping from the Sahara and driving to madness and suicide the residents of Algeria and even some who live staid, risk-free European lives. But Mary's European cheeks are left behind: the African eyes and the Congolese hair are apparent. It is an African Heaven and an African Hell which now loom. This woman has not taken flight; she is not a Binswangerian manic zipping through the glancing, sliding element of air. She is sunk down, rooted. She is proof that spirit dwells in matter. Her Heaven is not populated by rosy-cheeked cherubs, bodyless little entities whispering messages, nor are the Hellish angels which demand equal attention the shadowy ghosts of a Limbo-like Sheol. She lives an altogether different world than that for which such "lightweights" exist. Hers is a rich world, a passionate world, the obverse of those cheeks and that chin which beguile the outsider into believing Mary is innocent only. If innocent, then passionately innocent, like the draped nun whose delicate gold wedding band is so paltry a disguise for a divinely inflamed heart. If innocent, then a daemonic innocence, like that which so frightened Herod, leading him to slaughter so much while even greater escaped. Indeed, Mary has been the victim of such slaughter: a husband divorced her, the three children were taken. Neither minister nor psychiatrist believed when she announced her truth: "I am the woman from Revelation clothed with the sun!" Thus she was driven and drove herself to an Egypt of the soul. To this land I follow, tracing a path marked by the strands and wave of her black hair.

Consider hair. Hair grows from a scalp. A scalp is the topsoil of a skull. A skull is the bedrock of the head. And a head is the very empyrean of a person's world, sheltering its needs and guiding its way with soulful constellations. So goes a phenomenological geography which doubles as a lived anatomy. Multiple levels of meaning spall from its mountain faces, variegated experience exfoliates from its vegetation. But note the oddity: vegetation is set atop the empyrean, plants grow from the sky, bedrock rests on air. This is ordinary geography turned topsy-turvy, a tectonic anomaly not a bit ordinary. Or so it seems. One has only to recall the cosmology of so many ancient peoples to know that this phenomenological geography, which is applicable to micro- and macrocosmos alike, is of longer duration and was more thoroughly worked than that which has left us empty-handed with stellar whorl in the eyes and a Big Bang in the ears. Think of the Babylonians, of the Biblical Jews, of others, all of whom settled on a tripartite cosmos with the top stair resting on the empyrean. In most cases, that top stair was little different from our stair: plants grew there, gods tilled, waters rushed over the surface of heaven and passed through celestial sluice gates, thus giving us rain. Given this antique geography and the anatomy which is its reflection, much is to be said for the meaning of hair.

Hair is Heaven's vegetation. Hair is the cornstalks planted and harvested by the gods. Hair is the sinuous turn of thought which occurs spontaneously. Hair is the conscious reflection of the body's impulses. Hair is either treated or unruly, is either an emotional storm or a false placidity governed by social morays. To lose hair is to lose strength, if not one's mind. Samson and Medusa are brother and sister.

Given all this, much is to be said for Mary's hair. It is of special significance. How her world is, has bearing on the fall of her hair. And on the basis of an antique symbolic logic, it may also be said, *mutatis mutandis*, that how her hair falls, has bearing on how her world is. To Egypt, then, following the trail traced by her hair.

Who lives in Mary's world, there on the top stair of her tripartite cosmos? The hair is somewhat dry. There are not "split ends," as the advertisements say, but neither are there greased patches with clinging and bunched strands. Each strand is separable from the others. Likewise there are many distinct inhabitants of her world, many voices, all masculine except for one, which are recognizable on the basis of their tone and manner of address. There are the angels of Hell, a soft-spoken bunch, normally gentle in their treatment of Mary, the one exception being years before when they claimed to hold captive her children. But they have changed since then. They needed only to be introduced to the ordinary world, helped along as one would a 2-year-old just learning to walk. "The truth changed them," Mary said, that truth being composed of the many small truths which compose the affairs of her daily life. They were softened by her singing, and when she would stop, would say, "Sing it again, sing it over." Softened, too, were these and other angels upon her invitation that they dine with her. "I take them to the Chinese restaurant," she said with the lilting melody of a bird's song, "and ask them to taste this for me and eat with me." Like the infant turning its head from a full spoon after only a few bites, the angels are filled quickly. "No more! I'm full!" they would say. And so Mary and the angels "cry together and laugh together." "They are my family," she said softly, "We have a lot of joy together."

The single feminine inhabitant of Mary's world, the cowlick which falls unhesitatingly from the left temple, thus blocking the line of vision, is Silvania. Silvania!--my Mary's own Lucifer, a darkling light in her otherwise bright world, an ancient light bulb twinkling in a modern firmament from which all meaningful stars have fallen, leaving a scattered array of black holes. Silvania!--she is the trouble-maker. Her voice is "loud," all others are "soft." She curses Mary. They wrangle, much to the amusement of Satan, who comments at such moments, "Those two are going at it again." In contrast to her love for God, Jesus, and the angels--the angels of Hell included--Mary described Silvania as a "bitch."

A bitch! Just now there is the tug, the reversion, the pull to acknowledge what memory brings spontaneously to the fore. Much earlier

I questioned the whereabouts of the wizened, taciturn woman who struck me with all her force, then walked away in silence. Is Silvania not that woman? Is Silvania not the acerbic backside of that passionate woman who relentlessly faces the Egyptian world of angelic voices? And is the Raggedy Ann doll not the balance point, the fulcrum which mediates between a mundane world of ordinary experience and the extraordinary one of Silvania and the angels? Is it not true that the experential residue of Mary's world is an innocent, doll-like sweetness once her taciturn aggressiveness is stifled and her desire for spirit is denied confirmation?

Speculation springs forth instantly with this last question. Is not contemporary faith often maudlin and sentimental, while behind it lurks a cryptic and snappish denial of hair-raising vitality and spiritual inebriation? From Nietzsche's announcement of God's death and his substitution of a will to power for the paper lion of the old divinity--from this to Freud's Thanatos, buried, and yet powerfully present, in a spiritually discontented civilization relying on a pasteboard faith: from one to the other, the message is the same, and here we see it with Mary. She has leapt and struggle is required for discernment of the remaining footprint, the sweetly innocent figure who meets a contemporary world which hobbles spirit and stifles the consequent rage. Our Mary, could she be a tragedy of classical proportion, a person set out like Prometheus for having reached too high by the standards of a spirit-denying civilization. A saint might very well seem a sweet innocent, if not a Raggedy Ann doll, for the striding businessman of Manhattan who blitzes whole continents with his video game and is puzzled completely by the motivation of the pamphleteer dispersing religious tracts. It must be said, what Mary has so painfully made obvious: madness is prophetic. Madness is the showing forth of spirit, whether good or evil, for a world which tolerates only a maudlin spirituality and a firmly stifled cry of rage over precisely this loss.

Who, then, has lost, and who has gained? I would have our loss of Mary be seen as her gain, her gain as our loss. Which is not to say our loss is irrecoverable. Now reappears the path, occasionally cut with speculative detours, which leads deeper into the Egyptian world of angelic voices and so closer to recovery of our loss. Her hair and eyes have been the guide to this point. So it will remain.

Beautiful hair invites a caress, it lends itself to pampering. Consider how the young woman's head inclines itself toward the brush. The brush is as a hand in blessing, the arm raised and the fingers positioned just so. The head bends, it subdues itself willingly. And at the moment it sways to the side, the hair falls, weighting the head unevenly. Sensations are rampant then, cohering in a single impression of svelte silkenness. A lovely moment, a moment of beauty which is not only sensed but simultaneously imaged--imaged as is a dancer whose doubly mirrored reflection transforms the one lonely body into a _pas de trois_ of gestural melody. The lived body, with even its smallest gesture, creates worlds, miniworlds, which are not simply sensory, but imaginary as well. From the inclined head with its silken weightiness arises the vague presence of a self-observing point, from which point then arises the desired viewer, the viewer capable of receiving and matching the embodied desire which is the inclined head with its silken weightiness. But such a moment is the mature fruit of long years of growth: Mary did not come to know and love God in so complete a manner until late in their lengthy relationship. The tousled head of the young girl is the precedent for such a moment. Without it, the woman knows not the inclined head, nor the effect of such a moment on the other. And between times, were it not for the self-absorption of the adolescent in whose head alternates frigid isolation and sultry dissolution, there would never appear the spontaneously modulated bearing of the woman's head. As with femininity and hair, so with Mary in her relationship with God. Step by step they have come to know one another.

In their early days, neither God nor Mary was skilled in speaking with one another, much less in the intimate emotional interchanges which characterize their later relationship. "Tell me! Tell me!" God would say, encouraging Mary to speak and nearly speechless Himself. But not only Him: Mary also tiptoed into the relationship, asking questions to satisfy her curiosity, relying on brief simple sentences. It was an awful and wondrous event to speak with God then. But as with ordinary relationships, especially those marked with the demands of romance and still seesawing between mature companionship and the tyranny of adolescent love, Mary and God's trepidation turned to a testing of loyalty. God would make demands Mary recognized were outlandish. His soft-spoken requests puzzled and embarrassed her. Could it serve any purpose to obey this command: "Scream my name!" But what is the alternative? An intense guilt over God's having been "let down." "He trusts me," she has said, "and I don't want to fail Him." But not only

Him. The successful working of the divine economy rests partly on Mary's enacting such requests. By such deeds, she participates with the angels in ensuring the salvation of others. For the same reason, she has struck other persons. Such behavior she finds reprehensible.

The testing of their relationship has its more subtle and painful side. Mary has known God to vanish for months at a time, promising beforehand to return on a specified date. Once He told her 2 years, another time 5 years, and she would "wait and wait, mark the calendar and count the days," only to find He had "tricked" her and had been "playing" with her. She would become frustrated and angered eventually. Finally, she resigned herself to His ways, refusing to acknowledge she missed him, and discovering in the interim periods that boredom was not a problem after all since the angels were always present.

But God is not only a voice. He is known to be much more. Mary knows Him to be an invisible tide of love, a rich shower of love, a fluttering of gold coins as from Zeus to Danae. This has been the ultimate fruit of their relationship. Her words: "Three years ago--it was the most beautiful experience of God I ever had, like nothing I have felt in my entire life. I had been praying when God showed His feelings for me. Oh, my God, it was so beautiful! They were just feelings, not my own. They could only come from Him. His feelings for me were good and beautiful, perfect, clean and good. Just like when you hold a baby, like when you take your son and hold him on your lap and squeeze him and love him and kiss him and he does it back to you. Then he feels your love for him, knows you love him. Your wife loves you. It's how you feel about your wife. When God did that to me, it was

His feelings toward me. I can't describe them. I didn't know what to do. I said out loud to him, 'I give it all back!' I went on and a couple of days later an angel came. A man was suddenly standing there--it was an angel--and he said, 'You gave it all back.' Then he disappeared."

Our Mary: A Rubens, a Tintoretto; a baroque concerto with a rich continuo; a Chartrian Virgin, even a pieta! Her hair is fiery spirit.

John

History

John is a 31-year-old, black Filipino-American. The psychiatric history is complete and reads like a veritable textbook of the most recalcitrant, violent cases of paranoid schizophrenia. The social history is less thorough; it revolves mostly around his relationship with his mother and stepmother. His "difficulty in separating from his mother" was remarked upon in a note from 1970, for example; and a discharge summary following an inpatient hospitalization in 1979 said, "he lives between two houses--his mother's and step-mother's." The mother would seem to have invaded his inner world as well: during conversation he referred to his "telepathic" ability "to turn people into living corpses and eat their flesh"--a skill which he has lost since his "mother telepathically turned off his power."

The first schizophrenic diagnosis was given in 1970, when John was 19 years old. His career as a mental patient began in earnest after discharge from the military in 1973, the year of his first hospitalization. Since then there have been nearly 40 inpatient admissions, some in long-term facilities and the great majority on acute wards. Drug abuse of most kinds and "sexual identification problems" had been noted prior to 1973.

A gleaning of psychiatric notes over the years gives a vivid picture of John's behavior and some of the symptomatology. On many occasions he has "killed" or "battered" family pets. He seems to favor cats, having "smashed one against the wall and killed it" in 1977. Dogs are not treated particularly well either: the mother wrote in 1979 that he "tried to kill my dog by hanging him, but changed his mind and cut him down." His mother's parakeets have long since fallen from John's good graces: he has "decapitated" at least two of them with a "meat cleaver." Humans fare only a little better: he has tried to "poison his mother and adolescents" by putting psychotropic medicines in their "coffee" and "hamburger patties"; he has struck his 1½-year-old nephew; and on certain occasions he has broadened his scope, remarking, "Now I am finished with animals and will start on humans--I'm here to wipe out the human race!" Despite claiming to have come from "another dimension than normal human beings," his homicidal aspirations would seem also to include himself since he has been known to "cut his wrists" on at least two occasions. He has "destroyed furniture and televisions" at his mother's and sister's homes and sustained "stab wounds to the chest" as a consequence of fighting. The history is replete with notes concerning his auditory hallucinations. An early chart makes the interesting remark that as a child he "would hyperventilate and compress his carotids because it made his head buzz and he felt good."

John was not an unattractive looking person, although the topknot of hair tied at the crown of his skull, his long red robe, and his peculiar Groucho Marx style of walking gave an odd impression. His features and coloring are more Filipino and white than black. His articulation and word usage seemed subtly indicative of subclinical temporal lobe dysfunction of the dominant hemisphere, perhaps more than the somewhat similar paraphasic, grammatically disordered talking in chronic schizophrenia. John dealt with each question conscientiously, even when asked to return several times to points which had been completely incomprehensible initially. I drew our conversation to an abrupt close after an hour when he began to "hear my voices talking to him, cussing at him because he wanted to listen to God." I assured him of my good intentions and he recanted, supposing that it could really be "Satan playing tricks on him."

Narrative

John's only experience of God occurred "3 years ago" after awakening from a "dream." The entire experience may be divided easily into three parts, all of them integrally related. The sequence would include the dream, the direct experience of God's voice "talking through the thunder," and a series of visions involving his activities immediately after hearing God. The visions are complex in their own right; voices and bodily sensations accompany most every one.

John had "slept all day," and "about 6:30" he began "waking up from a Soviet Union dream." The dream was "about the whole country chanting a witch chant--'Aahh.'" He remembers few details, but presumes "they had been practicing witchcraft." This was his "race" which was involved since he is a "quarter Russian," and he closely identifies with its spiritual orientation of "Satanism." He recalls "running from something" in the dream, an "execution squad or something like that," after which he "hid." Upon hiding, the chant began. Then he awoke "feeling proud of his religion" and grateful to the "Soviet Union" for "having given him dreams like that." After all, John does not fall asleep or dream "on his own": "other people put him to sleep."

John then lay awake in bed "thinking about his dream" for "15 minutes to half-an-hour." Outdoors a thunder storm was in progress. Suddenly he heard "God's voice crackle in the thunder," saying, "John, O.D.!" The "strength" of God's voice was great; only "Satan's voice" rivals God's in volume. It was "like a giant screaming out loud." The meaning of God's words was that John should die--should "overdose." John understood His words not as a command to take a fatal dose of some drug, but rather as a declaration of God's then acting in a manner which could be fatal for him. "God is an O.D. creature, an overdose creature, an overdose giant, and He was going to O.D. him for straying from the United States' beliefs and going with Satan." And what makes God an "O.D. creature?" "He has the power of life and death." His desire was to "threaten" John and make him "turn chicken."

What exactly was the relationship between God and His voice? The voice was that of God Himself, and its specific form was that of thundering words. It was "in the thunder" and spoke "through the thunder"; it was thundering itself, but worded. It was the thundering voice of God--"the same way He talked to Adam and Eve," John believes. "God used the thunder to speak with, to talk, like a ventriloquist voice with thunder." But this is not to say God is unable to speak in other ways, John thinks.

And what of John's feelings immediately upon hearing God speak? He was "shocked and afraid." And after feeling afraid? He felt

> an emotion as if I took part in a science fiction movie, except the science fiction movie turned real. The reality shocked me, of there being such a creature--the reality of God. It was like some kind of miracle. I felt like a miracle happened. I didn't believe in Him, that there was such a creature. It shocked me into the reality of God, shocked me into belief--gave me a belief feeling, a belief emotion. I found something new to believe in. God showed me He was such a creature, that He existed. It made me want to go to war with God. After I started believing in God, I wanted to destroy Him.
>
> And through what means did you set out to destroy God?
>
> I sent out vibrations to all eternity for God and every living creature to feel suicidal. When I sent out that vibration, God felt suicidal and every creature on earth started feeling suicidal. I saw God slipping into unconsciousness. When God turned suicidal, when He started dying, everything around me started to die. I felt my body starting to die along with Him. It was the emotion of dying. A physical feeling--my spirit started not to exist. I've seen it, experienced the feeling of dying. It's scary, the spirit leaving the body. God showed me what would happen if He dies: everything else would cease to exist.
>
> But how did you know all this was coming about?
>
> After sending the suicidal vibration, I telepathically asked alien beings and creatures how many got killed with my suicidal vibration. They can see forever. They said there is a whole forever-ness of dead bodies by letting me get into the minds of them and watch how they feel when they're dead.

Once more, please.

> When I asked, a boy I call Frog Face because his hands have suction cups like a frog, I saw him from a distance talking to me, saw him in my mind, and he showed me their dead bodies and let me feel the emotions of the dead bodies. Then other aliens told me how they were killed. I saw the creatures from the dark side, that's what they call themselves because they come from a universe of darkness.

They were voices, then, too? "Yes. Then I saw the lightning sector, the aliens from the white light sector, and after that the one from the hole in the universe. The creature that lives there, its emotions are so dark they eat up the whole universe." These names, where do they come from? "They gave names to themselves."

The feeling of dying, of everything dying--could you say more? "It's hard to describe some emotions. It was as if human life were nothing but toys."

The poetics of John's cosmogony set him on par with the mythic imagination of such Gnostic thinkers as Valentinus and Basilides. He fails in comparison when such criteria as intellectual rigor and systematic coherence are brought to bear on his thinking. "I got beliefs about God," he explained, "how I see how He came into existence." And what are they? "In the beginning I believe there was a vacuum of nothingness, and it was compressed nothingness that created something like coal turned into diamond. That compressed-ness of nothingness turned into God."

Satan and the anti-Christ are central figures for John's cosmology. Their names are used in different ways and at different times; never do they seem interchangeable. While John himself may be the anti-Christ, he harbors no such suspicions with regard to Satan. The latter is an object of affection. As John said: "I love Satan. I call him 'Honey Lamb.' It means 'O.D. heterosexual.' The Soviets call him that because of his horns and face; he looks like a lamb." "Satan forgives better than God"; "He allows sin, and God doesn't." Satan was gracious enough to "camouflage" John, thus providing protection by causing him to look "as if he is one of God's creatures." The basis for John believing he may be the anti-Christ is certain experiences which demonstrate his Satanic power. For example, he is able "to control the weather telepathically." "It was my brain that caused the rain to wash away that mountain that killed all those people," he said, referring to recent mud slides in the northern part of the state. Several days before then, he "looked at the ground and saw colors coming up into his eyes, and then he looked up into the sky, straight up, and then he saw clouds leaving his eyes and going into the air." Such was the source of the clouds from which fell the rain causing the slides. The weather could have turned even more nasty were it not for John "pulling the sunshine out of the earth and putting it into the sky again." Another reason for his suspecting he is the anti-Christ is the "cannibalistic moods" he experiences. His "skin turns colors": when "red," he is "drinking someone's blood," and when "purple," he is "eating someone's corpse." These "telepathic powers are Satanistic."

Considering John's cosmic significance, one would expect him to have very high goals. Indeed, he does: "My goal," he said, "is to destroy everything in sight telepathically. I won't turn real murderer, because that's why I'm in here, because I don't want to turn real."

The Portrait

A membrane, silken and translucent, softens John's appearance, and such a partition is fortunate, for its penetration opens an abysmal depth too vacuous for even lingering coals to ignite. Imagine the sight and sound of black wisteria blossoms tumbling through moonlight, disappearing beneath the lower border of an open window. Imagine stepping outdoors unclothed, the blossoms caressing one's flesh, clinging momentarily before sliding toward luscious succulent plants bearing the impression of feet. Would you step into that night? Or think of a magazine photograph of a spider's velvety face magnified with the enormous acuity of an electron microscope. Would you wish for it to actually be so big, such that you might examine it with the naked eye and without benefit of lense? Or recall Debussy's musical portrait of the sea, but replace this theme with the distant rumbling of the night of Armageddon. The first movement of Mahler's Resurrection symphony carries one toward an imaginative neighborhood proximal to John's, but there remains too much of human tragedy for the listener to slice through to John's vacuum. The divine dyads of Basilides' _gnosis_ conceive a world in proportion to John's and of similar mood, but with John there is not a benevolent Father waiting for the overthrow of a vicious demiurge. Nothing waits--or is it that he is weighted with nothing human and so finds his world an inhuman waiting? For what, then, could he be waiting? But the question is mine, not his. And so it must be asked: For what does description wait? John's figure is to be carved from the cool black marble of his world; his world is to be discerned from the hollows and gestures of his body. The call is for a suitable knife, for a darkening light, a light which snuffs the outlines of the daytime world while brightening the darkness of John's world. Description awaits its own light, its own momentum.

The silver edge of a knife now slices the partition. But there is not blood. Mary would rot in this vacuum like a precious specimen of love left exposed in a scientist's petri dish. In contrast, John thrives, for he is not human. He has said his appearance is only "camouflage" granted by Satan, who thus protects him by allowing him to look "as if he were one of God's creatures."

But does he even appear human? Perhaps John is a clown, a clown become man, a man who would attain the condition of quintessential clownishness. So he appears. His head bobs side to side as he paces the corridor, his chin resting ponderously on the chest. A nearly perfect circle circumscribes his face; his skin is dark olive, the texture flawless. Recently he shaved his scalp: fine, dark bristles create a prickly aureole which is surmounted with a topknot of hair jutting straight from the crown of his skull. Hands clasped behind his back. A bright scarlet robe reaches to his knees, fluttering with the rocking-horse motion of his gait and contrasting nicely with the muslin texture of the white hospital pajamas reaching from knee to ankle. His feet are bare; the cutaneous ridges of the soles clutch the linoleum momentarily, then release, thus recalling Frog Face, an inhabitant of John's world whose hands, he says, "have suction cups like a frog."

Clowns are of several kinds. There is the circus clown, the mime, the harlequin. To know if John is a clown, each must be considered in turn.

Consider the circus clown. He entertains. He wears a sad, painted face. If he lopes and frolics at the rodeo, he jeopardizes his own safety for that of the bull-riding cowboy. He is the parody of cleverness and agility, the paradigm of carefully avoided formality and of caring attention to the sensitivity of the audience. The clown is a careful man, a man of care, for his world is one of sadness. His landscape is patched with flowery meadows, drawing animals from the fitful starts and scratching underbrush of the veld. A soft horizon is almost within reach when mist arises, obfuscating sky and horizon. Never a squall, only a sudden graying of color, like greasepaint blurred with tears. Then the clown's mood melts, is washed clean, just as a deep well is bathed continuously with fresh water from its underground spring. And so the clown is moved, moved to tears, moved to protect us, not from raging bulls but from the despair he has overcome, his feet buoyed from the surface of some deep well. Buoyed and bobbing, for the clown is a dancer, not of ordinary rhythm dictated by an aesthetic conscience, but of unpredictable rhythms, like the gesticulating dance of the exposed roots of a banyon tree. Francis of Assisi was a clown; Kazantzakis says his dancing frightened the pope.

With John, there are not animals. A tiger would slink away, a giraffe would lunge and tilt toward the plateau, an elephant's sense of propriety and kindness would be offended. John has decapitated his mother's parakeets, dangled her dog from a noose, and smashed the head of a pet cat against the wall. The velvet texture of a purring cat's fur he has matted with blood; the docile warmth of a dog he has rendered absolute, cooling it with the rope; and the source of a caged bird's insouciance he has muted with death. There are not animals with John, and he would have there not be humans either: "Now I am finished with animals," he once said, "and will start on humans--I'm here to wipe out the human race!"

There may not be animals surrounding John, but are there hints of dance, suggestions of sadness and of concern for an audience? To dance is to be danced. Nijinski shouted from the snowy cliff above St. Moritz that he was God: he was danced by satyric madness. His audience, a dapper Parisian crowd wearing top hats, stormed from the theater when he was the Rite of Spring heard by Stravinsky. And they were right in leaving, for their hats would have been left askew and tattered by that rite. Nijinski, a sad marionette, appearing here and there among the drooping bodies of the asylum's inmates. Nijinski: a mad clown.

But there is not spring to John's step: the soles clutch the smooth surface of the rubbery floor, then release; the thighs are thrown forward, off-center from the trunk, and the recurrent flex of the knees accentuates the right angle of the legs to an unusual degree. Only the head bobs free of this march.

"March"--yes! The word is a door, for John's motion is not the gangly floating of Francis, nor the spindly madness of a Nijinskian marionette: his is the goose-stepping march of the Third Reich, the rushing saurian motion of hate, the swooping howl of animated corpses led to Valhalla by Wotan's Valkyrie. Yes, his dance is a reptilian march, his dancer is Wotan. And it was Wotan who noticed the bobbing head which refused the bridle of loyalty, which refused the company of valiant warriors, which became intoxicated on the mead of its own self-created madness, and which acclaimed its own mouth to spout wisdom surpassing that from the soothsayer Mimir's decapitated head. And so Wotan saddled eight-legged Sleipnir, yanking John from the company of the brave and dragging him to the eternal cold of Hel, there to sit in isolation near the deepest root of Yggdrasil, a tree not unlike Sartre's oak, which vaporizes consciousness and sends the mind swirling in a viscous tangle of sap.

In Hel, one's only audience is of one's own creation, and sadness is useless because it is too late for recantation. No, John is not a clown, at least not a circus clown. But could he be a mime?

Consider the mime. To mime is to live the body with absolute purity. The Nijinskian satyr-body of _Umwelt_ is not in question, nor the impoverished, spirited Franciscan body of _Eigenwelt_. It is rather the cultured, gestural body of _Mitwelt_ which one mimes. But mime is not mimicry. The transposition of invisible meanings to the arena of muscular activity has little to do with mime; even less does the replication of another's body with mine. For mime is not to make something mine, in the sense of possessing what is other than my body. Rather, mime is to make nothing of what could be mine, for mime is to be what is simply gesture. "An impossible task" is the critic's retort, since gesture is only what happens between persons. After all, gesture in itself is nothing. Precisely. Mime is impossible--impossible for a person isolated from his fellows; but for one whose communication with others reaches boundless proportions, mime is the only suitable form of expression for charity. The ludicrous gesture of the Zen master, the symbolic shard-scattering of the Biblical prophet, the ranting artist of Dada announcing the madness of the First World War--this is mime, just as is the transubstantiation of Marcel Marceau's seemingly normal human body. To mime is to embody that which is present for all because it is that which is the being of the other for each person. To mime is to fall in love without speaking.

In Hel, there are not mimes because there is an absence of community. There are puppets, however, creatures whose strings are pulled by hallucinated powers. John knows of such powers. He has said he does not fall asleep or dream "on his own." "Other people" do these things to him. The Soviet masses are responsible for his more inspiring experiences; he is allied with them, and together they follow Satan. Satan is dear to John. "I love Satan," he said, "I call him Honey Lamb. It means 'overdose heterosexual.' The Soviets call him that because of his horns and face. He looks like a lamb." The chief benefit of following Satan is his forgiveness. "Satan forgives better than God," John said, "he allows sin and God doesn't." The geopolitics of John's world is itself puppetry: Satan is the manipulative force responsible for the activities of the Soviet Union, God the force responsible for the United States. The boundaries of his world extend yet further; they are extraterrestrial. Sweeping into the vast expanse of interstellar space, one comes upon "the creatures from the dark side." "They call themselves that," John said, "because they come from a universe of darkness." And further still are "the aliens from the lightning sector." And beyond that is "the one from the hole in the universe." "The creature that lives there," John said, "its emotions are so dark they left a hole in the universe--he's a whole universe in himself." These creatures are "mental images," he said. John speaks to them, they appear and answer.

John is a puppet of Hel, not a mime. He is the opposite of a mime, just as the creature from the hole in the universe is the perfect complement to the illuminating, creative *Logos* of another John. Rather than the *logoi spermatikoi* disseminated throughout the world, embracing their matter with multiple creative forms, John is the broadcasting of countless hates. But Cerberus does not howl in warning near the gate of this Hades; there is only the quiet working of John's visionary powers. It required 3 days for him to create the rain clouds which caused the mud slides in northern California. Many persons were killed, and more would have been had not John "pulled the sunshine out of the earth and put it into the sky again." "It was my brain which caused the rain to wash away that mountain that killed all those people," he said. In "controlling the weather telepathically," John functions as a magical tube. Several days before the rain, he "looked at the ground and saw colors coming up into his eyes, and then he looked up into the sky, straight up, and then he saw clouds leaving his eyes and going into the air." Such was the source of the clouds from which fell the rain causing the slides.

No, John is not a mime. He is the perfect mime's worst nightmare. But could he be a harlequin?

Consider the harlequin, a Renaissance king's Fool. Recall Lear, a Fool's king, if not the king of foolishness. For he became enraged with spite and embittered with regal vanity when Cordelia spoke honestly, without flattery or contrived solicitude, while the two remaining daughters milked him of kingdoms and wealth. "Milked him"-- yes, because Renaissance medicine identified this kind of rage with femininity, frequently with pregnant women, and called it *hysterica passio*. Lear so names his disease when he chokes with anger upon seeing the righteous steward Kent:

> O, how this mother swells up toward my heart!
> Hysterica passio, down, thou climbing sorrow,
> Thy element's below.

Lear is a ripe teat of sour milk, a sagging container of fiscal pulchritude, and the two daughters know an unhappy mother desires relief from her double burden. Thus Lear is milked of kingdoms and money. But he refuses the liberating pain associated with drained coffers: kingly men do not cry over wounded pride and broken heart, nor does a powerful ruler revoke his wish for vengeance. Rather, he is liberated by default--liberated with madness. To the Fool he first announces the impending shipwreck:

> You heavens, give me that patience, patience I need!
> You see me here, you gods, a poor old man,
> As full of grief as age; wretched in both!
> If it be you that stirs these daughters' hearts
> Against their father, fool me not so much
> To bear it tamely; touch me with noble anger,
> And let not women's weapons, water-drops,
> Stain my man's cheeks! No, you unnatural hags,
> I will have such revenges on you both
> That all the world shall--I will do such things,
> What they are, yet I know not; but they shall be
> The terrors of the earth. You think I'll weep:
> No, I'll not weep.
> I have full cause of weeping; but this heart
> Shall break into a hundred thousand flaws
> Or ere I'll weep. O, Fool! I shall go mad!

And he does. Kent's informer sees him upon the stormy plain

> tearing his white hair,
> Which the stormy blasts, with eyeless rage,
> Catch in their fury, and make nothing of;
> Strives in his little world of man to out-scorn
> The to-and-fro-conflicting wind and rain.

The foolish king is a charred banner flapping over the night of a decimated battlefield, a bloated teat of regal vanity, the prey of darling daughters. The foolish king is a dry womb which has absconded from its "element below" and choked the heart with enraged need. The foolish king is but "a paltry thing, a tattered coat upon a stick." But Yeats's Byzantium is beyond reach for those who "strive in their little world of man to out-scorn the to-and-fro-conflicting wind and rain." For their transportation is wrecked; their burnt hands and choked heart are unable to "clap and sing, and louder sing for every tatter in their mortal dress."

Not so the harlequin, the king's Fool, whose very costume is an orderly panoply of color, a skin-tight adherence of design and flesh. His belled cap, floppy points jutting here and there, belies the bright mind's creative intuition with its flaccid tips. Momentarily they stand erect: the Fool is a scattering of bright stars in the king's dark chaos. Toting his wand tipped with a puppet head resembling his own, the Fool seems a masquerade of kingly order, while in truth he is the discernment of the king's foolishness and the patterning of his downfall. The Fool is a vicious joke, not to be taken seriously, otherwise the listener would be swept beneath orderliness altogether. The Fool's presence is dry ice in the open palm of our innocence: one laughs while the skin is seared.

The Fool is larger than a puppet of Hel, though he knows of the worm which hollows the root of the cosmic tree Yggdrasil, just as he knows the words spoken by the sybyline raven circling Wotan's head. The Fool is larger than life--or is he beyond life? He grows before one's eyes, a giant. He is the gallow's humor of God, the gasp of the hanged man which is confused with laughter. But which god is in question? Certainly a dark one. How might one describe a god capable of sporting for aeons among the shards left when the primordial nothingness of medieval Kabala exploded into the 10 Sefiroth? John has words, for this god is his: "In the beginning, I believe there was a vacuum of nothingness, and it was compressed nothingness that created something like coal turned into a diamond. That compressed-ness of nothingness turned into God."

Yes, John is a clown after all, but of a certain kind. He worships the Fool, and is himself struck from the image of this god. Even the patterned color of the harlequin's dress is part of John's camouflage. He has described "cannibalistic moods" when his "skin turns colors," either red or purple depending on whether he is "drinking someone's blood or eating their corpse." This is the voracious appetite of a hungry well, one filled with brackish water rather than the cool influx of the circus clown's well. It is the rotten, toothy grin of a hovering _vagina dentata_. It is to thrust one's tongue deep into a vulture's mouth, allowing the beak to close repeatedly while the two creatures--an oily carnivorous bird and Satan's puppet--swill the warm blood. Yeats said Troy burned with the passion of Helen because Zeus' beak held Leda prostrate, but John's concupiscence engenders nothing, for he is a cold fire and his mate is the void.

But is it possible for a world such as this to exist for any length of time? Augustine said evil is the privation of good, and the Good equivalent to Being. Another Neo-Platonist, devoted more to the soulful plasma of imaginative phantasms than to the etheral forms of refined intelligence, might ask: Is John's world to shudder like a crumbling tenement, reduced to inchoate matter? Are his features to be smudged, leaving a faceless digestive tract with mossy scales? Indeed, could it be this world is nonexistent, some sort of mirage appearing before the intoxicated imagination of description? I have met this man--once when he wore his bright scarlet robe and once more in description: he lives, if this may be called living. Thus the question remains: Is it possible for a world such as this to exist for any length of time? Binswanger said the hole named Ellen West demanded the oblation of her life, which she gave in suicide. Is John to commit suicide? He has slit his wrists twice, but this was in the past. Von Gebsattel has referred to a quivering dread in the face of anti-eidos, a primal fear of how life-forms decay, sinking away into meaninglessness. Is John to quiver in shock upon seeing that his world is populated with bloodless eidolons? Perhaps he is beyond conversion, unshakable and fearless even in the face of death. So he seems. But _Dasein_ becomes present in absences, just as flowing water fills hollows and as _Tao_ turns the empty to use. John is such an absence; his world is a faceted transparency of cosmic proportions ruled by a god who appeared _ex nihilo_. But he was filled when God spoke to him 3 years before our conversation.

John had woken from a dream he found pleasurable: running from "an execution squad" in the Soviet Union, he hid, when there suddenly began a "witch chant" sung by the "whole country." He grew proud and felt grateful to the Soviet Union for "giving him dreams like this." He then lay awake in bed "thinking about his dream" for "15 minutes to half-an-hour." A thunder storm was in progress outdoors. Suddenly he heard "God's voice crackle in the thunder," saying "John! Overdose!" This was the voice of God Himself, "like a giant screaming out loud," and its specific form was that of thundering words. God's voice was worded thundering. Its intent was not simply to threaten John with death, but was itself an enactment of deadly power. "God is an overdose giant," said John, "because He has the power of life and death."

John was "shocked and afraid" upon hearing God speak. Describing his experience after this fear, John said:

> I felt an emotion as if I took part in a science fiction movie, except the science fiction movie turned real. The reality shocked me, of there being such a creature--the reality of God. It was like some kind of miracle. I felt there was such a creature. It shocked me into the reality of God, shocked me into belief--gave me a belief feeling, a belief emotion. I found something new to believe in. God showed me He was such a creature, that He existed. It made me want to go to war with God. After I started believing in God, I wanted to destroy Him.

To kill God, John "sent out vibrations to all eternity for God and every living creature to feel suicidal." He spoke to "alien beings" capable of "seeing forever" and requested to know "how many got killed." They allowed him to see heaps of dead bodies and to "enter their minds" in order for him to experience "how they feel when they're dead." Sweeping into darkest space, he saw the creatures from the "dark side" and from the "lightning sector," and finally the abysmal creature whose "emotions are so dark they left a hole in the universe." The radiating center of these far-reaching spokes of hate was itself dying. John experienced his own death: "I felt my body starting to die. It was the emotion of dying. A physical feeling--my spirit started not to exist.

I've seen it, experienced the feeling of dying. It's scary, the spirit leaving the body."

Ezekiel's valley of dry bones is a verdant pasture compared with this decimated world. When asked what is the feeling of everything dying, John said: "It's hard to describe some emotions. It was as if human life were nothing but toys."

But it was not only creaturely death which John envisioned, nor was his death wish the fundamental cause of their dying. For creatures have a ground upon which they are, and without which they are annihilated. The sequence of John's experience was of God's dying _followed_ by that of creatures. His words: "When God turned suicidal, when He started dying, everything around me started to die. God showed me what would happen if He dies: everything else would cease to exist."

After this epiphany, John retracted the spokes of hate. Once more the world hub began to turn, wheeling deeper into space, further from the shore of those whose feet are planted in the common ground. But we would be foolish to assume this is a lost soul. Hear this: John retains the wish to destroy the world, but has chosen to work out this purpose magically with full recognition that this leads to his remaining cast out from the world of sanity. "My goal," he said, "is to destroy everything in sight telepathically. I won't turn real murderer, because that's why I'm in here, because I don't want to turn real."

God has broken the Fool, reduced him to a foolish king, and transformed his hate into an altruism of madness.

Luke

History

Luke is a muscular, 20-year-old Caucasian with a ruddy complexion and long blond hair. There have been 17 psychiatric hospitalizations since his first in 1978, two of them at long-term residential facilities. The events preceding the initial hospitalization at age 17 all but set the pattern for later ones. A thorough history was taken from the parents following his admission in 1978. I will rely largely on this information, later having reference to subsequent hospitalizations.

Luke was brought to the hospital "by the police on a 72-hour hold" after becoming "unmanageable at home." There had been a course of "social deterioration for the previous 3 years" with him "abandoning longtime and stable peers" and eventually "dropping out of school." More recently he had become "totally apathetic"; "sleeping and watching TV were his sole activities." He had ceased "eating for a week" and lost "15 pounds." To "simple and direct questions" he would reply with "surly and cryptic giggling." He made "exaggerated claims of his strength" and "invited his father to do battle." "Catalepsy" became apparent "2 to 3 weeks" prior to the 1978 hospitalization with Luke "assuming static postures," such as "standing on one leg for long periods of time" and "resisting being moved." He "salivated excessively" and engaged in "ritualistic and constant spitting." He "poured cereal on the floor and would eat it like a dog." At the table he would "eat without using his hands." He would "lie on the floor in the hallway for as long as 24 hours and refuse to move."

The psychiatric evaluation at admission mentioned that he was oriented and admitted to auditory hallucinations. A toxic screen was without positive findings except for the suggestion of "possible valium ingestion." He was known to have used alcohol and marijuana in the past. He has a 10th grade education. The admitting diagnosis was acute psychotic reaction. Other diagnoses over the past years have been schizophrenia, typically of the paranoid variety. A diagnosis of chronic paranoid schizophrenia seems indisputable to me.

The dramatic and violent character of Luke's first admission is echoed throughout his other hospitalizations. For example, several months prior to our conversation he lept from a telephone pole and fractured the thoracic spine. In the emergency room he cried out: "I have to die! Let me alone! People are going to kill me!" Four months later he was found tying a "hangman's noose from a tree." He has been thought a danger to others, and a move was afoot to certify him for this reason during the hospitalization when our conversation took place.

With an air of condescension and only upon careful consideration did Luke agree to share some of his "wisdom." He was the very image of a coiled spring, squirming tensely, at least within the narrow bounds allowed by the cast surrounding his entire midsection. The tremor and awkwardness from heavy doses of major tranquilizer compounded the poor coherence of his movements. He spoke softly; the self-assurance conveyed with street argot was much at odds with the quivering tone of his talking. This was a young man making a valiant effort to control and contain himself. He interrupted our conversation about his "seeing God" by saying:

> You got to keep down tighter. You don't belong in a heavy place. Get your words a little lower to what's going on because I can't handle it. What I'm letting go is private. Talk more sensible about the things that are going on. Talk a little more careful to what's going on. Not every little fine detail. Not every detail, but coordination what you're saying to the right thing. When you see God, you don't ask people such things. The baddest thing a human can do on earth is to see God.

Luke's case is unique in the series and especially valuable because we talked at length about the initiation of his subsequently ongoing "communication" with God. This initial experience coincides with the outbreak of the psychosis in 1978, as will be apparent from the link between the admission note referring to his waiting in the "hallway" and what Luke himself says about God's first "communication" to him in the "hallway." It was not, however, his most powerful experience of God. The latter occurred when he "saw God," but he refused to talk about this because God commanded him to be silent at that moment during our conversation. The narrative, then, will detail his first experience of God, followed by several more general considerations of Luke's about his nearly constant "communication" with Him for the past 2½ years.

The wealth of Luke's knowledge of God is due to his being a "special and powerful person." He is "Moses." God "told him he was suppose to be Moses from a baby, but things got in confusion with his parents and he wasn't named Moses." The proper sequence of events would have been for the "United States to have had charge of him" and for him then to have been "in the hands of Prince Charles."

<u>Narrative</u>

Luke was "walking down the hallway at home where he used to live."

While passing "this picture of Jesus on the wall," he said to himself, "I wish I was into religion--it would be nice to be into religion." Passing it another time later, he thought "he wanted to be as bad as Jesus was, to have that kind of bad." On the 5th day following his first thinking about his, he again passed down the hallway and "the picture winked at him." This was strange. He "didn't know quite what to think of it." He knew "it was God doing it, but couldn't sense it out, didn't know." He asked the picture, "Is that you, Jesus?" and it nodded its head from side to side. He then asked, "Is it God?" and the figure nodded affirmatively. This "happened a few more times" before the instance when God spoke, saying either "Turn on the music and I'll meet you there" or "Turn it on and see what happens." Luke proceeded down the hall and turned to his right, passing into the living room where the stereo was placed against the opposite wall. He turned on the music and God "introduced Himself," saying "This is God" and "You're a favorite ol' person of mine." This was their "first communication and they just progressed from there." Luke "felt at ease, very comfortable, not frightened."

God and Luke have been in "communication" and have had "closeness" since then. Only once during the past 2½ years has God left. This contrasts with other voices heard by Luke. They might be present for a "month at a time, then leave and then they'd come back and now they're gone." It contrasts also with the voice of Jesus, who is "different from God." Jesus has been present to Luke "going on almost 8 months, maybe 10 months--9½ months." As with God, Jesus introduced himself, saying "I am Jesus." A phrase of Jesus' spoken concurrently with our conversation was "doo-da, doo-da," which would seem to have been in character since Jesus is "very cool." God's voice and to a lesser extent Jesus' are those heard most frequently by Luke. Occasionally he will "talk to some people who die." In the past he heard a greater number of voices.

Investigation of the differences between the various sounds heard by Luke--ordinary and otherwise--brings one close to the auditory dimension of his world. "A very good way" of listening to God is "through the stereo." "This is the main way" Luke and God talk--"through the radio." How, then, is God's voice distinguished from the sounds broadcast over the radio, or is it? God's voice is "like programming on top of the other words." Evidently this makes it difficult to attend to music since Luke "really never finds out all the words to the songs." And how does God's voice differ from that of a radio announcer? God's voice has "more harmony, more characteristics." "Newscasters have sharper endings and God's is more smooth and mellow." Aside from His introducing Himself, how might it be possible to recognize God's voice? "Not everyone talks to you through the air. You can tell by the vocal cords--not the vocal cords but the vibration of the words into a person." Considering that other voices come through the air, how did you know it was God's? "Because it wasn't in my mind: it was in my ear, like you're talking to me there, just like anybody else talks, same as when you talk to your wife and your friends--it's the same thing." But other voices come through the air. "Yes, occasionally other voices come from outside, but really they're in my mind. God talks to you on the outside, not the inside. And besides, you feel God's words strongly."

And Jesus? "He says his words, and the words combine what he wants to say and what I want to say. That's the only way Jesus likes talking to me." What? "He's to my body and he'll look through what I say and speak words out of what I say through the vibrations of after-talking. The vibrations that go out would be him." As if He were in you? "He speaks out of my mouth through the vibrations of after-talking." But it's not that you speak his very words? "No."

God's talking would seem to have a certain affinity for objects, generally impersonal and mechanical objects which are moving, although Luke once mentioned His talking coming from "flying birds." The "radio" has been mentioned, but as well God talks "from a piece of machinery: a tractor, airplanes, jet airplanes--anything! It's just communication. No big deal what He uses. He uses what's convenient." Does He have a favorite thing from which to talk? "He probably does, but I wouldn't know that." Evidently there is little stability in the loci of God's talking. Luke "used to stay up all night talking with God, cracking jokes, having a good time." He "would turn off the radio," say "I'll check you outside," and once in the front yard would hear God "talking from a passing car."

Luke's "closeness" to God is such that I was able to pursue the question of God's experience of Luke and of our conversation. I was able to learn a little, but this was an exceptionally delicate matter. Luke resisted and occasionally refused to answer questions pertaining to God's present experience. To my request to talk directly to God, Luke said: "God wouldn't do nothing like that. It's out of order, not right at all, it's impossible." I could only learn "the words God already gave Luke." After all, it "takes someone very special for God to talk to him." And what of God's wishes for Luke and His thought of our conversation? God wanted for Luke "to discuss the right things in an orderly manner, not to go overboard and be embarrassed." God was "checking out Luke to see how he handled himself," which evidently he did rather poorly in that our conversation ended abruptly after Luke said: "I don't want to talk no more. I'm getting in trouble." He had already informed me he "gets into trouble if he says the wrong things." Once before, God spoke a word which led to Luke's interrupting conversation and announcing that "God said to 'care.'" Some while later he informed me that "God doesn't like pity."

In the broadest scope, what does God and Luke's "closeness" mean for Luke's life? He hinted at having a mission. "I'll be talking to other people," he said, "some ministers would probably like to talk." But first he "needs to get hold of himself and devise his words in more technical ways." His experiences are a matter of "testing," a way of increasing his "power and his closeness" to God. With more "closeness" comes "more power." In the process, "love grows." And despite God's "wanting him to have a happy life," which he "hasn't," God and Luke do have their "controversies." When presented with an especially unbearable test, Luke simply "turns away because some things I don't like to see, experiences he puts me through."

The Portrait

The fledgling crushed beneath a boot heel cries the faintest whimper, but the echo resounds with horrible volume, awakening a hundred objects to its pain, each of which takes voice and spreads the rumor of death to an entire world. The pained whimper has become the shrapnel of hallucinated sound; a new world has appeared, and deep within rests an egg, an Orphic egg, nestled with the assurance of complete impassivity and speaking with the voice of God. The etiology of divine hallucination is the filling of Elliot's hollow men, for what began as a whimper ends with a bang.

Now comes Luke, a scraggly rooster sitting on the egg which is God's voice. It rustles beneath him, but without engendering the kind of warmth a mother feels when her baby turns within. Rather it pricks him, torments him, swells him with power. There is "closeness," too, as he said; pride and power are not the only consequences of roosting with God.

Consider an old rooster, or rather a young one with premature senescence. The bright red feathers, the pendular tic-toc of the alert neck, the momentary lunge of the head, the aggressively spiked feet and the sudden gouging of hens--all are unattainable dreams for the cock dwarfed too early. The clock stops for the young rooster prematurely judged unfit for competition. It recognizes dawn, but sleeps in. In the henhouse it remains cooped, bypassing safely the clippers of the king of the roost.

But impulse may drive the rooster and raise its ire. It becomes cocky, believing itself fit for the fight, imagining its dew claws pointed with sharp metal tips. Thus Luke became stiff for long periods before his first admission 2½ years ago: standing erect on one leg, he refused to move. And to his father he boasted of his great strength, challenging him to battle.

The young cock with sparse feathers sorts the gravel for decent feed. It has all been taken; what remains are jagged pebbles which grate in the throat and puncture the craw. Acid leaks into the peritoneum from the ulcerous burn of the punctured throat; a burning reflux flushes the slender tongue with a slurry of granular fire. Thus Luke is said to have salivated excessively before his first admission, spitting almost constantly. This is heartburn of an esoteric kind; it flavors saliva with gall and transposes one's voice from a shriveled throat to a palatial egg resounding with a baritone bass.

The frightened little rooster confuses the dawn with moonlight. He remains on his roost, having eaten crow too often to greet the day. But he dreams of a lattice feathered with the brilliance of a Mayan priest's hummingbird headdress. The scraggly rooster confuses the dawn with moonlight as the adolescent Luke confused manhood with the dreams of youth. Thus he slept for days before his first admission, neither waking nor eating. Abulia is the strong man's nightmare, but the bed which cradles the little rooster's best dreams.

Goya said the sleep of reason breeds monsters, and he portrayed the same. What of Luke, who has lost his reason, and would have another reason for living than that held by reasonable persons? Without reason, one regroups, recuping his losses, stealing away toward the dimly lit shell of a new fortress. Timpani resound, trumpets blare, the gate swings open: from the dusty bricks of Jericho rises the New Jerusalem, built on rocky plains and centered about an altar trickling with rooster blood. The armored soldiers clatter over the fortress's porcelain courtyard, drawing near the altar. The rumpled feathers breathe a final sigh. The apparition of a stark fist fades; in its place stands an enormous man with a coarse brown cape and flowing white beard. Michelangelo gave him horns, for he is the dictation of God's Law and the power of its enforcement. A whisper descends from on high. Luke awakens to his new identity. He is Moses. God Himself whispered this: "God told me I was suppose to be Moses from a baby, but things got in confusion with my parents and I wasn't named Moses." The plan Luke thought was foiled has come true: the proper sequence of events, he thinks, was for "the United States to have had charge" followed by him being given over to "the hands of Prince Charles." So it is: the egg has hatched, its union fractured, and there stands forth a nation's righteous prince saddled with the golden yoke of kingly responsibility.

Moses was a foundling prince rescued from the rushes of the Nile and raised in pharaoh's court. Years would pass before he escaped, and even longer before he returned with Aaron to escape again in company with his people. Why Aaron? Because Moses was in need of an Egyptian voice: he was of another people and spoke with an antique pidgin echoed in Luke's own street argot. Why Aaron? Because Moses' arm was weak: Aaron braced his elbow while the Amalekites fled before the upraised staff. But the Psalms say Yahweh's arm is mighty, a glowering face leading the Ark into battle. It was a burden for Moses to be the horn of God, a ponderous load for him to support the arm of Yahweh. Without a voice, Moses might have been silenced permanently, even before he cowered beneath the rock while the ageless roar of the divine Shekhinah passed ominously overhead. Without a staff, even Moses' world would collapse, its axis--around which the Hasidim danced centuries later--reduced to a ribboned Maypole blown down by a Spring storm. One needs a staff, a flail for beating the chaff which deprive one of the bread of life. One needs a staff, a rod for punishing those unable to recognize the strength of one's arm. One needs a staff, a walking stick to navigate life's rocky terrain. One needs a staff, a sceptre to wield before the miserly face of those blind to greatness. Yes, one needs a staff, a firm back aligned perfectly with the world's upright support. But Luke's back was broken when he leapt from a telephone pole and fractured his spine. In the emergency room, he cried: "I have to die! Let me alone!"

Since jumping, Luke's midsection has been girthed with a chalky saddle. It aligns his spine, keeping it rigid, while constricting his breath, cutting it short. When excited, he gasps, but the constricted lungs do not fill adequately. When he walks, he lopes like a crippled horse. Yes, Luke is a horse, a battered horse--or is it an embattled horse? For he was pulled to the edge of an abyss of faith, like the hollow seduction shoved in front of war torn Troy; and rather than assay the cost of entering the fortress gate, he forged ahead, or fell, tumbling deeper than Kierkegaard's man of faith would fall.

More than a staff is needed for one who would bear the horn of God: a voice is necessary also, even if rent with the wheezes of a crushed chest. But if one's education is limited to the 10th grade, and if one's speaking is muffled by that of a crowd of soldiers milling about while awaiting its hallucinated leader, language is not as it should be.

Written Hebrew is composed of consonants. Some say Moses forgot the vowels of his langauge after seeing God, and was thus left to stammer gutteral vocatives addressed to Him only. His white veil would flap gently as if he were sneezing while actually he was mumbling incoherent penance for the entire tribe. Luke has seen God, but refuses to talk about it. His language reflects Moses' brush with the eneffable:

> You got to keep down tighter. You don't belong in a heavy place. Get your words a little lower to what's going on because I can't handle it. What I'm letting go is private. Talk more sensible about the things that are going on. Talk a little more careful to what's going on. Not every little fine detail. Not every detail, but coordination what you're saying to the right thing. When you see God, you don't ask people such things. The baddest thing a human can do on earth is to see God.

Luke: a Mosaic phoenix rising from a sacrifice of rooster blood, arising like Yahweh from His Ark, rising like vapor from the moist lips of a raped child. Luke, to whom God spoke during our conversation, saying "Care!" Care? Luke explained the word's meaning: "He means to care about things, and care about clothes you wear, the way you talk to people, the way you treat animals--anything! He only says that to people who care about everything!" But people who care about everything are delicate creatures, sensitive to hurts, pained even when watching a multitude of the enemy caught in the vindictive swirl of collapsing walls of seawater. A person too full of care is pitiable because he is without spine. This is why God spoke to Luke moments after saying "Care!" but this time with an indictment addressed secretly to me: "God said He doesn't like pity." Luke: so badly in need of loving care, whether it be the ministrations of another Luke, one such as Paul called a beloved physician, or the tender kindness of Yahweh Himself, which the Psalms liken to a hen gathering her brood. Luke, who says his "experiences of God are a matter of testing," his testing a way of their growing in "closeness," their closeness a way of his gaining "more power," and each of these a contribution to the growth of "love." Love? Perhaps the word should be "loyalty," for Luke attempts loyalty at any cost. He explained that despite God "wanting him to have a happy life," he "hasn't," since there are occasionally unbearable tests. At these moments, Luke "turns away because some things I don't like to see, experiences He puts me through." The cost of disloyalty is high. Moses turned away from Yahweh at Meribah, thus sacrificing the vision of the Promised Land. And Luke--what is the cost of his turning? What is the dream of a wooden horse broken against the rocks of faith? To be embraced by Troy, to enter the warm gates opened by Helen's wink.

Two-and-a-half years before our conversation, Luke "was walking down the hallway at home where he used to live," and while passing "this picture of Jesus on the wall" he said to himself, "I wish I was into religion--it would be nice to be into religion." Passing it another time, he thought how he "wanted to be as bad as Jesus was, to have that type of bad." Five days later, passing down the hall, "the picture winked at him." Strange, indeed, he thought, not knowing "quite what to think of it." "I knew it was God doing it," he said, "but couldn't sense it out. I said, 'Is that you, Jesus?'" and the figure nodded its head from side to side. Then Luke asked, "Is it God?" and the figure nodded affirmatively. This occurred a "few more times" before God spoke, saying "Turn on the music and I'll meet you there." Luke proceeded to the stereo in the living room and turned on the music. God "introduced Himself": "This is God," He said, "You're a favorite ol' person of mine." This was their "first communication and they just progressed from there." From there, Luke progressed through the city's resplendent gates, awaiting an escort to shoulder his festooned dais and listening for the spangled blare of trumpets. But the city would not be as he imagined, for within 2 years he would festoon a tree branch with a hangman's noose and enter the hospital alone on bare feet.

The New Jerusalem is a mirage for one unable to shake the dust of crumbled Jericho. The traveler chokes from the dust of his own cape; his chest feels constricted. It is not the shofar he hears, but his own whimpering cough. Rather than the tumult of victorious soldiers stomping across the rubble, the sporadic sounds of broken thoughts crowd his ears. But as with other adolescents, Luke did not easily forget the inviting wink. To roost with Helen--to become a man! To waltz across the fortress's porcelain courtyard, arm-in-arm with some young thing, surrounded by proud soldiers bearing silver shields. A wink opens a world! Who can resist peeking behind the red velvet curtain festooning the blank screen which promises every wish with its empty whiteness? But the city would not be as he imagined. Rather than loyal soldiers, the men heard by Luke come and go: they might be present for "a month at a time," he said, "then leave and then they'd come back and now they're gone." An unruly mob of brigands, this is, not a platoon of devoted followers. Luke was shucked of rank instantly, the stripes torn from his shoulder. He was taken to the edge of the desert and sent with the goat to the crusty arms of Azazel. It is a demonic face with slit pupils which winks in the desert, not green eyes set in an eiderdown face.

Life in the desert is difficult. One tends to grumble--for water, from boredom, for something green. Once into Sinai, the Jews grumbled. Moloch hovered at the edge of their camp; green sheaths were raised to Astarte. What better sport when faced with the tedium of an angry god who salts the pain of those embittered over their lot? For Yahweh is a jealous god: one has only to wink and His mind is changed. He shows mercy to the thousandth generation on those who return his love and obey his commandments, but those less distantly related to the wicked and hateful are punished. Of what is Yahweh jealous? Lilith knows, since she mothered Moloch, the fruit of her union with Azazel. Beneath some desert bush, this spiteful Shulamite was mounted by the demon. Thorns pricked her back. She bit at the goat's neck, but musky fur kept her from drawing blood. Some say her cry is heard to this day when a vortex of hot air brushes against a desert canyon. In such a canyon, she raised the hungry little god who would later mount to royalty in the enemies' pantheons. Of this Yahweh was jealous. Lilith once winked at him--his own sister! And he never forgot the pulsing french horns which flushed his neck with a crescendo of rage. He sent her wandering in the desert. In cemeteries she searched fresh graves for an infant still breathing. If her king would not give her a king, she would find her own. She pressed her lips to those of many tiny corpses, but in vain. Then one evening, with Ishtar just on the horizon, she noticed the unsettled earth begin to move: a fresh grave, one with life! On hands and knees she dug, clawing beneath the surface for warm flesh. She recoiled from the touch: could a creature be so cold and yet live! Azazel stood upright, uncircumcised--the earth's own phallus! Yes, to give birth by Azazel, what better way to vent one's spite over Yahweh's rejection? What better than to raise a child who would deprive Yahweh of his first-born? To mother a god to lead the enemies, one from whose brassy arms Yahweh's sons would slide into flame. This father who kept even Moses from entering the Promised Land--He would know a son had been born! He would know from the howls released by children who could have been his own.

A child may be sacrificed in many ways. It may be buried alive, drowned, or consumed by flames; it may be throttled before drawing breath. The task is more difficult the longer the father waits. Isaac was an exception because of his passivity under Abraham's knife. A mind may be sacrificed in many ways as well. It may be buried in the brittle earth of senility; drowned in the toxic flush of metabolic encephalopathy; consumed with manic rage; or wizened with permanent innocence by congenital retardation. Luke, like Isaac, is an exception, for he yielded to the knife trusting his father would behave as a righteous god rather than as Moloch. But the horizon of Yahweh's world is littered with tiny, bleached skeletons: they gleam at sunset, barely visible, and each spark reminds him of the lascivious antics of the bride he rejected. A god cannot be too careful: the seemingly perfect child may betray origins not one's own. Sheepish women, humble and obedient by day, are known to slip beyond the camp site during the evening. Some join the enemy's throng; what sounds like muffled drums are their feet beating a round dance to the time of struck bones. No one speaks in the morning, all ignore the evening's passage. At the well, women mention fresh goat prints at the back of their tent. A god cannot be too careful. Some must die; the stock must be kept clean. *Lex talionis* dictates that Moloch be dealt with in the way he deals with his own. The knife which circumcises the heart may slip, cutting deeper than its aim, severing the mind from good sense. A child may be sacrificed in many ways, one of them being to tear it limb-from-limb. A mind may be sacrificed in many ways, one of them being to tear it apart, letting its words depart to the desert--wrangling, disparate, and lost.

There they live, a thousand jangling words. Some roost with desert birds. Loud curses straddle the eagle's neck; soft whispers nestle in the down of sparrows; whimpers settle to earth with feathers. Birds of a kind flock together, selecting the appropriate bush. The carnivorous eagle, having little need for protection, chooses a burning bush or stumps standing starkly against the noonday sky. The sparrows prefer a sandy patch where seed might have fallen. Their pecking is idle chatter. And the feathers? They drift about, liberated from bloody entrails left by eagle beaks. A whimper signals victory for some birds.

Life in the desert is difficult, but Luke's exile has allowed close acquaintance with desert birds. He has become an ornithologist of the soul. He knows how and where to listen. For birds of spirit, he listens inside. "Occasionally they come from outside," he said, "but really they're in my mind." For the royal eagle of divinity, which the Psalms say shields the faithful beneath its pinions, Luke listens to the medley rising from happy caravans. "A very good way of listening to God," he said, "is through the stereo." But how is God's voice distinguished from the sounds broadcast on the radio? "God's voice is like programming on top of the other words," he said. "God's voice has more harmony, more characteristics" than the radio announcer; "newscasters have sharper endings and God's is more smooth and mellow." How is it possible to recognize God's voice? "Not everyone talks to you through the air," said Luke. "You can tell by the vocal cords--not the vocal cords but the vibration of the words into a person. It isn't in my mind: it is in my ear, like you're talking to me there, just like anybody else talks, same as when you talk to your wife and your friends--it's the same thing."

But the royal eagle is not so easily located as Luke leads one to believe. Prometheus knew, for the same bird swooped to dip from the dark red cells of his liver, while the hero was left wondering whether the fulminating screech was the bird's or his own shrill gasp. Lashed to the rock, he watched the floating wings recede toward the blue vault as a vortical wind lifted olive branches skyward and funneled pebbles beveled from the mountainface. The bird tore a burnished flap from the solar disc; the sky's dark pupil winked as it entered the blackness beyond. Rarely has the eagle been seen since its skimming attack on the roosting Prometheus. Once more, when Zeus tired of Hera's flabby goading and yearned for younger flesh more taut than his motherly queen's, did the eagle herald the god's voracious appetite--and that was when handsome Ganymede sunned on Crete's white shore, his milky flesh reddening with excitement as a dozen men pawed the sand like bulls while circling their catch. Mortals deserve less, bellowed the king, and certainly not such pearls as Ganymede. Thus he was dropped at the throne, thighs bloodied with eagle talons. Rapt from the common ground, he served as cupbearer to the king, his boyish beauty subdued by the gouging plunge of the old man's vindictiveness. The god has since spoken from any surface which collects sunlight, but those objects and sounds which mimic his rapacious cupidity and emotive blast serve best. "God talks from a piece of machinery," said Luke, "He uses what's convenient--a tractor, a car, airplanes, jet airplanes--anything!"

A bird with which Luke is little acquainted first appeared 9 months before our conversation. It has flesh rather than feathers; its ugliness belies the accuracy of its flight. Some liken it to the flapping edge of black material which serves as the opening for tents. It is rumored to feed on mites from the scapegoat's back, thus serving charitable ends for the most forlorn of creatures. Adulterous women are frightened when it alights near camp, since its wings remind them of hair tousled in wantonness. But they have been known to protect it from men, for it shades infants left abandoned in the desert and feeds them from its own mouth. Luke knows this bird as Jesus.

Jesus' voice has kept Luke company more closely than others, so closely as to confuse his very speaking with its own sounds. Neither "in his mind" nor "in his ear," Jesus is "to my body," said Luke, "and he'll look through what I say and speak words out of what I say through the vibrations of after-talking. The vibrations that go out would be him." "He says his words," Luke explained, "and the words combine what he wants to say and what I want to say. That's the only way Jesus likes talking with me." Close, indeed, is the voice of Jesus, as if one's self were mismatched with one's body, such that the mouthing of words was followed instantly by their internally worded afterthought. But this is not mimicry--those who speak of <u>echo de pensée</u> may not have heard, for Luke answered "No" to my question of whether he spoke the very words of Jesus. If not, then what kind of words are in question, and of which body are they the vibration? Jesus is "to his body," Luke says, peering through the knowing eyes of his words, and speaking within the delayed resonance of his own speaking. What kinds of speaking are in question, and of what body, or bodies, are they the vibration? The phenomenological grammar of hallucination is a hall of mirrors. One enters carefully, quietly. The dim candle of description is preferable to the beacon of abstract discourse. While the former lightens shade and accentuates sound in accordance with their experiential outlines, the latter constricts the pupil and blinds the heart. To enter, the body which speaks ordinarily must be known first. Only then may the reverberating presence of hallucinated sound be understood.

But how is it possible to sing the dense silent body? Our world is a reticulum of spoken meaning, created and sustained by the chirping presence of a thousand words. Should the net tear, we fall... Into what? Yes, this is an opening: we fall, or drift, into the body. We shrink toward the pliable outline of the cover of flesh. We return home--not like prodigals to feed on fatted calves, but as children napping on the mother's breast. For the body is the womb of speech, the mouth its pelvis. The body is the sad mother of dumb meaning, gesturing in anticipation of the echoed joy of its spoken children. The body is a recurrent sleep, lulled by the whir and noisy bruises of the world of sound, until the trilling tongue and the rippling sonority of throaty contractions mirror its presence in words. The body is the earth's very presence, the mouth its Lourdes. Rinsed in the grotto's bubbling springs, rows of pilgrims file from the fenced gate, some ponderous and heavy, others buoyant and light, some prepared to quicken the stubborn silence, others to form and reform the ragged fringes of the world of sound. Like a blind woman molding clay, the body is the unspoken builder of the common world of spoken meaning. How is it possible to sing the dense silent body if not by whispering in veneration of a Herculean task for which the shoulders of a gentle virgin must suffice?

But who smiles for the newly crowned words? An innocent Joseph trustful of his wife's intentions, or a grimacing Herod waiting with murderous forceps? Luke's god is known: the fate of his words is equally certain. His tongue will be circumcised, marking its bearer as an oracle of God. His words' wings will be clipped upon rising from their mouthy roost; tumbling back, they flutter like sparrows in the cave of the mouth. Fatherless in the common world of sound, unwelcome and poorly received, the orphaned words retreat, trailing a hollow resonance like tinseled wishes. For unwelcome words neither fade nor die--there is not an audiometry so sensitive as to record the body's call for birth. They return home--foiled pilgrims with needs unmet. The leprous words banging a belled staff cluster in the entrails; the elevated words spoken with hyphens and capitals occupy the skull; the brusque speech of elisions and exclamation marks clings to the throat;

the makeshift chatter of the marketplace settles lightly in the mouth. A second body is thus created; a speaking within a speaking, a life within a life, a son within a mother, a word within the silence.

Life in the desert is difficult. The wail of a broken cello is heard from the rubble of Jericho.

Chapter 5

DISCUSSION

The advances of the present study are many, and as with explorative work of any kind, these advances are marked with questions and probes for further investigation. The concluding chapter considers such matters with the guidance provided by the following format. The methodology is discussed first; several serendipitous findings born of the invention of the methodology are given afterward. The critical literature review is discussed briefly, followed by a lengthier consideration of the portraits. The points belonging to each of these four sections are numbered, not to indicate relative importance but merely for ease of organization. The study concludes with a description of the nature of God's presence as experienced during schizophrenic psychosis.

The Methodology

1. The methodology of the present study is a psychologically coherent and philosophically attuned means for the phenomenological investigation of the experience of schizophrenic psychosis. It has extended the reach of phenomenological-psychological investigation to the experience of actively psychotic patients. Persons diagnosed schizophrenic have, of course, been the central figures of the study, but the addition of a person suffering with the acute effects of a cycling affective illness suggests that the method may be applicable

for varieties of psychoses other than schizophrenic. The methodology demands critical attention and more instances of application in order to determine the validity of its claims, its utility for different varieties of mental illness, and the emendations which may be warranted given a subject matter different from the religious experience of persons diagnosed schizophrenic.

2. The methodology has clarified the nature of data for phenomenological-psychological research (pp. 46-48; 83-93). The twofold distinction between factual data and phenomenological description, and between the states of consciousness pertinent to each, is basic to this research and advocated for future phenomenological-psychological investigations. Distinguishing between levels of factual data is an equally important advance, especially because it allows one to organize data in accordance with a hierarchy based on such phenomenological criteria as intensity of presence, kinds of temporal experience, and degrees of negative and positive affective involvement with the patient. The idea of a hierarchy of factual data could be extracted from the present study and utilized in other kinds of phenomenological or empirical research.

3. The methodology offers a means of questioning which preserves maximum flexibility while allowing careful clarification of the content material gathered during patient interviews (pp. 54-58). This involves shifting from a focus on content alone and reestablishing one's perspective in accordance with the formal outline of the experience under investigation and the logical principles to be employed during questioning. The problems associated with using protocols or a

completely unstructured interview format are thus obviated. The basic idea of the formal outline of an experience and the equally simple procedural matter of employing the principles of symbolic logic during questioning could be adopted for other kinds of phenomenological research, although the particular logical principles and the specific features of the outline would probably require change given a subject matter different from the experience of God.

4. The call for a new attitude is an important advance (pp. 58-64; 66-76). The following are some of its implications and ramifications. The new attitude links traditional Buddhist psychology with Western phenomenological psychology and does so in the context of psychological research. A step is taken beyond simply noting one or another parallel between traditional Eastern psychologies and certain elements of Western psychology, or advocating the utility of Eastern psychological techniques for achieving the vaguely defined goal of personal growth. The context is psychopathological research; the gulf between Buddhist and Western psychologies is spanned by the enterprise of phenomenological-psychological investigation. But this is not to say the new attitude is without personal repercussions. Indeed, there is an ethical dimension to the new attitude as well as an invitation to psychological transformation. An instance of the transformation advocated by the methodology is the call for a change of consciousness such that certain phenomena become apparent which might not otherwise. The ethical dimension of the new attitude is especially prominent in the discussion of the morally repugnant and aesthetically revolting features of the severely disturbed schizophrenic patient. The present study faces

squarely the ethical dimension of psychological research; its methodology pays particular attention to the impact of the researcher's own psychology on the specific features of his attitude toward the patient. Such matters deserve further consideration; they complement the strongly utilitarian, explanatory, or theoretical emphasis of much psychological research past and present.

5. The presentation of communication and recollection draws upon a variety of psychological procedures and philosophical ideas which seem not to have been linked before (pp. 76-81; 93-107). A degree of scholarly interest accrues from the jostling of such ideas and procedures; each is clarified in their mutual contact. The invention of phenomenological-psychological research techniques is another result of such an undertaking. These techniques demand critical attention and more instances of application. The more varied the psychology of those who employ them, the better, since this would allow a clearer understanding of such questions as the interaction of the psychological predisposition of the researcher and the results obtained from application of the techniques. The experience and results of communication and recollection probably vary, depending on such factors as the naturally favored perceptual modalities of the researcher and the kinds of stimuli offered by the patient during conversation and recollection.

Of the varied experiences to which the method provides access, communication is one of the most valuable, despite its not being an essential step for the collection of factual data or the portrayal of the patient. Progress has been made in understanding the psychology of communication with the discussion of eidetic intuition and the ambivalence of portraiture. More clarification is in order. This would be a theoretical endeavor to some degree. Of those phenomenologists who might provide guidance because of their having given attention to human encounter, Gabriel Marcel comes to mind immediately. The distinctly psychological perspective of Husserl's intentional analysis of the intersubjective world might provide a sound complement to study of Marcel's existentialism. Further theoretical developments based on the work of such scholars would need to go hand in hand with application of the evolving methodology for experiencing communication.

6. The wording of recollection ranks alongside communication as one of the more elusive elements of the methodology. The presentation of the wording of recollection involves a tacit phenomenology of creative verbal expression. A hermeneutic is in question; its chief concerns are the power of words to elicit imaginative imagery, the epistemological status of words relative to imagery, the kinds of consciousness implicated by different kinds of word usage, the perceptual features of spoken and written words, and the stylistic features of language which is not predominantly denotative and univocal. In some cases, the presentation of wording spans the distance between offering its ideas with the kind of language governed by simple, denotative word usage, on the one hand, and the poetic display of the kind of evocative, polyvalent word usage of portraiture on the other. This tacit phenomenology of creative verbal expression requires elucidation; this would be an essential step toward fully understanding the language of the portraits. A fully developed phenomenology of the wording of recollection might

also provide fresh insights with regard to the peculiarities of language in schizophrenia.

7. The presentation of the methodology breaks down the insularity of phenomenological-psychological research by linking the concerns specific to phenomenological psychology with a broad range of material from a variety of psychological subdisciplines. The "hard" data of neuropsychology, physiological psychology, and learning are not an exception. The theoretical developments of phenomenological psychology reflected in its methodologies must be marked by exceptional rigor, otherwise the entire endeavor floats away on a sort of insubstantial, conceptual haze. One way of preventing this is to link the elusive and often esoteric concerns of phenomenological psychology with its neighboring disciplines while preserving the integrity of the special phenomenological concerns. The present methodology models the effort of meeting these goals.

Serendipitous Findings

1. The near equivalence of the prevalence figures for the experience of God in schizophrenia and for normals was a surprising and interesting finding (pp. 51-54). Needless to say, the validity of these data rests on gathering additional information from a larger sample of persons diagnosed schizophrenic. The meaning of these prevalence figures for the question of the normality of God-experience was given close consideration; its value for determining what was called the "phenomenological integrity" of the experience of God was emphasized strongly. The question of "phenomenological integrity" seems a new and important idea since it helps guard against the vagaries of

phenomenological-psychological research which has not determined whether its subject matter is a discrete and integral phenomenon.

2. An outgrowth of the development of the method which was unplanned and striking is the discussion of the "ambivalence" of recollection and the "bi-vocal" nature of portraiture (pp. 101-107). This discussion allows Emmanuel Levinas to assume a place of importance for phenomenological-psychological research which has been occupied previously by Husserl, Binswanger, or others. The depths of inter-subjective experience assume a place of importance concomitantly--a place which would seem to have lain vacant. This is one of the frontiers of phenomenological-psychological investigation; the present research has advanced haltingly into this territory by discussing the stylistic ramifications for portraiture of the kind of communication which is marked with the experience of the expanding meaningfulness of the other communicant.

The Literature

1. The literature presented in the first section of the second chapter is highly varied and drawn from a broad range of subdisciplines clustered under the labels of psychiatry and the psychology of religion. Furthermore, the presentation of this material is necessarily critical; the paucity of literature with bearing specifically on religious experience in schizophrenia, and the implicit adoption of a phenomenological perspective, demand such a stance. The outcome is an informative overview which clears the stage for the specifically phenomenological orientation of the remainder of the

study; the disadvantage is that relevant and significant literature may have been overlooked or swept aside due to the declarative tone of the critiques and a quite general analysis which neglects a fine-grained attention to specific studies.

2. The second section of Chapter 2 is more substantive than the first. Some traditional terms of phenomenological psychopathology are restored to currency, thus linking the present study with the roots of phenomenological psychopathology and anticipating the use of these terms in the portraits. Questions of significance for the study are addressed, not the least of which involves the presence, in comparison with the existence, of God. Straus's psychology of sensory experience is given close attention. Besides providing an informative evaluation of several important notions from the phenomenological psychopathology of schizophrenia, the second section gives a sense for the historical development of this field. The latter was felt to be a necessity because the present study is situated academically in the European branch of phenomenological psychology known as phenomenological psychopathology.

The Portraits

1. The value of the portraits rests in their impact on the reader. Just as description is an encounter with the patient, so the portrait is meant to evoke the reader's encounter with the patient. These are intersubjective matters, as was discussed at length in Chapter 3, and are not entirely explicable in terms of the language and states of consciousness common for the evaluation of empirical data. The portraits are capable of eliciting an experience like that of the actively psychotic person diagnosed schizophrenic. Those who fall into

the portraits, wittingly allowing themselves to experience the moods, feelings, images, the appeal for fantasied sensory experience, and other dimensions of the experience of portraiture--these readers may have a new experience of themselves and of the patients. They may be able to sense the outlines of the patient's world and see how the particular experience of God is congruent with this world. This is not to say the satisfaction of such possibilities is a necessary consequence of reading the portraits. For some readers, the portraits may be an obscure, black net without sense, without power, and without any provision for common sense. For such persons, in other words, the portraits share the obfuscation and meaninglessness they find in the experience of psychotic persons diagnosed schizophrenic.

The variables which influence the reader's ability to fall into the portrait are several. Those versed in mythology and archetypal psychology have a decided advantage in that this background spares them having to refer often to the glossary; a certain name--say, "Athena"--elicits a response instantly, allowing them to proceed without losing the development of the portrait. An interest in the language of schizophrenia and a readiness to adopt a form of word usage other than the denotative are helpful also. Perhaps most important is a willingness to sacrifice the modulatory power of dominant hemisphere language functions for the flexibility of auditory, tactile, gustatory, olfactory, and especially visual imagination. The psychological typology of the reader is significant in this regard.

Those able to experience the portraits as other than a hazardous net of nonsense may find their world is more encompassing. The range of experience from which the psychotherapist may draw will have grown somewhat, and his ability to engage the actively psychotic person diagnosed schizophrenic will have become more efficient.

2. The portraits vary; they do not have the same kind or the same degree of evocative power. Paul's portrait, which was written first, has somewhat the character of a pilot study, a first effort in the application of the methodology. Its stylistic continuity is not so great nor its composition so intimately informed by recollection as the remaining three portraits. Its evocative power seems less intense as a consequence. The emphasis given perceptual experience, and the germinal force attributed to the lived body for the creation of a possible imaginative world, ally Paul's portrait with Mary's and signal the contrast of both of their portraits to the later, more mythopoeic portraits of John and Luke. The four portraits illustrate an interesting development in this respect: they range from the portrait of Paul and to a lesser extent that of Mary, both of which are phenomenologies of perceptually oriented world-building based on the lived body, to those of John and Luke, which illustrate the creation of imaginative worlds in which the patient seems almost to shrink away as a figure will vanish when one focuses upon its ground. This development recalls the gradual change in phenomenological philosophy from the perceptual emphasis of early Husserlian constitutional analysis to the poeticized philosophy of late Heidegger. The implications of there being a parallel between the sequence of the portraits and the development of phenomenological philosophy, should it prove itself under careful examination, would be interesting. One might ask what

elements are common to the methodology of the study and of the philosophies in question, thereby coming to understand the psychology basic to the creation of phenomenological philosophy. The psychological links between myth and some kinds of phenomenology might also become more apparent.

4. Paul's portrait adopts Straus's seminal idea of the upright posture, extends its use to the domain of psychopathological experience, and enriches its meaning through treating it as a dynamic structural reality rather than a static interpretive symbol. A degree of predictive force accrues to the idea once it has been understood as a structural reality comprising a systematic set of organizational changes. An instance of this is the way in which the basic form of Paul's experience of God could be anticipated and outlined simply on the basis of using the idea of the upright posture as a hermeneutic key to understand his experience of the body and of the world. That phenomenological description might have predictive power is a fascinating idea which deserves more attention. One might ask what other keys there are beside the idea of the upright posture.

The role of the upright posture in Paul's portrait recalls the discussion of Jung and Binswanger in Chapter 2. Jung's idea of _enantiodromia_ was linked with Binswanger's conceptualization of the development of schizophrenic existence; a polarized structure which reverses itself in a dialectical fashion was seen to underly both men's thinking. This similarity may now be extended to include the interpretation given the idea of the upright posture in Paul's portrait, since Paul, too, undergoes a dramatic reversal of the anatomical-cosmic axis based on his accentuation on one pole of the upright posture over and against the other. Jung's enantiodromia, Binswanger's conceptualization of the dialectical turn which plummets schizophrenic existence into oblivion, and the interpretation given the upright posture in the present study--all share a basic insight into a dynamic, polar structure which reverses itself in a dialectical fashion at certain moments of schizophrenic existence.

5. The portraits use traditional religious ideas and images in a manner which remains psychological without thereby accruing the marks of reductionistic psychologism. The images typically have the status of imaginative analogies. Some of the ideas, especially for the first portrait, are without the spontaneity, suddenness, and aesthetic appropriateness evident with an adequate imaginative analogue; their effect is different as a result. Consider, for example, the difference between the idea of incarnation in Paul's portrait and the figure of Lilith in Luke's. The first is a technical theological term which carries considerable interpretive and organizational power in understanding Paul's world and his experience of God. Lilith, in comparison, is a vivid and disturbing imaginative presence. She is a member of the divine and semidivine mythological lineage of which Luke's god is also a part. She is less an interpretive key brought to bear upon the factual data of the narrative of the experience of God, and more the result of discerning intuitively a haunting anima figure which appears given the archetypal constellation of Luke's world. One might expect Luke to actually know such a figure, either through hallucination or in the form of an overpowering and menacing mood.

Here, then, are two examples of the way traditional religious ideas and images function within the portraits. Careful examination would yield other functions for such ideas and images. In neither case does the image or idea escape the bounds of psychology and assume a role with strictly doctrinal, metaphysical, or theological import. That traditional religious material may be used in this manner, as demonstrated by the portraits, has significance for the psychotherapy of schizophrenia, since the treatment of such patients often stumbles upon just this kind of material. The patient exaggerates and concretizes his dear, hallucinated, godly powers; the psychotherapist accepts at face value the patient's claim to have experienced perceptual realities other than ordinary and yet denies on metaphysical grounds that they have a reality other than mere fantasy. A tacit battle ensues based on the unspoken and poorly understood field of conflicting assumptions about the nature of reality. In some cases, a phenomenological perspective on the part of the psychotherapist toward the religious ideas and images of schizophrenic psychosis might provide the saving link of communication with the hallucinated and deluded patient. The portraits, and the methodology which establishes the psychological conditions for the creation of the portraits, embody such a perspective.

6. Another value of the portraits, and of the psychological condition which allows their spontaneous creation, rests on their being used as archetypal templates from which hypotheses about the patient's personal history and the structure of his family of origin may be derived. The derivation of hypotheses is a matter of interpretation, not unlike the psychotherapist's effort to interpret

a dream; its validity corresponds to the degree of spontaneity which marks the mythopoeic portions of the portrait to be interpreted. Such is the nature of imaginative analogy: the analogy for some element of the experience of God, or for some feature of the patient's lived body, is assumed to embody and express the same archetypal constellation found in other, unexamined aspects of the patient's life. The mythopoeic phenomenology of the experience of God and of the lived body is accorded a special status in this respect: it epitomizes the patient's world, real or imagined, and may thus be used as the primary material to be interpreted in the context of the patient's personal history and family structure.

To illustrate this process of interpretation, Luke's portrait may serve as an example. Let the imaginary figure of the rooster, the legend of the scapegoat, the mythological place the portrait identifies as the New Jerusalem, and the mythological figures of Yahweh, Lilith, Azazel, and Helen be the primary material which is assumed to yield the personal-historical and familial hypotheses. The first step of interpretation requires one to link Luke and the central family members to certain of the portrayed figures. This is a matter of identifying these persons and figures in a static fashion: interpretation has yet to move to the level of psychodynamic process. Luke may thus be identified as the family scapegoat; his mother as the two-faced feminine presence resembling the loving and lovely Helen, on the one hand, and a bitter demon like Lilith on the other; and the father as a mighty, authoritarian, Yahweh-like presence so thwarted by his son's masculinity that he would castrate him emotionally.

The second step of interpretation proceeds on the level of psychodynamic process and allows one to delve speculatively into the predominant patterns of the family process. For example, the Lucan myth suggests that the marital relationship is terribly one-sided, with the father's threatened, jealous, legalistic personality contributing to the wife's displeasure and flirtatiousness toward the son and perhaps other men. The son, Luke, abounds with need for the mother, but finds her face turned, resembling Lilith's more often than Helen's. The lordly father oversees these episodes; his thoughts turn to circumcision and his jealousy to greater acquisitiveness, as do Yahweh's when He is possessed with suspiciousness over the sneaking, nightly activity of the women of the portrait. Not only are the mother-son and the husband-wife bonds troubled due to the faulty marital relationship, but one is able to discern what is ordinarily called an identity problem based on the faulty father-son relationship. Recalling the early section of the portrait, Luke may be understood as the helpless, strutting little rooster who is sacrificed to the father. Luke's fantasies of assimilating the father's power, ruling the roost, and acquiring the bodily and emotional accouterments of manhood grow to enormous proportion due to the father's thwarting of Luke's filial needs. This is psychosis--the very breaking forth of psychosis, reflected clinically in Luke's identifying with Moses, the mightiest of Biblical fathers, as Freud (1953/1975d) knew, and reflected imaginatively in the New Jerusalem, obedient soldiers, military victory, and the winning of Helen. An orthodox Jungian would notice a dialectical process of compensation occurring at this moment: the sacrificial death of the measly rooster triggers the emergence of a mighty father archetype in full psychotic display.

Even this bundle of hypotheses may be enlarged, and more refined ones discerned. For example, given this sketch of the probable father-son relationship, it is no wonder that Jesus winks. This is the initial seduction into psychosis, and it occurs due to the wink of a son (Jesus) who was loved, loved right into the heavenly court of the mightiest of all fathers (God the Father). But women wink at men customarily, or vice versa, thus we see Luke's gender confusion, a psychopathology associated commonly with adolescent identity disorder, paranoid personality disorder, and according to early Freudian formulations (Macalpine & Hunter, 1956), paranoid schizophrenia. The wink, then, is congruent with Luke's diagnosis as well as the interpretation of the father-son relationship based on the Lucan myth.

Luke's is a deeply tragic portrait. There is not a history of schizophrenia in the family, and the outbreak of Luke's first episode occurred at the expected age and with the florid, agitated, and religious symptomatology associated commonly with schizophreniform psychosis. Yet the illness has continued for several years and over many hospitalizations. Luke continues to plummet into an abyss stirred with the gale force of madness. The intellect searches in vain for causative factors; it grasps at straws when intent on explaining Luke's downfall. But imagination forges ahead, drawing closer to Luke, his world, his experience. If the psychotherapist is to meet this young man, or others of his kind, on territory governed by mutual understanding rather than major tranquilizer, then he must master unusual forms of cognition which grant a quick grasp of the basic outlines of the psychotic material and an efficient means of generating personal-historical hypotheses. The methodology of the present study attempts a definition of such forms of cognition; the portraits display their application; and the brief interpretation of the Lucan myth illustrates the possibility of this method and its results yielding an efficient means of generating personal-historical hypotheses.

7. A fruitful extension of the present research would be to gather additional factual data on the basis of which would be constructed a typology of religious experience in schizophrenia. This is a different kind of endeavor than portraiture; in some respects its utility would be greater. A typology would allow for the creation of numbered and clearly delineated questions to be used in a formal protocol. On this basis, correlations could be established between kinds of religious experience and psychodiagnosis. Mary's narrative suggests that God may be experienced during schizophrenic psychosis in a developmental fashion, such that the patient's ongoing experience of God parallels both the developmental sequence of adolescence and various phases of the psychotic process. Ideas of this nature could be pursued with a protocol which provided a standardized set of content responses to questioning.

Additional benefits of a typology would be the following. Provision would be made for the psychotherapist without imaginative leanings but with a sincere interest in the psychotic experience of the schizophrenic patient. The typology would gather an array of the most popular images and ideas linked with psychotic religious experience and would indicate those most commonly associated; the unusual terrain of religious madness would become less foreign as a result. The typology would indicate common sequences of religious experience without implicating a theoretical bias, thus enabling the psychotherapist to encourage, frustrate, or anticipate the patient's continued involvement in his religiously deluded or hallucinated world. The psychologist and phenomenologist of religion would both find a typology useful. The one would be able to pursue in greater detail and on an empirical basis the question of the normality of religious experience; the other would have at hand a means for expanding his work to include the experience of persons diagnosed schizophrenic.

8. Another extension of the present research would be the creation of a series of essays devoted to findings apparent from unexamined factual data. These findings have the sense of germinal ideas; with further investigation, they may assume the status of incipient discoveries with considerable organizational and interpretive power for religious experience, schizophrenic or otherwise. The essay format would allow for the development of these ideas and the creation of various hypotheses which could then be addressed in formal research projects. At this point, four essays could be written. The first would discuss the finding that the majority of patients associate the experience of God with dying. Certainly this is a matter of significance, not only because it is congruent with the Judeo-Christian tradition, but also because the intensity of the patient's confrontation with death seems to correspond with the extent to which the experience of God is personally transformative. This kind of transformation is not uniform, however: John, for example, sets out to kill God with

renewed hate after he has nearly died himself, while Sarah is converted to a vigorous and staunch ethical stance after she experienced near-death during her horrendous nocturnal experience of God.

The second essay would be a phenomenological analysis of the kinds of intentionality apparent within psychotic experience. This would be based on the decidedly simple observation that God and other psychotic figures address the patient by name as well as name themselves and each other. If naming is assumed to be a chief mark of intentionality, then this simple observation leads to the idea that some kinds of psychosis are experiences of poly-intentionality. This provides a new phenomenological view of the fundamental principle of psychosis: rather than its being simply an instance of unitary intentionality gone awry, or a disordered mode of Dasein, it may be that psychosis is an engulfing self-referential system organized at its most basic level by poly-intentionality.

A third essay would address the function and meaning of number during schizophrenic psychosis. Mark Thomas would be the key informant, although I have known another patient who also used numbers to ascertain divine truths. The oddity is that both of these men are Jewish, but the second patient was clearly a case of cycling bipolar affective disorder, not schizophrenia. Neither of them knew of Kabalism and the importance attributed to numerology by this mystical Jewish sect; neither of them had heard or read that Kabalistic numerology understood the esoteric meaning and function of numbers in a way similar to their own. Furthermore, the second patient was not told of his peculiar logic of number at all: it entered his mind spontaneously with the eruption of mania. This is highly speculative material which points toward such questions as the psychohistory, or perhaps even the psychobiology, of varying mystical traditions.

The final essay would discuss the religious hallucinations of schizophrenic psychosis in relation to distortions in the perception of the material world of ordinary reality. By holding constant the subject matter of the hallucinations, one may isolate and focus specifically on the formal properties of the hallucination and the distorted perception. Teresa would be the key informant since her narrative includes two visions of Jesus which occurred a year apart. These visions show that the surface and depth of material objects have varying degrees of transparency and porosity relative to the power of hallucinated realities to intrude upon the material world. There also seems to be a correspondence between their transparency and porosity, on the one hand, and the affective response of the patient on the other. With Teresa, for example, the initial vision was the most frightening because of the intrusion of Jesus' presence within the surface of the wall and the sharp contrast between the ordinary world and the black mandorla surrounding Jesus. One might suppose that the mandorla signals the presence of an extraordinary reality, as it does when surrounding saints and legendary figures in the iconography of the major religious traditions. That a greater fear accompanies this kind of vision, in contrast to Teresa's second vision, in which Jesus' presence does not distort the perceptual features of material reality, is understandable, since it displays with greater impact the disintegration of her perceptual contact with the customary physical laws of the material world. A reflection following this line of thought could prove valuable clinically; such questions as the degree of the patient's reality contact, whether the psychosis is advancing or resolving, and how to direct the patient to alter the place of his hallucination to eliminate some of his fear--each would receive a tentative answer.

God's Presence

A description of God's presence as experienced during schizophrenic psychosis is not the ultimate goal of the present study. Ideas spall from this kind of phenomenological work as flakes of stone slide from a rocky surface. Something fresh awaits at each turn of thought, some new experience which may be emotional and intuitive as readily as purely conceptual. And yet it is apropos that a study focusing on the experience of God should end with a description of His presence, no matter how tentative. It is necessarily brief; a description which could be generalized with confidence and assumed to have greater validity awaits the creation of a typology. With these qualifications, then, God's presence during schizophrenic psychosis may be described in the following manner.

God is not experienced pantheistically. He is transcendent, much more so than immanent. Generally, God is experienced as a person in the theological sense of the term. He is a divine subject, in other words, and is able to enter into relationship with humans in a way not totally unlike that in which humans enter into relationships with one another. The same may be said for the possibility and capability of persons diagnosed as schizophrenic to enter into relationship with Him. He is not only a benevolent God of love, but also a wrathful, horrendous, punitive force. Whether He appears as one or the other seems partly, but not totally, dependent on the condition of the patient. "Hubris" is an appropriate word in this respect. An inflated stance seems conducive toward an experience of God as a wrathful force. Witness John, Paul, and Luke, and contrast their experiences with those of Mary, Sarah, and Teresa. Finally, God is experienced as autonomous; there is not a simple correlation between the credulity of the patient, on the one hand, and either His presence or its form on the other.

All of this recalls certain basic notions about God held by the Judeo-Christian tradition, and it is tantamount to saying that the phenomenological integrity of the experience of God extends beyond the simple matter of prevalence and includes His nature as experienced during madness and sanity alike. If there were a feature of God's presence more common during the religious experience of schizophrenia than for those who have not been given a schizophrenic diagnosis, it would be His horrendous, convulsive power. This may be viewed in at least two ways. It could be considered a manifestation of underlying psychopathology specific to schizophrenia, or a reflection of the schizophrenic experience having retained a more complete array of the primordial features of the experience of God than that preserved and offered by most contemporary currents within the Judeo-Christian tradition. The phenomenological integrity of the experience, the prominent link between dying and experiencing God for both schizophrenic persons and the Judeo-Christian tradition, and several other pieces of evidence tend to rule against the former alternative. The latter alternative seems more convincing, especially when one adopts an historical perspective and seeks to determine whether the God of antiquity was experienced in a more complete manner than the experience of divinity promised and represented contemporarily. The horrendous divine images which grasped the Biblical prophets come to mind immediately. Also within the Jewish tradition and occurring much later is the current of mysticism which occasionally went askew from Hebrew orthodoxy in asserting strange notions about the nature of God and the degree of His tolerance for ethically questionable behavior. The Christian tradition has also been marked with persons and ideas which complement the graciousness of a benevolent deity with a God whose goodness is not beyond question. Jacob Boehme's name springs to mind, and there is still theology being written which speaks of the hiddenness and inscrutibility of a _deus absconditus_.

The phenomenological psychopathology of the experience of God may now be raised to the level of a cultural critique which focuses attention on the poverty of an era which restricts the psychological scope of religious experience to an incomplete shadow of its former outline. Limbs which atrophy from inactivity give pain during the early stages of their recovery: the religiously hallucinated person called schizophrenic may be viewed as a psychologically impoverished culture's pained organ of religious experience.

REFERENCES

REFERENCES

Allport, G. W. The individual and his religion: A psychological interpretation. New York: Macmillan, 1961. (Originally published, 1950.)

Ambrose, A., & Lazerowitz, M. Fundamentals of symbolic logic. New York: Rinehart, 1948.

American Psychiatric Association. Diagnostic and statistical manual of mental disorders (3rd ed.). Washington, D.C.: American Psychiatric Association, 1980.

Arcaya, J. M. A phenomenology of fear. Journal of Phenomenological Psychology, 1979, 10, 165-188.

Assagioli, R. Psychosynthesis: A technique for the use of intuition. In R. E. Ornstein (Ed.), The nature of human consciousness: A book of readings. New York: Viking Press, 1971.

Avens, R. Imagination is reality: Western Nirvena in Jung, Hillman, Barfield, and Cassirrer. Irving, Texas: Spring, 1980.

Bachelard, G. The poetics of reverie (D. Russell, Trans.). Boston: Beacon Press, 1968.

Bachelard, G. The poetics of space (M. Jolas, Trans.). Boston: Beacon Press, 1969.

Bakan, D. The duality of human existence: Isolation and communion in Western man. Boston: Beacon Press, 1966.

Bakan, D. Paternity in the Judeo-Christian tradition. In A. W. Eister (Ed.), Varying perspectives in the scientific study of religion. New York: Wiley, 1974.

Bateson, G. (Ed.). Perceval's narrative: A patient's account of his psychosis, 1830-1832. New York: William Morrow, 1974.

Beshai, J. A. Psychology's dilemma: To explain or to understand. Journal of Phenomenological Psychology, 1971, 1, 209-233.

Beshai, J. A. Is psychology a hermeneutic science? Journal of Phenomenological Psychology, 1975, 5, 425-439.

Binswanger, L. On the relationship between Husserl's phenomenology and psychological insight. Philosophy and Phenomenological Research, 1941-1942, 2, 199-210.

Binswanger, L. Schizophrenie. Pfullingen: Neske, 1957.

Binswanger, L. Existential analysis, psychiatry, schizophrenia. Journal of Existential Psychiatry, 1960, 1, 157-165.

Blauner, J. Existential analysis: L. Binswanger's Daseinsanalyse Psychoanalysis and the Psychoanalytic Review, 1957, 44, 51-64.

Bly, R. (Trans.). Selected poems of Rainer Maria Rilke. New York: Harper & Row, 1981.

Boisen, A. T. Out of the depths: An autobiographical study of mental disorder and religious experience. New York: Harper & Brothers, 1960.

Boss, M. Psychoanalysis and Daseins-analysis (L. B. Lefebre, Trans.). New York: Basic Books, 1963.

Brand, G. Intentionality, reduction, and intentional analysis in Husserl's later manuscripts. In J. J. Kockelmans (Ed.), Phenomenology: The philosophy of Edmund Husserl and its interpretation. Garden City, N.Y.: Doubleday, 1967.

Brown, N. O. Life against death: The psychoanalytic meaning of history. Middletown, Conn.: Wesleyan University Press, 1959.

Buber, M. Tales of the Hasidim: The early masters (O. Marx, Trans.). New York: Schocken Books, 1947.

Buckley, P. Mystical experience and schizophrenia. Schizophrenia Bulletin, 1981, 7, 516-521.

Buytendijk, F. J. J. The mind of the dog (L. A. Clare, Trans.). New York: Houghton Mifflin, 1936.

Callanan, E. Emergence and analysis: A brief sketch for an underlying model of "psycho"-pathology. In A. Giorgi, R. Knowles, & D. L. Smith (Eds.), Duquesne studies in phenomenological psychology (Vol. 3). Pittsburgh, Penn.: Duquesne University Press, 1976.

Campbell, J. Hero with a thousand faces. Princeton: Princeton University Press, 1968.

Campbell, L. B. Shakespeare's tragic heroes: Slaves of passion. New York: Barnes & Noble, 1930.

Cargnello, D. From psychoanalytic naturalism to phenomenological anthropology (Daseinsanalyse): From Freud to Binswanger. Human Context, 1968, 1, 70-92.

Casey, E. S. Comparative phenomenology of mental activity: Memory, hallucination, and fantasy contrasted with imagination. Journal of Phenomenological Psychology, 1976, 6, 1-26.

Cassirer, E. The philosophy of symbolic forms (R. Manheim, Trans.). (3 vols.). New Haven, Conn.: Yale University Press, 1955-57.

Castedo, L. A history of Latin American art and architecture: From pre-Columbian times to the present (A. Freeman, Trans.). New York: Praeger, 1969.

Chan, W. (Trans.). The way of Lao Tzu (Tao-te ching). Indianapolis, Ind.: Bobbs-Merril, 1963.

Christou, E. The logos of the soul. Dallas, Texas: Spring, 1976.

Clark, R. A. Religious delusions among Jews. American Journal of Psychotherapy, 1980, 34, 62-71.

Clark, W. H. The psychology of religious experience. Psychology Today, 1968, 1(9), 42-47, 68-69.

Clark, W. H., Malony, H. N., Daane, J., & Tippett, A. R. Religious experience: Its nature and function in the human psyche. Springfield, Ill.: Thomas, 1973.

Coe, G. A. The psychology of religion. Chicago: The University of Chicago Press, 1916.

Colaizzi, P. F. Reflection and research in psychology: A phenomenological study of learning. Dubuque, Iowa: Kendall/Hunt, 1973. (Originally published, 1948.)

Colaizzi, P. F. Psychological research as the phenomenologist views it. In R. S. Valle & M. King (Eds.), Existential-phenomenological alternatives in psychology. New York: Oxford University Press, 1978.

Conze, E. Buddhist thought in India: Three phases of Buddhist philosophy. London: George Allen Unwin, 1962.

Corbin, H. Mundus imaginalis or the imaginal and the imaginary, Spring, 1972, pp. 1-19.

Delius, H. Descriptive interpretation. Philosophy and Phenomenological Research, 1953, 13, 305-323.

Downing, C. Poetically dwells man on this earth. In C. E. Scott (Ed.), On dreaming: An encounter with Medard Boss. Chico, Calif.: Scholars Press, 1977.

Draper, E., Mayer, G., Parzen, Z., & Samuelson, G. On the diagnostic value of religious ideation. Archives of General Psychiatry, 1965, 13, 202-207.

Dublin, J. E. Lived-taste: Hors d'oevre or entree? Existential Psychiatry, 1967, 6, 361-378.

Dublin, J. E. Language as expression of upright man: Toward a phenomenology of language and the lived-body. Journal of Phenomenological Psychology, 1972, 2, 141-160.

Edwards, D. G. Existential psychotherapy: The process of caring. New York: Gardner, 1981.

Eliade, M. The sacred and the profane: The nature of religion (W. Trask, Trans.). New York: Harcourt Brace Jovanovich, 1968.

Eliot, T. S. Collected poems 1909-1935. New York: Harcourt, Brace, 1936.

Ellis, H. C., & Hunt, R. R. Memory: The processing of information. In M. H. Marx & M. E. Bunch (Eds.), Fundamentals and applications of learning. New York: Macmillan, 1977.

Eng, E. Locating Erwin Straus. Journal of Phenomenological Psychology, 1976, 7, 1-14.

Epstein, S. Natural healing processes of the mind: Acute schizophrenic disorganization. Schizophrenia Bulletin, 1979, 5, 313-321.

Fenton, W. S., Mosher, L. R., & Matthews, S. M. Diagnosis of schizophrenia: A critical review of current diagnostic systems. Schizophrenia Bulletin, 1981, 7, 452-476.

Fischer, W. F. Erwin Straus and the phenomenological approach to psychopathology. Journal of Phenomenological Psychology, 1976, 7, 95-115.

Flor-Henry, P. Commentary on theoretical issues, neuropsychology, and electroencephalographic issues. In J. Gruzelier & P. Flor-Henry (Eds.), Hemispheric asymmetries of function in psychopathology. Amsterdam: Elsevier/North-Holland, 1979.

Freud, S. Civilization and its discontents. In J. Strachey (Ed.), The standard edition of the complete psychological works of Sigmund Freud (Vol. 21). London: Hogarth Press, 1975. (Originally published, 1961.) (a)

Freud, S. The dynamics of the transference. In J. Strachey (Ed.), The standard edition of the complete psychological works of Sigmund Freud (Vol. 12). London: Hogarth Press, 1975. (Originally published, 1958.) (b)

Freud, S. The interpretation of dreams. In J. Strachey (Ed.), The standard edition of the complete psychological works of Sigmund Freud (Vols. 4 and 5). London: Hogarth Press, 1975. (Originally published, 1953.) (c)

Freud, S. Moses and monotheism: Three essays. In J. Strachey (Ed.), The standard edition of the complete psychological works of Sigmund Freud (Vol. 13). London: Hogarth Press, 1975. (Originally published, 1953.) (d)

Freud, S. Obsessive actions and religious practices. In J. Strachey (Ed.), The standard edition of the complete psychological works of Sigmund Freud (Vol. 9). London: Hogarth Press, 1975. (Originally published, 1959.) (e)

Freud, S. On beginning the treatment (Further recommendations on the technique of the psycho-analysis, I). In J. Strachey (Ed.), The standard edition of the complete psychological works of Sigmund Freud (Vol. 12). London: Hogarth Press, 1975. (Originally published, 1958.) (f)

Freud, S. The psychopathology of everyday life. In J. Strachey (Ed.), The standard edition of the complete psychological works of Sigmund Freud (Vol. 6). London: Hogarth Press, 1975. (Originally published, 1960). (g)

Freud, S. A religious experience. In J. Strachey (Ed.), The standard edition of the complete psychological works of Sigmund Freud (Vol. 21). London: Hogarth Press, 1975. (Originally published, 1961.) (h)

Freud, S. Totem and taboo. In J. Strachey (Ed.), The standard version of the complete psychological works of Sigmund Freud (Vol. 13). London: Hogarth Press, 1975. (Originally published, 1953.) (i)

Giorgi, A. Psychology as a human science: A phenomenologically based approach. New York: Harper & Row, 1970.

Giorgi, A. An application of phenomenological methods in psychology. In A. Giorgi, C. T. Fischer, & E. L. Murray (Eds.), Duquesne studies in phenomenological psychology (Vol. 2). Pittsburgh: Penn.: Duquesne University Press, 1975.

Goldstein, L. Some relationships between quantified hemispheric EEG and behavioral states in man. In J. Gruzelier & P. Flor-Henry (Eds.), Hemispheric asymmetries of function in psychopathology. Amsterdam: Elsevier/North-Holland, 1979.

Greeley, A. M. The religious imagination. New York: Sadlier, 1981.

Grene, M. Approaches to philosophical biology. New York: Basic Books, 1965.

Grimal, P. (Ed.). Larousse world mythology. New York: Hamlyn, 1965.

Gruzelier, J. H. Synthesis and critical review of the evidence for hemispheric asymmetrics of function in psychopathology. In J. Gruzelier & P. Flor-Henry (Eds.), Hemispheric asymmetries of function in psychopathology. Amsterdam: Elsevier/North-Holland, 1979.

Gruzelier, J. Hemispheric imbalance masquerading as paranoid and nonparanoid syndromes? Schizophrenia Bulletin, 1981, 7, 662-674.

Gruzelier, J. H., & Hammond, N. V. Schizophrenia: A dominant hemisphere temporal-limbic disorder. Research Communication in Psychology, Psychiatry, and Behavior, 1976, 1, 33-72.

Gudeman, H. E. The phenomenology of delusions. Review of Existential Psychology and Psychiatry, 1966, 6, 196-210.

Guenther, H. V. Philosophy and psychology in the Abhidharma. Berkeley, Calif.: Shamahala, 1976.

Gunderson, J. G. A reevaluation of milieu therapy for nonchronic schizophrenic patients. Schizophrenia Bulletin, 1980, 6, 64-69.

Hall, G. S. Adolescence: Its psychology and its relation to physiology, anthropology, sociology, sex, crime, religion and education (2 vols.). New York: Appleton, 1904.

Hall, G. S. Jesus, the Christ, in the light of psychology (2 vols.). New York: Doubleday, 1917.

Halling, S. The implications of Emmanuel Levinas's Totality and Infinity for therapy. In A. Giorgi, C. T. Fischer, & E. L. Murray (Eds.), Duquesne studies in phenomenological psychology (Vol. 2). Pittsburgh, Penn.: Duquesne University Press, 1975.

Hecaen, H., & Albert, M. L. Human neuropsychology. New York: Wiley, 1978.

Heidegger, M. Being and time (J. Macquarrie & E. Robinson, Trans.). New York: Harper & Row, 1962. (Originally published, 1927.)

Heidegger, M. Early Greek thinking (D. F. Krell & F. A. Capuzzi, Trans.). New York: Harper & Row, 1975. (Originally published, 1943-1954.)

Henry, J. Pathways to madness. New York: Random House, 1965.

Hillman, J. Suicide and the soul. Zurich: Spring, 1964.

Hillman, J. Re-visioning psychology. New York: Harper & Row, 1975.

Hoeller, K. The phenomenological psychology of Erwin Straus. Review of Existential Psychology and Psychiatry, 1975-1976, 14, 94-107.

Hoenig, J. Karl Jaspers and psychopathology. Philosophy and Phenomenological Research, 1965, 26, 216-229.

Holt, H. Schizophrenia: A contribution from existential psychiatry. American Journal of Psychoanalysis, 1971, 31, 182-191.

Horton, P. C. The mystical experience as a suicide preventive. American Journal of Psychiatry, 1973, 130, 294-296.

Howard, D. Hallucination: A phenomenological analysis. Review of Existential Psychology and Psychiatry, 1966, 6, 211-229.

Howe, L. Review article (Rizzuto, Ana-Maria. The birth of the living: A psychoanalytic study. University of Chicago Press, 1979.). Perkins Journal, Southern Methodist University, 1981, 34, 34-40.

Hume, R. E. The thirteen principal Upanishads: Translated from the Sanskrit with an outline of the philosophy of the Upanishads (2nd ed.; rev.). New York: Oxford University Press, 1975.

Husserl, E. The phenomenology of internal time consciousness (J. S. Churchill, Trans., M. Heidegger, Ed.). Bloomington: Indiana University Press, 1964. (Originally published, 1928.)

Husserl, E. Cartesian meditations (D. Cairns, Trans.). The Hague: Mijhoff, 1968. (Originally published, 1950.)

Husserl, E. The crisis of the European sciences and transcendental phenomenology: An introduction to phenomenological philosophy (D. Carr, Trasn.). Evanston: Northwestern University Press, 1970. (Originally published, 1954.)

Husserl, E. Ideas: General introduction to pure phenomenology (W. R. B. Gibson, Trans.). New York: Macmillan, 1975. (Originally published, 1913.)

Ihde, D. Listening and voice: A phenomenology of sound. Athens, Ohio: Ohio University Press, 1976.

Ihde, D. Experimental phenomenology: An introduction. New York: Paragon Books, 1979.

Jager, B. Horizontality and verticality: A phenomenological exploration into lived space. In A. Giorgi, W. F. Fischer, & R. von Eckartsberg (Eds.), *Duquesne studies in phenomenological* psychology (Vol. 1). Pittsburgh, Penn.: Duquesne University Press, 1971.

Jager, B. Dionysos and the world of passion. In A. Giorgi, R. Knowles, & D. L. Smith (Eds.), *Duquesne studies in phenomenological psychology* (Vol. 3). Pittsburgh, Penn.: Duquesne University Press, 1976.

James, W. *The varieties of religious experiences. A study in human nature*. New York: The New American Library, 1958. (Originally published, 1902.)

Jaspers, K. *General psychopathology* (J. Hoenig & M. W. Hamilton, Trans.). Chicago: University of Chicago Press, 1963. (Originally published, 1913.)

Jaynes, J. *The origin of consciousness in the breakdown of the bicameral mind*. New York: Houghton Mifflin, 1977.

Johnasson, R. E. A. *The psychology of Nirvana*. London: George Allen & Unwin, 1969.

Jonas, H. *The gnostic religion*. Boston: Beacon Press, 1963.

Jung, C. G. The psychology of the unconscious. In R. F. C. Hull (Trans.), *The collected works of C. G. Jung* (Vol. 7). Princeton: Princeton University Press, 1966. (Originally published, 1953.)

Jung, C. G. Aion: Researches into the phenomenology of the Self. In R. F. C. Hull (Trans.), *The collected works of C. G. Jung* (Vol. 9ii). Princeton: Princeton University Press, 1968. (Originally published, 1956.) (a)

Jung, C. G. Psychology and alchemy. In R. F. C. Hull (Trans.), *The collected works of C. G. Jung* (Vol. 12). Princeton: Princeton University Press, 1968. (Originally published, 1953.) (b)

Jung, C. G. Answer to Job. In R. F. C. Hull (Trans.), *The collected works of C. G. Jung* (Vol. 11). Princeton: Princeton University Press, 1969. (Originally published, 1958.) (a)

Jung, C. G. On the nature of the psyche. In R. F. C. Hull (Trans.), *The collected works of C. G. Jung* (Vol. 8). Princeton: Princeton University Press, 1969. (Originally published, 1960.) (b)

Jung, C. G. Psychology and religion. In R. F. C. Hull (Trans.), *The collected works of C. G. Jung* (Vol. 11). Princeton: Princeton University Press, 1969. (Originally published, 1958.) (c)

Jung, C. G. The transcendent function. In R. F. C. Hull (Trans.), The collected works of C. G. Jung (Vol. 8). Princeton: Princeton University Press, 1969. (Originally published, 1960.) (d)

Jung, C. G. Mysterium coniunctionis: An inquiry into the separation and synthesis of psychic opposites in alchemy. In R. F. C. Hull (Trans.), The collected works of C. G. Jung (Vol. 14). Princeton: Princeton University Press, 1970. (Originally published, 1963.)

Jung, C. G. Psychological types. In R. F. C. Hull (Trans.), The collected works of C. G. Jung (Vol. 6). Princeton: Princeton University Press, 1971.

Jung, C. G. Symbols of transformation: An analysis of the prelude to a case of schizophrenia. In R. F. C. Hull (Trans.), The collected works of C. G. Jung (Vol. 5). Princeton: Princeton University Press, 1974. (Originally published, 1956).

Jung, C. G. The Tavistock lectures. In R. F. C. Hull (Trans.), The collected works of C. G. Jung (Vol. 18). Princeton: Princeton University Press, 1975.

Kaplan, B. The inner world of mental illness. New York: Harper & Row, 1964.

Kasamatsu, A., & Hirai, T. An electroencephalographic study of the Zen meditation (Zazen). Folio Psychiatry and Neurology Japanoica, 1966, 20, 315-336.

Kasanin, J. S. Language and thought in schizophrenia. New York: Norton, 1944.

Kazantzakis, N. Saint Francis (P. A. Bien, Trans.). New York: Simon & Schuster, 1962.

Keen, E. Three faces of being: Toward an existential clinical psychology. New York: Appleton-Century-Crofts, 1970.

Keen, E. A primer in phenomenological psychology. New York: Holt, Rinehart, & Winston, 1975.

Kockelmans, J. J. Husserl's original view on phenomenological psychology. In J. J. Kockelmans (Ed.), Phenomenology: The philosophy of Edmund Husserl and its interpretation. Garden City, N.Y.: Doubleday, 1967.

Koehler, K. Critical remarks on the symptom of "thought insertion." Archiv fur Psychiatrie und Nervenkrankheiten, 1976, 221, 369-382.

Koestenbaum, P. The vitality of death: Essays in existential psychology and philosophy. Westport, Conn.: Greenwood, 1971.

Kolle, K. Karl Jaspers as psychopathologist. In P. A. Schilpps, *The philosophy of Karl Jaspers*. New York: Tudor, 1957.

Kruger, D. *An introduction to phenomenological psychology*. Pittsburgh, Penn.: Duquesne University Press, 1981.

Kuffler, S. W. Neurons in the retina: Organization, inhibition and excitation problems. *Cold Spring Harbor Symposia on Quantitative Biology*, 1952, *17*, 281-292.

Kuffler, S. W. Discharge patterns and functional organization of mammalian retina. *Journal of Neurophysiology*, 1953, *16*, 37-61.

Kugler, P. Image and sound: An archetypal approach to language. *Spring*, 1978, pp. 136-151.

Kugler, P. *The alchemy of discourse: An archetypal approach to language*. Lewisburg, Penn.: Bucknell University Press, 1982.

Kullman, M., & Taylor, C. The pre-objective world. In M. Natanson (Ed.), *Essays in phenomenology*. The Hague: Martinus Nijhoff, 1966.

Laffal, J. *A source document in schizophrenia: Whoever had most fish would be lord and master*. Hope Valley, R.I.: Gallery Press, 1979.

Laing, R. D. Minkowski and schizophrenia. *Review of Existential Psychology*, 1963, *9*, 195-207.

Laing, R. D. *The politics of experience*. New York: Pantheon Books, 1967.

Laing, R. D. *The divided self*. New York: Pantheon Books, 1969.

Landsberg, P. L. The experience of death. In M. Natanson (Ed.), *Essays in phenomenology*. The Hague: Martinus Nijhoff, 1966.

Lauer, Q. *Phenomenology: Its genesis and prospect*. New York: Harper, 1965. (Originally published, 1958.)

Leach, M., & Fried, J. (Eds.). *Funk and Wagnall's standard dictionary of folklore, mythology and legend*. New York: Funk & Wagnalls, 1972.

Lefebre, L. B. The psychology of Karl Jaspers. In P. A. Schilpp (Ed.), *The philosophy of Karl Jaspers*. New York: Tudor, 1957.

Lettvin, J. Y., Maturana, H. A., McCulloch, W. S., & Pitts, W. H. What the frog's eye tells the frog brain. *Proceedings of the Institute of Radio Engineering*, 1959, *47*, 1940-1951.

Lettvin, J. Y., Maturana, H. A., McCulloch, W. S., & Pitts, W. H. Two remarks on the visual system of the frog. In W. A. Rosenblith (Ed.), Sensory communication. Cambridge, Mass.: MIT Press, 1961.

Leuba, J. A. A psychological study of religion: Its origins, function, and future. New York: Macmillan, 1912.

Levinas, E. Totality and infinity: An essay on exteriority. (A. Lingis, Trans.). The Hague: Martinus Nijhoff, 1979. (Originally published, 1969.)

Lingis, A. The void that awaits the force of anxiety. Journal of Phenomenological Psychology, 1976, 6, 153-168.

Loewenberg, R. D. Karl Jaspers on psychotherapy. American Journal of Psychotherapy, 1951, 5, 502-513.

Luria, A. R. The working brain: An introduction to neuropsychology (B. Haigh, Trans.). New York: Basic Books, 1973.

Lyons, J. An annotated bibliography on phenomenology and existentialism. Psychological Reports, Monograph Supplement, 1959, 5, 613-631.

Macalpine, I., & Hunter, R. A. Schizophrenia 1677: A psychiatric study of an illustrated autobiographical record of demoniacal possession. London: Dawson, 1956.

Magaro, P. A. Cognition in schizophrenia and paranoia: The interpretation of cognitive processes. Hillsdale, N.J.: Lawrence Erlbaum, 1980.

Magaro, P. A. The paranoid and the schizophrenic: The case for distinct cognitive style. Schizophrenia Bulletin, 1981, 7, 632-661.

Mamiya, L. V. From black muslim to Bilalian. Journal for the Scientific Study of Religion, 1982, 21(2), 138-152.

Marsh, M. Toward a framework for memory: Straus and some others. Journal of Phenomenological Psychology, 1976, 7, 34-53.

Matthews, S. M., Roper, M. T., Mosher, L. R., & Menn, A. Z. A nonneuroleptic treatment for schizophrenia: Analysis of the two-year post-discharge rate of relapse. Schizophrenia Bulletin, 1979, 5, 322-333.

Maugham, W. S. Of human bondage. Salem, N.H.: Ayer, 1977. (Originally published, 1915.)

May, R. On the phenomenological bases of psychotherapy. In E. W. Straus (Ed.), Phenomenology: Pure and applied. The first Lexington conference. Pittsburgh, Penn.: Duquesne University Press, 1964.

May, R., Angel, E., & Ellenberger, H. F. (Eds.). Existence: A new dimension in psychiatry and psychology. New York: Simon & Schuster, 1958.

McCasland, S. V. By the finger of God: Demon possession and exorcism in early Christianity in the light of modern views of mental illness. New York: Macmillan, 1951.

Melges, F. T. Time and the inner future: A temporal approach to psychiatric disorder. New York: Wiley, 1982.

Merleau-Ponty, M. Phenomenology of perception (C. Smith, Trans.). Atlantic Highlands, N.J.: Humanities Press, 1962. (Originally published, 1945.)

Merleau-Ponty, M. Structure of behavior (A. Fisher, Trans.). Boston: Beacon Press, 1963.

Merleau-Ponty, M. The primacy of perception and its philosophical consequences. In The primary of perception (J. M. Edie, Trans.). Evanston, Ill.: Northwestern University Press, 1964. (Originally published, 1947.)

Miller, P. L. The new polytheism: Rebirth of the gods and goddesses. New York: Harper & Row, 1974.

Minkowski, E. Bergson's conceptions as applied to psychopathology (F. J. Farnell, Trans.). The Journal of Nervous and Mental Disease, 1926, 63, 553-568.

Minkowski, E. Lived time: Phenomenological and psychopathological studies (N. Metzel, Trans.). Evanston, Ill.: Northwestern University Press, 1970. (Originally published, 1933.)

Misiak, H., & Sexton, V. S. Phenomenological, existential, and humanistic psychologies: A historical survey. New York: Grune & Stratton, 1973.

Mohanty, J. N. Phenomenology and existentialism: Encounter with Indian philosophy. International Quarterly, 1972, 12, 484-511.

Munson, T. N. The pre-objective reconsidered. Review of Metaphysics, 1959, 12, 624-632.

Naranjo, C. Present-centeredness in Gestalt therapy. In J. Fagan & I. L. Shephard (Eds.), Gestalt therapy now. Palo Alto, Calif.: Science & Behavior Books, 1970.

Needleman, J. (Trans.). Being-in-the-world: Selected papers of Ludwig Binswanger. New York: Basic Books, 1963.

Neumann, E. Origins and history of consciousness (R. F. C. Hull, Trans.). Princeton: Princeton University Press, 1954.

Neumann, E. Depth psychology and a new ethic (E. Rolfe, Trans.). New York: Harper-Row, 1973.

New American Bible. Camden, N.J.: Bishops' Committee of the Confraternity of Christian Doctrine, 1971.

Newlin, D. B., Carpenter, B., & Golden, C. J. Hemispheric asymmetries in schizophrenia. Biological Psychiatry, 1981, 16, 561-581.

New World Dictionary-Concordance to the New American Bible. New York: C. D. Stampley Enterprises, 1970.

Nijinsky, R. (Ed.). The diary of Vaslov Nijinsky. Berkeley: University of California Press, 1968.

Nowlis, D. P., & Kamiya, J. The control of electroencephalographic alpha rhythms through auditory feedback and the associated mental activity. In R. E. Ornstein (Ed.), The nature of human consciousness: A book of readings. New York: The Viking Press, 1973.

Ornstein, R. E. The psychology of consciousness (2nd ed.). New York: Harcourt Brace Jovanovich, 1977.

Otto, E. The idea of the holy: An inquiry into the non-rational factor in the idea of the divine and its relation to the rational (J. W. Harvey, Trans.). New York: Oxford University Press, 1950. (Originally published, 1917.)

Oxman, T. E., Rosenberg, S. J., & Tucker, C. J. The language of paranoia. American Journal of Psychiatry, 1982, 139, 275-282.

Patrick, M. M. The Greek sceptics. New York: Columbia University Press, 1929.

Pelikan, J. The Christian tradition: A history of the development of doctrine. Vol. 1: The emergence of the Catholic tradition (100-600). Chicago: University of Chicago Press, 1971.

Perry, J. W. The far side of madness. Englewood Cliffs, N.J.: Prentice-Hall, 1974.

Pickthall, M. M. (Ed.). Holy Quaran with English translation. Columbia, Mo.: South Asia Books, 1976.

Pope, K. S., & Singer, J. L. (Eds.). The stream of consciousness. New York: Plenum Press, 1978.

Price-Williams, D. R. Proprioception and personal identity. Philosophy and Phenomenological Research, 1957, 17(4), 536-545.

Prince, R. Religious experience and psychosis. Journal of Altered States of Consciousness, 1979-1980, 5, 167-181.

Ratliff, F., & Hartline, H. K. The response of limulus optic nerve fibers to patterns of illumination on the receptor mosaic. Journal of General Physiology, 1959, 42, 1241-1255.

Ratliff, F., Miller, W. H., & Hartline, H. K. Neural interaction in the eye and the integration of receptor activity. Annals of the New York Academy of Sciences, 1958, 74, 210-222.

Reed, D. Anna. New York: Penguin, 1977.

Ricoeur, P. The symbolism of evil (E. Buchanan, Trans.). Boston: Beacon Press, 1969.

Rizzuto, A. M. The birth of the living God: A psychoanalytic study. Chicago: University of Chicago Press, 1979.

Rokeach, M. The three Christs of Ypsilanti: A psychological study. New York: Alfred A. Knopf, 1964.

Roos, B. Theories concerning comprehensible and incomprehensible aspects of schizophrenic experiences. Nordisk Psykiatrisk Tidsskrift, 1974, 28(8), 577-587.

Russell, E. W. The pathology and clinical examination of memory. In S. B. Filskov & T. J. Boll (Eds.), Handbook of clinical neuropsychology. New York: Wiley, 1981.

Ruth, D. N. The social reference of body symbols. In A. W. Eister (Ed.) Changing perspectives in the scientific study of religion. New York: Wiley, 1974.

Sardello, R. J. Hermeneutical reading: An approach to the classic texts of psychology. In A. Giorgi, C. T. Fischer, & E. L. Murray (Eds.), Duquesne studies in phenomenological psychology (Vol. 2). Pittsburgh, Penn.: Duquesne University Press, 1975.

Sargant, W. Battle for the mind: A physiology of conversion and brain-washing. New York: Doubleday, 1957.

Sartre, J. P. Being and nothingness: An essay on phenomenological ontology (H. E. Barnes, Trans.). New York: Philosophical Library, 1956. (Originally published, 1943.)

Sartre, J. P. Nausea (L. Alexander, Trans.). New York: New Directions, 1964. (Originally published, 1938.)

Scanlon, J. D. The epoché and phenomenological anthropology. Journal of Phenomenological Psychology, 1972, 2, 95-119.

Schiller, G. Iconography of Christian art (Vols. 1 & 2). Greenwich, Conn.: New York Graphic Society, 1971. (Originally published, 1966.)

Schneider, A. M., & Tarshis, B. An introduction to physiological psychology. New York: Random House, 1975.

Schneiderman, S. (Ed. & Trans.). Returning to Freud: Clinical psychoanalysis in the school of Lacan. New Haven: Yale University Press, 1980.

Scholem, G. S. Major trends in Jewish mysticism. New York: Schocken Books, 1961.

Scott, C. E. Heidegger, madness, and well-being. Southwest Journal of Philosophy, 1973, 4, 157-177.

Scott, C. E. Daseinsanalysis: An interpretation. Philosophy Today, 1975, 19, 182-197.

Scott, C. E. (Ed.). On dreaming: An encounter with Medard Boss. Chico, Calif.: Scholars Press, 1977.

Searles, H. F. Schizophrenia and the inevitability of death. In Collected papers on schizophrenia and related subjects. New York: International Universities Press, 1965.

Sechehaye, M. Autobiography of a schizophrenic girl. New York: New American Library, 1970. (Originally published, 1951.)

Shakespeare, W. The tragedy of King Lear (T. Brooks & W. L. Phelps, Eds.). New Haven, Conn.: Yale University Press, 1919. (Originally published, 1608.)

Sheikh-Dilthey, H. Ritualisiertes Leiden als Gesundungsfaktor. Confinia Psychiatrica, 1976, 18, 48-54.

Sonnemann, U. Existence and therapy: An introduction to phenomenological psychology and existential analysis. New York: Grune & Stratton, 1954.

Spiegelberg, H. Toward a phenomenology of imaginative understanding of others. Proceedings of the 11th International Congress of Philosophy, Brussells, 1955, 7, 235-239.

Spiegelberg, H. Phenomenology through vicarious experience. In E. W. Straus (Ed.), Phenomenology: Pure and applied. The first Lexington conference. Pittsburgh, Penn.: Duquesne University Press, 1964.

Spiegelberg, H. How subjective is phenomenology? In M. Natanson (Ed.), *Essays in phenomenology*. The Hague: Martinus Nijhoff, 1966.

Spiegelberg, H. *Phenomenology in psychology and psychiatry: An historical introduction*. Evanston, Ill.: Northwestern University Press, 1972.

Spiegelberg, H. *The phenomenological movement: An historical introduction* (3rd rev. & enlarged ed.). The Hague: Martinus Nijhoff, 1982.

Starbuck, E. D. *The psychology of religion*. New York: Scribner, 1899.

Stark, R. A taxonomy of religious experience. *Journal of Scientific Study of Religion*, 1965, *5*, 97-116.

Strasser, S. *Phenomenology and the human sciences*. Pittsburgh, Penn.: Duquesne University Press, 1963.

Strasser, S. Emmanuel Levinas (born 1906): Phenomenological philosophy. In S. Spiegelberg, *The phenomenological movement: An historical introduction* (3rd rev. & enlarged ed.). The Hague: Martinus Nijhoff, 1982.

Straus, E. W. *On obsession: A clinical and methodological study*. New York: Nervous and Mental Disease Monographs (No. 73), 1948.

Straus, E. W. Phenomenology of remembering and infantile amnesia. *Acta Psychotherapeutics et Psychosomatic*, 1960, *8*, 334-351.

Straus, E. W. *Primary world of the senses: A vindication* (J. Needleman, Trans.). Glencoe, Ill.: Free Press, 1963.

Straus, E. W. Chronognosy and chronopathy. In E. Straus (Ed.), *Phenomenology: Pure and applied. The first Lexington conference*. Pittsburgh, Penn.: Duquesne University Press, 1964.

Straus, E. W. *Phenomenological psychology: The selected papers of Erwin W. Straus* (E. Eng, Trans.). New York: Basic Books, 1966.

Straus, E. W. Anosognosia. In E. Straus & R. M. Griffith (Eds.), *Phenomenology of will and action. The second Lexington conference on pure and applied phenomenology*. Pittsburgh, Penn.: Duquesne University Press, 1967.

Straus, E. W. Phenomenology of memory. In E. W. Straus & R. M. Griffith (Eds.), *Phenomenology of memory. The third Lexington conference on pure and applied phenomenology*. Pittsburgh, Penn.: Duquesne University Press, 1970.

Straus, E. W. (Ed.). Language and language disturbances. The fifth Lexington conference on pure and applied phenomenology. Pittsburgh, Penn.: Duquesne University Press, 1974.

Straus, E. W., Natanson, M., & Ey, H. Psychiatry and philosophy. New York: Springer-Verlag, 1969.

Stroll, A., & Popkin, R. H. Introduction to philosophy (3rd ed.). New York: Holt, Rinehart, & Winston, 1979.

Szasz, T. S. Ideology and insanity: Essays on the psychiatric dehumanization of man. New York: Doubleday, 1970.

Thines, G. Phenomenology and the science of behavior: An historical and epistemological approach. London: George Allen & Unwin, 1977.

Titelman, P. A phenomenological approach to psychopathology: The conception of Irwin Straus. Journal of Phenomenological Psychology, 1976, 7, 15-33. (a)

Titelman, P. Some implications of Ricoeur's conception of hermeneutics for phenomenological psychology. In A. Giorgi, R. Knowles, & D. L. Smith (Eds.), Duquesne studies in phenomenological psychology (Vol. 3). Pittsburgh, Penn.: Duquesne University Press, 1976. (b)

Torrey, E. F. Schizophrenia and civilization. New York: Aronson, 1980.

Tymieniecka, A. T. Phenomenology and science in contemporary European thought. New York: Farrar, Straus, & Cudahy, 1962.

Vallalonga, D. M. Straus on shame. Journal of Phenomenological Psychology, 1976, 7, 55-69.

Valle, R. S., & King, M. An introduction to existential-phenomenological psychology. Existential-Phenomenological Alternatives for Psychology. New York: Oxford University Press, 1978.

Van den Berg, J. H. The human body and the significance of human movement. Philosophy and Phenomenological Research, 1952-1953, 13, 159-183.

Van den Berg, J. H. A different existence: Principles of phenomenological psychopathology. Pittsburgh, Penn.: Duquesne University Press, 1972.

Van den Berg, J. H. On hallucinating: Critical-historical overview and guidelines for further study. Journal of Phenomenological Psychology, 1975, 6, 1-16.

Van den Berg, J. H. Phenomenology and psychotherapy. Journal of Phenomenological Psychology, 1980, 2, 21-49.

Van Dusen, W. A central dynamism in chronic schizophrenia. Psychoanalysis and Psychoanalytic Review, 1959, 46, 85-91. (a)

Van Dusen, W. Existential analysis: The English literature. Existential Inquiries, 1959, 1, 16-30. (b)

Van Dusen, W. The phenomenology of a schizophrenic existence. Journal of Transpersonal Psychology, 1961, 17, 80-92.

Van Dusen, W. The natural depth in man. New York: Harper & Row, 1972.

Van Dusen, W. The presence of other worlds: The psychological/ spiritual findings of Emmanuel Swedenborg. New York: Harper & Row, 1974.

Van Dusen, W., & Ansbacher, H. L. Adler and Binswanger on schizophrenia. Journal of Individual Psychology, 1960, 16, 77-80.

Van Kaam, A. Existential foundations of psychology. Pittsburgh, Penn.: Duquesne University Press, 1966.

Wallace, R. K., & Benson, H. The physiology of meditation. Scientific American, 1972, 226, 85-90.

Watson, J. B. Behaviorism. Chicago: University of Chicago Press, 1924.

Whitman, W. Leaves of grass. Ithaca: Cornell University Press, 1961. (Originally published, 1885.)

Wieman, H. N., & Westcott-Wieman, R. Normative psychology of religion. New York: Crowell, 1935.

Wild, J. Husserl's life-world and the lived body. In E. W. Straus (Ed.), Phenomenology: Pure and applied. The first Lexington conference. Pittsburgh, Penn.: Duquesne University Press, 1964.

Yeats, W. B. Collected poems (2nd ed.). London: Macmillan, 1956.

Zaner, R. M. The problem of embodiment: Some contributions to a phenomenology of the body. The Hague: Martinus Nijhoff, 1964.

Zoila, F. The fragmented time of schizophrenia: Study of intensive time and constructed time. Evolution Psychiatrique, 1976, 41, 973-991.

APPENDICES

APPENDIX A

GLOSSARY

The glossary is very nearly a complete listing of mythological figures and places, of historical persons and works of art, of technical terms from psychiatry and dance, and of bibliographic references and scriptures mentioned or quoted in the portraits. In some cases, the reference for the glossary item is given immediately following the listing. Major sources for the remainder are Grimal (1965), Leach and Fried (1972), and Schiller (1966/1971). The _New American Bible_ (1971) is used consistently, and the _New World Dictionary-Concordance to the New American Bible_ (1970) is a reliable resource for biblical figures and events. The translation of the _Koran_ used is Pickthall's (1976).

The format for each listing is as follows: the item is given as it appears in the text of the portrait, then the name of the patient portrayed and the page on which the item occurs. Occasionally a quotation is given when recall of the item's place in the portrait would prove helpful in understanding its meaning. A definition or explanation of the item follows; it is rarely interpretive, since the intent of the glossary is not to provide a skeleton key, as if the portraits were allegories awaiting a deeper reading, but rather to provide enough material to allow understanding of the item in its original context.

Aaron (Luke, p. 188): Appointed by God as Moses' spokesman with pharaoh (Ex. 4:14-16, 5:1-4), he supported Moses' arm and staff while Joshua fought the Amalekites in the valley below (Ex. 17:10-12). The

Hebrews emerged victorious because of this intervention. His own staff was the source of various prodigies which conveyed to pharaoh the divine inspiration of Moses' mission (Ex. 7:9-10).

Abraham (Paul, p. 133; Luke, p. 194): Hebrew patriarch (Cf. Isaac and Kaabah).

Adam's face (Paul, p. 127): The angelic faces which replicate Adam's in Paul's portrait are pictured often in books of Latin American art and architecture (cf. Castedo, 1969).

Apostles (Paul, p. 124): "the Spirit's fire above the _______ heads"): With wind and fire the Spirit descended on the apostles at Pentecost (Acts 2:1-13); then they spoke in foreign languages and were "filled with the Spirit."

Astarte (Luke, p. 193): The Canaanite fertility goddess whose cult was a popular Hebrew idolatry (2 Kgs. 23:13; Jgs. 10:5).

Ark (Luke, p. 188: "a glowering face leading the _______ into battle"; and p. 190): The ark of the covenant, a wooden chest covered with gold and containing the tablets given Moses (Ex. 25:10-22). Its history was lengthy, moving here and there with the wandering Jews before being deposited by David in Solomon's Temple (II Sam. 6:15-21; I Chron. 16:1-3). Its power was great: the Psalms describe Yahweh arising mightily from the ark and leading the Hebrews into battle, and rabbinical legend describes its power in a manner which recalls a recent popular movie which showed rippling, blue jets of energy rising from the ark and destroying its surroundings.

Athena (Paul, p. 128): Virgin goddess and daughter of Zeus. Fearful over the possibility of a more powerful son being born, Zeus swallowed her mother, Metis, after turning her into a fly.

Augustine (John, p. 175: "_______said evil is the privation of good, and the Good equivalent to Being"): Bishop Augustine of Hippo (354-540), Neoplatonist and Christian theologian. His doctrine of the privatio boni (privation of good) thoroughly riled C. G. Jung (cf., e.g., 1956/1968a). Whether John's evil intentions and his experience of God support or contradict the idea is one of the more interesting questions raised by the portrait.

Azazel (Luke, p. 193: "sent with the goat to the crusty arms of _______"): Cf. Goat.

Basilides (John, p. 166: "_______gnosis"): Along with Valentinus, one of the more systematic and powerful of Gnostic thinkers. For Gnostic cosmologies generally, a benevolent god awaits the redeemed soul after is has ascended past the celestial spheres guarded by evil gods (Jonas, 1963).

Baudelaire (Paul, p. 122): "the tantalizing sensuality and perfumed air of _______ poetry"): The French poet Charles Baudelaire (1821-1867), prophet of decadence and exquisite sensibility.

Boss (Paul, p. 127): The phenomenological psychologist Medard Boss, whose understanding of Dasein is discussed in Chapter 2.

Cerberus (John, p. 172): The dog-like guardian of the portals of Hades; he allowed Eurydice only to return to the realm of light.

Chartres (Mary, p. 150): "the heraldic seated madonna on the forehead of the portico at _______"; and p. 159): The stone relief above Chartres's west portico shows a massive, seated Virgin, legs splayed, the Christ child seated between them.

Cordelia (John, p. 172): Lear's child, neither avaricious nor cunning, as are her two sisters (Shakespeare, 1608/1919).

Crete (Luke, p. 196): Greek island and home of the Minosian dynasty; known for its bull cult, which would seem parallel to the Baal-Moloch cult of the Phoenicians (cf. Moloch).

Cyclops (Paul, p. 121): One-eyed giant visited by Odysseus; a wild, cannibalistic, uncivilized shepherd, linked traditionally with Hephaestus, smithy god of the underworld.

Dada (John, p. 170): The anarchistic pre-World War I artistic movement; founded in Zurich, where Hugo Ball, Hans Arp, and other Dadaists enacted weird and comical stage plays not unlike the happenings of the 1960s art scene.

Danae (Mary, p. 158): Locked in a tower by her father Acrisius, who feared the birth of a powerful grandson, Zeus took a liking to her and visited in the form of a shower of gold. Often portrayed lounging upon a couch--voluptuous, nude, and relaxed.

Dasein (Paul, p. 127; John, p. 176): Defined for this study as a concept totally inclusive of the modes and factical content of the openness which is human being in its concreteness. The term is discussed in Chapter 2.

Debussy (Paul, p. 125: "_______ faun"; John, p. 166: "_______ musical portrait of the sea"): The French composer Claude Debussy (1862-1918). His faun is from the ballet *Prélude à l'après-midi d'un faun*, choreographed by Nijinski (cf. infra) and produced by Diaghilev. His musical portrait is the impressionistic symphony *La Mer*.

Echo de pensée (Luke, p. 198): The descriptive diagnostic term for one's own thoughts taking the form of auditory hallucination. Typically associated with schizophrenia.

Eigenwelt (Mary, p. 150; John, p. 170): A Heideggerian term appropriated by Binswanger and subsequently used rather infrequently in phenomenological psychopathology; a mode of being-in-the-world or Dasein (cf. Mitwelt and Umwelt). It refers to one's own world, a being-to-itself, a personal world engaged in extending itself over time. As such, Eigenwelt is foundational for experiencing any world at all.

Elizabeth (Mary, p. 146: "a heart not unlike _______ unborn John, who lept with happiness in the double hidden presence of his Lord"): She was pregnant with John the Baptist, who was thus doubly hidden, when her cousin, the Virgin Mary, pregnant also with Jesus, came to visit. John lept with joy (Lk. 1:41).

Eliot (Luke, p. 186: "_______ hollow men"): Poet and Nobel laureate T. S. Eliot (1888-1965; Eliot, 1936). His hollow men are from the poem of the same name, of which the final stanza runs: "This is the way the world ends/ This is the way the world ends/ Not with a bang but a whimper." (Torrey [1980] prefaced his book on schizophrenia with the first three stanzas of the same poem: "We are the hollow men/ We are the stuffed men/ Leaning together/ Headpiece filled with straw." Those who have visited back wards will recognize the mood of chronic schizophrenia.)

Emptying (Paul, p. 131: "divinely initiated self-_______"; and p. 134: "'he _______ himself and took the form of a slave'"[Phil. 5:7]): The word is from the Greek kenosis, which figures importantly in the hymn describing Christ's emptying himself of divinity in order to become human (Phil. 2:5-11). An early theology of the Incarnation sprung from the idea.

Ex nihilo (John, p. 176: "his world is a faceted transparency of cosmic proportions ruled by a god who appeared _______ _______"): Developed during the 2nd and 3rd centuries by Christian apologists, the doctrine of creation from nothing--*ex nihilo*--ensured God's sovereignty over the natural world, dethroned polytheistic conceptions of divinity, and guaranteed the finality of salvation brought in Christ (Pelikan, 1971). This is a theological doctrine, not derivative strictly from the Genesis cosmogony. The counterpart from John's portrait is the credo: "In the beginning, I believe there was a vacuum of nothingness" (p. 175), which would have John's god appear *ex nihilo* rather than God create *ex nihilo*.

Ezekiel (John, p. 178: "_______ valley of dry bones"): The Old Testament prophet who envisioned such a valley (Ez. 37:1-14).

Ganymede (Luke, p. 196: "when handsome _______ sunned on Crete's white shore"): A beautiful boy ravished away by an eagle sent from Zeus, whom he then served as cupbearer. In time the story becomes one of pederasty, and on Crete King Minos replaces Zeus as the ravisher (cf. Crete).

Goat (Luke, p. 192f.: "taken to the edge of the desert and sent with the _______ to the crusty arms of Azazel"): The scapegoat of the Day of Atonement, sent with the Hebrews' sins into the desert for Azazel (Lev. 16:8-10). Whether the latter name refers to a demon or merely applies to the goat's departure is uncertain. For the portrait,

Azazel is the demonic presence of the Hebrew nation's evils; his mating with Lilith yields Moloch, the devouring god which is the darkest shadow of the jealous Yahweh. This part of the portrait progresses purely on a mythopoeic level, but the potential for there being a parallel with Luke's family process is acknowledged and thought probable (cf. Ch. 5, The Portraits, p. 213-217 ff).

Goethe (Paul, p. 118: "_______ mentioned these eyes"): The identity of a sensory organ with the qualitative properties of its percipients is presupposed by the German poet, dramatist, and scientist Johann Wolfgang von Goethe (1749-1832) in certain poems and in his work on visual perception, as it was by most thinkers prior to more current physiopsychological discoveries. The logic of apotropaic magic is based on such an identification.

Goya (Luke, p. 187: "_______ said the sleep of reason breeds monsters"): The Spanish artist Francisco Jose de Goya y Lucientes (1746-1828); his prints of this title show bat-like creatures hovering above the screaming faces of the newly awakened. But the thought is timeless; Freud's oeuvre could be given a similar title.

Hades (John, p. 172): Here used as a place name for the ghostly realm of the Greek underworld (cf. Cerberus).

Hasidim (Luke, p. 189: "the axis around which the _______ danced centuries later"): The Jewish mystical movement; its founder, the Baal Shem Tov (1700-1760), a leader in the spiritual lineage of Moses, was occasionally likened to the *axis mundi* (Buber, 1947). To this day, black-frocked Hasidim dance to celebrate certain festivals, the chief rabbi leading the twining line of men.

Hel (John, pp. 169, 170, 171, 174): For Teutonic mythology, the realm under the roots of the cosmic tree Yggdrasil (cf. infra); another Hades, not the place of punishment of the Christian Hell.

Helen (Luke, pp. 191, 192): The Helen of Greek legend, daughter of Zeus and Leda, the most beautiful of women; induced by Paris to leave Menelaus, thus triggering the Trojan War (cf. Yeats, 1956).

Hephaestus (Paul, p. 128): the Greek god of volcanic fire, and the fire of the smith's forge; thrown from heaven by Zeus, he injured his foot.

Herod (Mary, p. 152; Luke, p. 199): King of Judea at the time of Jesus' birth (Mt. 2:1; Lk. 1:5); he ordered the slaughter of male infants upon hearing of the birth of one greater than himself.

Isaac (Luke, p. 194): "_______was an exception because of his passivity under Abraham's knife"): The child born of barren Sarah; his father Abraham's hand was stayed when God interrupted the boy's sacrifice, which He himself had commanded.

Isaiah (Paul, p. 128: "the seraphim of his vision burns the tongue"): His visionary experience (Is. 6:1-7) is the best known of those reported in the prophetic books of the Old Testament. The seraphim sears his "unclean lips" with a coal, thus enabling him to prophesy.

Ishtar (Luke, p. 193: "with _______ just on the horizon"): The great goddess of Babylonia and Assyria, sharing many features with the Phoenician Astarte (cf. supra); she is a compassionate mother, a goddess of sex, war, and the underworld, and associated with the planet Venus--thus she appears "just on the horizon" at dusk.

Jericho (Luke, pp. 187, 192, 200): The ancient city crumbled when circumambulated by the marching Hebrews blowing the shofar. For Luke's portrait, the mirror image of the New Jerusalem (cf. infra).

Jerusalem (Luke, pp. 187, 192): Used always with reference to the New Jerusalem--the eschatological city described in the New Testament's book of The Revelation (Rev. 21:1; 22:5). The biblical city is centered about an altar which marks the victory of Christ's sacrifice, while the city of Luke's portrait is centered about one from which "trickles rooster blood." His victory is Pyrrhic, his booty, madness.

John (Paul, p. 134: "_______ sings the same with greater sophistication"; and p. 134: "his amazement . . . is apparent elsewhere"): John the Evangelist; from the Prologue of his gospel is drawn the verse: "The Word became flesh" (Jn. 1:14); and from the pastoral epistle assigned to his authorship comes the verse: "what he has heard" (1 Jn. 1:15).

Joseph (Luke, p. 199): The Virgin Mary's husband, the mirror image of Herod.

Kaaba (Paul, p. 133): The site of Islamic pilgrimage and the sacred shrine in the city of Mecca, containing in its walls a sacred, black, volcanic stone. It is the giblah--the point toward which the Muslim prays (Surah II, 144; et passim); its foundation was laid by the Hebrew patriarch Abraham (Surah II, 127; et passim).

Kabala (John, p. 175: "the primordial nothingness of medieval _______ exploded into the 10 Sefiroth"): The mystical tradition of Judaism; rooted in the visionary mysticism of the first few centuries of the common era and reaching a peak of theosophical sophistication with Isaac Luria in the 16th century. The latter's cosmogony described the shard-like remnants of evil left from the explosion of divinity into the nodal points of creative power called Sefiroth (Scholem, 1961; for Sefiroth, cf. infra).

Kazantzakis (John, p. 168): The Greek author Nikos Kazantzakis (1885-1957); his *Saint Francis* (1962) is the opposite of sentimental portraits of saintly mystics.

Kierkegaard (Luke, p. 189): "tumbling deeper than _______ man of faith would fall"): The Danish philosopher and theologian Søren Kierkegaard (1813-1855); often credited with founding existentialism; his man of faith must risk the so-called "leap of faith," thus plunging helplessly into an abyss (Stroll & Popkin, 1979).

Laing (Paul, p. 126: "Laing has spoken of the danger of embodiment"): The British psychiatrist and phenomenological psychopathologist R. D. Laing (1969, p. 173).

Lear (John, p. 172): Shakespeare's Lear, the Fool's master in the tragedy of the same name (1608/1917). In sequence, the quotations from John's portrait are II, iv, 56-8; II, iv, 274-89; and III, i, 7-11. For *hysterica passio*, cf. Campbell (1930).

Lex talionis (Luke, p. 195): The law of talion, spoken of in the Pentateuch; the principle that retaliation should correspond in degree and kind to the original offense--"an eye for an eye."

Lilith (Luke, p. 193): Traditionally Adam's first wife, the queen of demons, and sometimes the Devil's wife. Refusing to acknowledge Adam as master, she was turned out of Paradise, say the early rabbis. For the Moslem tradition, she cohabitated with the Devil and birthed evil spirits, but many of them died because of her recalcitrance with

Adam. A complex image overlapping many traditions and reaching to Medieval Jewry, for which she is the succubus par excellence, the temptress of righteous men, the cause of nocturnal emissions, and a child stealer.

Limbo (Mary, p. 151: "a _______-like Sheol"): The borderland of Hell in medieval Christian cosmography.

Logos (John, p. 172: "the perfect complement to the illuminating, creative _______ of another John"): John the Evangelist is in question (cf. supra); his Logos is the divine creativity imaged as the power of worded thinking; as such, it illuminates human nescience (Jn. 1:1-5).

Logos spermatikos (John, p. 172: "the _______ _______ disseminated throughout the world"): A concept closely related to that of Logos, a fruit of late Neoplatonism, and meant to stretch philosophically across the gap between the spiritual nature of the unitary Logos and the multiform reality of material nature. The logoi spermatiko inform the many objects which compose the natural world.

Lourdes (Luke, p. 199): The site of Christian pilgrimage in southern France, and much earlier a grotto dedicated to the mother goddess; its cave and springs are famous for healing.

Lucifer (Mary, p. 154: "Silvania!--my Mary's own _______"): The rebellious prince of demons, the antagonist of Christ and Lord of this world; as the "morning star" (Is. 14:12), he, too, is a light, just as "Silvania" names a brand of light bulb.

Mahler (John, p. 166): The Austrian composer Gustav Mahler (1860-1911); the initial movement of his choral Resurrection symphony is intolerably bleak, dark, and cacophonous.

Marcel Marceau (John, p. 170): The French mime, still living, who is largely responsible for revitalizing the art form.

Maugham (Paul, p. 120): The English novelist William Somerset Maugham (1874-1965); his hero is the protagonist of Of Human Bondage (1915-1977).

Mayan (Luke, p. 187: "a lattice feathered with the brilliance of a _______ priest's hummingbird headdress"): Such sacerdotal vestments still retain their color in modern museums; typically they are scapular-like, not headdresses.

Medusa (Mary, p. 153: "Samson and ________ are brother and sister"): A mortal gorgon with boar tusks, glaring eyes which turn the observed to stone, and, more importantly for Mary's portrait, snakes for hair.

Meribah (Luke, p. 191: "Moses turned away from Yahweh at _______"): Here the Hebrews murmured against Moses, who showed little faith and consequently was not allowed to enter the Promised Land of Canaan (Num. 20:1-13).

Michelangelo (Luke, p. 188: "_______ gave him horns, for he is the dictation of God's law"): The Italian artist Michelangelo Buonarrati (1475-1564). His enormous statue, surmounting a fountain in Rome, shows Moses holding the tablets of the commandments, of which he is the dictation because of his responsibility for transmitting the Law. Two horns of light grow from his curly hair. (Cf. Moses' veil.)

Mimir (John, p. 169: "the soothsayer _______ decapitated head"): A gigantic god of Teutonic mythology whose home is a well beside the roots of Yggdrasil; having drunk from the well, he is wise and able to recall the past and tell the future. He is also a smithy god. (Cf Odin and Yggdrasil).

Mitwelt (John, p. 170): A Heideggerian term appropriated by Binswanger; another of the three modes of being-in-the-world (cf. Eigenwelt and Umwelt). It refers to the world of sociality or inter-relationship, the with-world in the sense of being-with-others.

Moloch (Luke, pp. 193, 194, 195: "brassy arms"): A non-Israelite god venerated with human sacrifice by having children pass through fire or slide into it along his metal features (Lev. 18:21; 20:3-5; 2 Kgs.23:10; Jer. 32-35). For the psychohistory and psychology of Moloch and infanticide, which figure so prominently in Luke's portrait, cf. Bakan (1966, 1974).

Moses' veil (Luke, p. 190: "His white _______ would flap gently"): Conversing with God, Moses' face became radiant, which frightened the Israelites. Thereafter he wore a veil over his face (Ex. 34:29-35).

Nijinski (John, p. 169: "_______ shouted from the snowy cliff above St. Moritz"): The renowned Russian ballet dancer Vaslav Nijinski (1890-1950) who became schizophrenic according to the diagnosis of Jung and others. His autobiography (1968) recounts his discovery on the mountain above St. Moritz, Switzerland, that he was God.

Odin, Wotan (John, p. 169): The one-eyed patriarch of the Teutonic gods; all-seeing, all-knowing, god of wisdom and war; the two ravens of thought and memory perch on his shoulders as he sits enthroned in Valhalla (cf. infra) surrounded by chosen warriors. With an insatiable thirst for knowledge, he sacrificed an eye for a drink from soothsayer Mimir's well (cf. supra) and hung entranced for 9 days from Yggdrasil all the while peering into the depths of Hel. Thus he learned the runes.

Orphic (Luke, p. 186 "an _______ egg"): The primeval matter of our Big Bang theory would be comparable to the cosmic egg of Greek Orphism. The cult's theme is death-and-resurrection. In some accounts Orpheus loses his head, which is oracular like Mimir's.

Pas de trois (Mary, p. 156: "a _______ _______ _______ of gestural melody"); A dance for three persons.

Paul (Paul, p. 134: "consider the letter of another Paul"; and p.131: "Echoing the feeling of another Paul who said"): The apostle Paul; the letter is his epistle to the church at Phillipi (cf. Emptying); the feeling in question is conveyed in the quotation from Rm. 8:28.

Prometheus (Mary, p. 155; and Luke, p. 196: "_______ knew, for the same bird swooped to dip from . . . his liver"): Son of a titan and unwilling to submit to Olympian authority, he was finally chained to a Caucasian mountain by Zeus. There he suffered a monstrous eagle tearing his liver, which regrew to be torn again.

Prophet (John, p. 170: "The symbolic shard-scattering of the biblical _______"): More than once Yahweh directs an Old Testament prophet to shatter a clay flask in front of the people, thus announcing divine judgment (cf., e.g., Jer. 19:10-13).

Revelation (Mary, p. 152: "the woman from _______ clothed with the sun"): Always used with reference to the concluding, visionary book of the New Testament--the book of The Revelation (cf. Jerusalem). Its author says "a great sign appeared in the sky, a woman clothed with the sun, with the moon under her feet, on her head a crown of twelve stars" (Rev. 12:1). She is the gathering of the lost Israel in the bosom of the church victorious, the counterpart to Eve, and the same celestial accouterments are sometimes shown with the Virgin Mary.

Ricoeur (Paul, p. 129): The French phenomenological philosopher Paul Ricoeur (b. 1913); the book is The Symbolism of Evil (1969).

Rilke (Paul, p. 125: "_______ conveys the boggling effect of His appearance"): The poem is "Imaginary Biography" (Bly, 1981), the poet is the German Rainer Maria Rilke (1875-1926).

Rubens (Mary, p. 151; and p. 150: "a _______ in appearance, but floridly alive like a Madonna of Tintoretto only wishfully"): The Flemish painter Peter Paul Rubens (1577-1640) and the Italian painter Jacopo Robusti Il Tintoretto (1518-1594) are in question. For Mary's portrait, distinguishing between the two is not a matter of technical art historical differences: it is based on a variety of impressionistic evaluations. While Rubens's figures, including the Virgin, are more heraldic in pose and more substantial and dense in their bodily presence, Tintoretto's figures are closer to the etherealization of bodily presence exemplified by El Greco. A greater floridness of color accompanies the transition from Rubens to Tintoretto and from Tintoretto to El Greco. This set of comparisons may be situated in a more extensive one ranging from the architectural Chartrian Virgin (cf. supra) to Rubens, from Rubens to Tintoretto, and from Tintoretto to El Greco. As with other analogies throughout the portraits, these have their parallels. For example, the Chartrian Virgin is to the heaviness of Umwelt as the Tintorettian floridness and passion is to an Eigenwelt posed on the edge of self-transcendence.

Samson (Mary, p. 153: "_______ and Medusa are brother and sister"): A judge of Israel known for his enormous strength and single-handed victories over the idolatrous Philistines. For Mary and her hair, Samson's significance rests in the link between hair and strength. "If I am shaved, my strength will leave me" (Jgs. 16:17). Delila does, and the Philistines then gouge out his eyes. Coincidentally, Mary likewise damaged her eye; medical staff believes the injury was self-inflicted. (Cf. Medusa.)

Sartre (Paul, p. 126: "_______ furtive voyeur stands upright, blanching and dehumanized"; and John, p. 170: "________ oak, which vaporizes consciousness and sends the mind swirling in a viscous tangle of sap"): The oak triggers Roquentin's enlightenment to the nauseating meaning of existence in Sartre's novel (1938/1964); it depersonalizes consciousness and is imaged vaguely as a viscous tangle of bark. The voyeur is a critical figure for Sartre's analysis of the lived body (1943/1956), which figures as background for some of the portraits.

Sefiroth (John, p. 175: "when the primordial nothingness of Medieval Kabala exploded into the 10 _______"): The 10 nodes of divine power, both immanent and transcendent. Their formation coincided with the explosive cosmogonic event (cf. Kabala).

Shekinah (Luke, p. 189: "he cowered beneath the rock while the ageless roar of the divine _______ passed ominously overhead"): The 10th Sefirah (cf. Sefiroth); the kingdom of God; the eschatologically reassembled community of Israel; the pillar of fire which guided the exiled Hebrews; and most importantly for Luke's portrait, the Shekinah is at times identified with the presence of God, the backside of which Moses was able to see without dying (Ex. 33:18-23). The link between seeing God and dying is explicit in the majority of the nine patients of this study. Once again Harold Searles (1965) was correct; he emphasized the unusual importance of death for persons diagnosed schizophrenic. But the whole matter opens like the Grand Canyon when great thinkers remind us of the link in such pithy apothegms as this one of Meister Eckhart: "He who is not dead from the ground up knows absolutely nothing of the holiness which God has always revealed to his dear friends" (quoted in Landsberg, 1966, p. 231).

<u>Sheol</u> (Mary, p. 151: "a Limbo-like _______"): The subterranean place of postmortem existence for biblical Judaism, a gray place of dust and darkness where social differences are leveled. (Cf. Limbo.)

<u>Shulamite</u> (Luke, p. 193: "This spiteful _______ was mounted by the demon"): Originally the lovely bride of the Old Testament erotic poem "The Song of Songs"--a woman "dark but lovely" (Songs 1:5), of which the bridegroom says, "You are an enclosed garden . . . a fountain sealed" (4:12) and "Turn, turn, O Shulamite, that we may look at you!" (7:1). The "spiteful Shulamite" of Luke's portrait is the mirror image of the original and identical to Lilith.

<u>Simoon</u> (Mary, p. 151: "The _______ wind whipping from the Sahara"): The dry, gritty, Saharan winds which sweep from North Africa across parts of Europe. The incidence of suicide correlates with the wind's activity.

<u>Sleipnir</u> (John, p. 169): Odin's powerful and loyal eight-legged gray horse.

Straus (Paul, p. 118: "_______ elucidation of the upright posture"; and pp. 123f: "Words blend with other kinds of sounds" and "'Sensing is to know as a cry is to words'"): The psychiatrist whose work is given lengthy consideration in Chapter 2. His "elucidation of the upright posture" refers to his best known essay "The Upright Posture" (1966). The presentation of the gnostic moments of sensory and perceptual experience is treated at length in Chapter 2. And the quotation may be found in Primary World of the Senses (1963, p. 312).

Stravinsky (John, p. 169: "The Rite of Spring heard by _______"): The Russian-born composer Igor Stravinsky (1882-1981), whose work introduced the 12-tone scale, and whose ballet Le Sacre de Printemps was danced by Nijinski (cf. supra). The "dapper Parisian crowd" was scandalized by his rhythms and intensity; some left the theater before the end of the first staging in May 1913.

Sunni (Paul, p, 118): The Sunni Black Muslims. This is the original and more conservative branch of the Black Muslim movement (Mamiya, 1982). It does not push for a revolutionary militancy, thus Paul's notions of a revolutionary uprising may be viewed as his own rather than a borrowing from his religious sect.

Tao (Paul, p. 124 "the _______ forest haunted by the valley spirit"; and John, p. 176: "as flowing water fills hollows and as _______ turns the empty to use"): The spiritual discipline and religion of Taoism, but specifically the teachings of its founder Lao Tzu, from whose writings is taken the images of water filling hollows, the usefulness of the useless, and the valley spirit, a feminine presence of gentleness which conduces to wisdom, inactivity, and passivity (Chan, 1963).

Theotokos (Paul, p. 129): The Greek theological term which translates as "God-bearer"; the title attributed to the Virgin Mary at the Council of Ephesus in 431 (Pelikan, 1971).

Tintoretto: Cf. Rubens.

Troy (Luke, p. 189: "an embattled horse"; "the hollow seduction shoved in front of war torn _______"): Troy of the Trojan War, which was finally captured when the hollow horse filled with soldiers was accepted within the gates of the embattled city. (Cf. Helen and Yeats.)

Umwelt (Mary, p. 150; John, p. 170): A Heideggerian term appropriated by Binswanger; another of the three modes of being-in-the-world (cf. Eigenwelt and Mitwelt). It refers to the natural world, of which the body is an aspect and for which spatiality is a necessity; the world of objects; the world into which one is thrown.

Uroborus (Mary, p. 148: "the _______ of imagination"): "Tail-eater" in Greek, the title for the dragon devouring itself tail-first; one of Western alchemy's most basic images; a symbol for the alchemical opus, which, says Jung (1953/1968b), required the alchemist to harbor his imaginative images, ply them with amplifications, and thus generate the emotional intensity and symbolic insight required to bring the opus to completion.

Vagina dentata (John, p. 175: "the toothy grin of a hovering _______ _______"): Toothed vagina; a motif common especially to the American Indians. Many die before the hero smashes the teeth. So it is the days of the hero and trickster before civilization, just as with John we inhabit an uncivilized, barbaric world lorded over by a cannibalistic pit.

Valhalla (John, p. 169): Odin's favorite home where he entertains warriors chosen from the slain. Surrounded by trees with golden leaves, the great hall has spears for rafters and polished shields for a roof. Its hundreds of doors can accommodate hundreds of soldiers passing through shoulder-to-shoulder. For this and all Teutonic mythology linked with John, one would do well to recall the architecture of the Third Reich and the "rushing saurian motion" of Hitler's "goose-stepping" soldiers. (Cf. Odin.)

Valkyrie (John, p. 169): Teutonic battle maidens and attendants of Odin who ride to retrieve the bodies of fallen warriors and return with them via the rainbow bridge to Valhalla. They approach the warrior destined to die in battle; their golden hair and lily white arms surround him during a kiss.

Valley Spirit: Cf. Tao.

von Gebsattel (John, p. 176: "_______ has referred to a quivering dread in the face of anti-eidos"): The German phenomenological psychopathologist Freiherr Viktor E. von Gebsattel (b. 1883). Anti-eidos is the meaningless, soiled, morbid residue of becoming (May et al., 1958, p. 179).

Vivaldi (Mary, p. 150: "Are _______ concerti imbalanced because of the dully present continuo?"): The Italian cleric and musician Antonio Vivaldi (1695-1741). The sound of the "dully present continuo" is common to much Baroque music; it provides a bass and a rhythm.

West (Mary, p. 150: "She is the reverse of Binswanger's Ellen West"; and John, p. 176: "the hole named _______ _______"): Ellen West is the subject of what is perhaps Binswanger's greatest case study

(May et al., 1958). He described her mode of existence as a "hole." She finally commits suicide.

Whitman (Paul, p. 117: "the electric body _______ sang"): The American poet Walt Whitman (1819-1892); the poem is "The Body Electric," although "Song of Myself" and many others from Leaves of Grass (1885/1961) would provide an equally appropriate lyrical background for the effort of constructing phenomenological landscapes based on the lived body.

Wotan: Cf. Odin.

Yeats (John, p. 174: "the foolish king is but 'a paltry thing, a tattered coat upon a stick'"; p. 174: "_______ Byzantium is beyond reach"; p. 174: "their burnt hands and choked heart are unable to 'clap and sing, and louder sing for every tatter in their mortal dress'"; and p. 175: "_____ said Troy burned with the passion of Helen because Zeus's beak held Leda prostrate"): W. B. Yeats (1865-1939; Yeats, 1956), the Irish poet. "Leda and the Swan" describes Zeus's visitation of Leda in the form of a swan, a coupling which "engenders there/ The broken wall, the burning roof and tower/ And Agamemnon dead" (cf. Helen). "Sailing to Byzantium" described "an aged man" unable to reach the bountiful kingdom of Byzantium because he is "but a paltry thing,/ A tattered coat upon a stick, unless/ Soul clap its hands and sing, and louder sing/ For every tatter in its mortal dress."

Yggdrasil (John, p. 170: "the deepest root of _______"; and p. 174): The world tree of Scandinavian mythology; its roots and branches bind heaven and Hel; an eagle roosts on its top, a serpent gnaws its roots; it supplied the branch from which Odin's sword was made.

APPENDIX B

CASE HISTORIES AND NARRATIVES OF THE EXPERIENCE OF GOD

Sarah

History

Sarah is a 28-year-old Caucasian. She is overweight and has brown eyes and straight, black hair. There have been three psychiatric admissions and numerous emergency room visits for various somatic complaints. The psychiatric history is moderately complete, the social history less so.

This is an exceptional case in that Sarah stands apart diagnostically from the rest in the series. There have been two recorded episodes of manic depression, with her entering the hospital during an acute manic phase, then falling into a severe depression before she once again recovered a moderately depressed state following the initiation of Lithium therapy. These bipolar episodes follow a nearly exact 2-year cycle. The 1980 admission occurred in March, while the 1982 admission occurred in February. A history taken from the husband suggests a manic-depressive phase with a similar pattern in 1978. In both 1980 and 1982, Sarah's experiences of God occurred during the affective crescendo of the escalating manic phase. As she said, "the same thing happened both times--I saw visions of Hell, of my being condemned to Hell"; consequently, only her first experience will be recounted.

Mentioned either in the medical charts or by Sarah herself are the following elements of her history. Her stepfather was "abusive" and there was "incest in the family." "Darvon, alcohol and sleeping medicines" have been "abused." She is "unable to have a baby because she doesn't have regular periods." She has worked periodically as a prostitute. I have met her husband personally, a foreign man smaller in build than Sarah and having the presence and interpersonal skills of a mouse. Some of her presenting medical complaints in the emergency room have been "duodenitis," "allergies," and "musculo-skeletal chest wall pain."

Sarah was brought to the hospital for the 1980 admission after her husband called the police. She had "jumped out of the car and began accosting strangers, jumping on the hood of their car." "She was preoccupied with religious thoughts, claiming she was dead and reincarnated and unable to make interpersonal contact." She was "totally disoriented but without a formal thought disorder." The depressive phase commenced "within a day after the patient's admission." She exhibited "*cerea flexibilitas* with flaccid posture although she was able to respond with her gaze." She was placed in a "wheel chair with soft restraints." The presentation in 1982 was not significantly different except for the absence of catatonia. She had been "walking in the rain screaming and yelling, jumping over strangers' fences, saying that she had to spread the Lord's Word, that she didn't live anywhere anymore and that there was no way to save herself from Hell." She was, however, "almost catatonic when first examined" for an admission 3 months later.

Narrative

Because of the complexity of Sarah's experience of God, it will prove helpful to mark out its three segments before proceeding. For "about three weeks" there were various voices, the most prominent being those of "God" and "Jesus." This segment ended with a "dream" in which she saw "Jesus coming on a cloud" with these words: "This is your Judgment Day." The second major segment was a day in length; it involved waking "visions," horrendous experiences involving a variety of unusual bodily sensations. The final segment involved voices only, this time "urging her to go out" and sell her belongings. The entire experience was occurring during a period of great upset: "One thing would lead to the next. I was getting more and more agitated. I kept pacing around my house. I didn't know what to do. I couldn't sit still. I couldn't get rid of the voices. The days blurred together because I wasn't sleeping right." Now to more detail.

They began as "whispering voices," and this was "terrifying"--it "scared her to death"--because "never in her life had she heard voices." "One voice in particular was different from the others. The others came and went, and they had all started out gentle, but this one got more urgent, more insistent." It was God's voice, saying: "You've been a sinner; you're going to die and you're going to Hell; I am condemning to Hell." She felt this was justified, and began "comdemning" herself as well. She "hadn't repented." She "had accepted Jesus Christ, but didn't take it seriously." Another voice, that of Jesus, was different in tone. It "never condemned" and was "always gentle." It asked in a questioning tone "why she was so afraid to do what He wanted her to do"; it asked, "Why don't you pick up your cross and follow me?" It was "embarrassment and fear" that kept her from "telling other people" about Him. Another voice, especially disturbing because "she didn't want to think things like that," came while Sarah was "driving to the store," saying "she was the anti-Christ." Reading the Bible compounded the intensity of her experience of condemnation: "Everything I was reading, I was getting condemned."

For some while she had been "praying to God to please kill her or heal her" of the "different physical things" that troubled her and which doctors could not explain. But she realized at this point during the experience that "she didn't want to die." (Some of these same "physical things" were present during our conversation. Her "tongue" began "pulling over to the side, feeling really weird" and like she was "going to swallow it," and causing her to talk periodically with slurred speech. Her explanation was that "Satan was trying to stop her from telling me this.")

The dream that brought the first segment of the experience to a close occurred during the evening when she was asleep. Its prophetic intent is plain: "Jesus came on a cloud and told me that this was my Judgment Day." And, indeed, it was.

The form of the experience of "Judgment Day" was that of waking "visions or hallucination or whatever you want to call them." Along with the "visions" was occasionally the voice of God announcing or describing the visions. Sarah:

> I was laying on my bed and I couldn't really go to sleep. I kept going to sleep but it was like I was half awake and half asleep. I wasn't even sure I was sleeping. Like dreaming, but I wasn't asleep. Wide awake and having these dreams. I dreamed that I was locked inside my body and it was like God showing me what Hell was like. I would be shown what the punishment will be for all the sins I committed against Him all my life. I couldn't move, I couldn't talk, I couldn't do anything, and I was dead on the outside. People would look at me and say, "She's dead," and they would take me and

> do an autopsy and I would feel it because He said, "Your spirit will be locked inside your body forever."

And more:

> God locked me inside; I was trapped in my body--for eternity, He said. My spirit was trapped in my body and everyone would think I was dead but I was really alive inside. You would be able to feel things, like when the autopsy cuts into you. I was in a dark cave, chained to the wall. I saw He was going to throw me into the ocean and I couldn't breathe. I saw all that! Yet I would still be alive. Locusts would eat your body, you'd feel bugs crawling on you, like I was buried alive--like I was looking on my body, not like a dream. I was seeing it in my mind, but it was like seeing it with my eyes too.

During this experience, "sores started breaking out all over Sarah's body." They did so "at the same time as the dreams." Not only that, she "started getting terrible pains in her bones, especially the legs and arms. Shooting, awful bone pain, deep inside her bones." Apropos of this, it was announced: "This is the pain Jesus felt when he got crucified on the cross. Christ felt this when He took on the sins of the world." Sarah understood this to mean that God "wanted her to feel the pain and agony His son went through for her." Consequently, she "felt remorse, really sad He had to go through that for her." "I suddenly realized that He loved me--He really loved me. The things He suffered, I went through, like in my mind, and it was awful!" Later she concluded: "If there's Hell, there's a heaven; and if there's a heaven, there's a God; and if there's a God, then everything in the Bible is true."

I asked Sarah about the possibility of her moving during the "visions." Yes, "she could have moved, if she had wanted to, but she had no urge to move." She "wasn't frozen." She was "writhing around, like a snake, in pain and extreme agony."

The experiences of the evening of the day of Hell are different in form than the earlier "visions." They do involve visual images, but without them being assimilated to the body and its sensory world. The evening visions do not have the lucidity of the earlier ones, nor are they linked with voices.

Still laying in bed, the room lit, Sarah noticed "the little silver ball, like a bell, at the end of the bedside lamp chain." On the ball she "saw the face of Jesus, really small, like seeing a movie almost, fading and coming clear again." He was "moving his lips, but she couldn't hear him, and she kept asking, 'What? What?'" She "tried to read his lips," and it seemed like he was saying, "'Come unto me,' like in the Bible." The vision ceased. She looked to the table and "saw another vision in the tin foil ashtray made from a little pie pan." It was "cleaned out," and she saw on its surface a "bunch of men standing in a row, lined up, and behind them was some kind of a monster that was under water--there were bubbles coming up in back of the men." She thought the men were "the apostles"; the monster, which was an "octopus that kept waving its arms," she thought was "God." The "men kept changing: their faces would fade and a new face would come--they were kind of smiling." They spoke, but Sarah could not hear them. The vision ceased and another of Jesus' face replaced it. Jesus spoke also, "His lips moved," but she was unable to hear. He "kept changing--he looked like Jesus, but looked like a different person." How did He look? "You know, you see pictures of how he is supposed to look--beard, moustache, long hair." Again he seemed to be saying, "Come to me." During the evening, she was "terrified and thought she was going insane." She searched for explanations, "trying to find some reason for it, to explain it away." Perhaps it was the "anti-histamines, the nose spray she uses all the time--it's suppose to make you see things."

With the coming morning, Sarah

> felt the urge to go out and leave her husband--go out and tell others to turn back go God. First she was going to take all her clothes and give them away, take her rings and jewelry and sell them. She did manage to get rid of her rings.

All of this was at the instigation of divine command; she simply "tried to follow what the voices were telling her." Hospitalization interrupted her plan.

Of significance are the reservations Sarah has now about her previous interpretation of these experiences. Certain of the voices could well have been Jesus, since they were similar or duplicated phrases and directions in the Bible. Other elements are less certain--for example, the identity of the octopus in the later vision. She has since adopted the humble attitude conveyed in this statement:

> I refuse to say whether it was God's voice because it's not my place to say whether it's God or not because I don't know. It got my attention! I'll put it that way! So whether it was Him or not, it was His purpose that it happened, because it brought me to where I am now, which is a higher level of understanding. I can't tell Him anything. He's the great God of everyone. He is so great! You have to come trusting like a child.

To my question of whether she felt forgiven after this experience, Sarah answered, "Not then, but I do now." And since then? Fifteen months later she experienced God in a different way. While "the first time it was more terrifying," she "cried from joy" during this next experience. She had been troubled with "a guilty conscience" for some while, partly due to childhood "incest." And while "listening to a record about Jesus" one afternoon--a record which "really hit me where I live"--she "prayed the 'Sinner's Prayer': 'Lord, have mercy on me a sinner.'" Then she experienced "the feeling of God's love" and "cried from joy." The experience was as powerful as it was simple.

Mark Thomas

History

Mark Thomas is a dark-haired, 28-year-old Caucasian. His actual first and middle names have been retained since they figure prominently in the numerical system he employs to derive certain religious truths. Little information about Mark is available. He has been hardly more than a passer-by in the county where our conversation took place and in which he has been hospitalized on three occasions. He either simply appears at the emergency room or is brought in by the police for disruptive behavior. It was discovered during his earliest stay that he is a resident of a more northern county, and on the occasion of each hospitalization he has been transported to psychiatric facilities in that county almost immediately. It seems the reason for his spontaneously traveling south is to escape from a homosexual lover. The event prompting the admission during which we conversed was his reporting to the emergency room staff that he had come to collect his "inheritance of three million dollars some family had stolen." The admitting diagnosis was chronic undifferentiated schizophrenia.

The soft-spoken quality of Mark's talking was quite at odds with the coarseness of his features, posture, and gestures. He wore a loose fitting, white hospital robe, slouched in his chair with legs akimbo, and scratched his genitals periodically. A tic upset the balance of his mouth at regular intervals and gave the impression of a smirk. He seemed only minimally present though intent on making sure he was understood. Whether his amused preoccupation was a matter of erotic self-stimulation or attending to hallucinations, I am not sure, although he denied hearing voices during the course of our conversation.

Mark's is a unique case in the series because he is the only one who identifies himself with God. It is not that he has never experienced God as other than himself: he has "seen Jesus in a white robe"--a kind of "miniaturized" homunculus who "appeared to him in a room"; he has been "annointed" through "seeing the rod of God--a rod of light--come down and go right through his forehead"; and he has "prayed to see heaven," as a consequence of which he "got zapped by a robot-like creature" who he "thought was God." But none of these experiences has ranked with the great boon he discovered with the "A-B-C-1-2-3" system of numerical transformation. It was this system that allowed him to learn "the fact that he is Jesus Christ the Lord" and "God." The intricacies of the system follow. Its implications will be detailed in the narrative.

The "A-B-C-1-2-3" system is based on first establishing an identity between the cardinal numbers and the letters of the alphabet. Thus 1 = A, 2 = B, and 3 = C. For each number there is one letter. Beyond this fundamental feature of the system are the following rules of number-letter transformations. Contiguous digits of a single numeral, even when it is composed of more than two digits as with letters beyond "I," are to be added, thus reducing the original numeral to a single-digit numeral. For example, the letter "L," which is matched with the number "12," is to be reduced to "3" (12 = [1 + 2] = 3) during the process of calculating number-letter equations in which it happens to figure. The number "0" is to be dropped since "it is nothing." When working with more than one name or word at once, one is not to treat the group of names or words as if they, too, could be collapsed initially. The individual name or word retains a measure of independence in this respect. This holds true even when the numerical equivalents of the group of names are reduced for the purpose of establishing the identity of that group with another name or group of names. For example, M-A-R-K = J-E-S-U-S C-H-R-I-S-T, not because M-A-R-K = "7" and J-E-S-U-S C-H-R-I-S-T = "7," but because the reduction of J-E-S-U-S and C-H-R-I-S-T, when each name is reduced individually before both are collapsed, is also equivalent to "7." Another significant feature of the system is its allowing one to run either direction, from letters, words, and names to numbers and vice versa. With this final element of flexibility, the field is wide open and yet governed by strict rules. "It's logic," Mark Thomas assured me, "no game-playing."

Narrative

A "rock musician in Oregon" first told Mark Thomas of the system which allowed him "to understand numerological values." He then "expanded" its usage, realizing its true importance when studying "a book of the mystical classification of certain people." There he "found his name written in the book--St. Thomas--and there was a letter right next to it: 'Q 14.'" "Q 14" is reducible to "God Aquinas Thomas," and consequently, Mark Thomas discovered that he had "been classified as being God." Since then other secrets have been "revealed" to him, the most prominent being those associated with his "social security number," his "property code" number, and his "4-F" classification when he was released from the military in 1974. Some of these many secrets, all of which he demonstrated to me with the "A-B-C-1-2-3" system, thus "proving" their truth, are the following: he is capable of "decoding military intelligence" and will be a "five star general"; he is "the messenger of the ark of the covenant of the Lord," as was Jesus; he is "Douglas McArthur" according to "code 74"; he became able retroactively, so to speak, to decipher "past codes," even those which "reveal" his "identities in past lives." In each case, the applicable "code" refers to the equivalence between certain names and their respective numerals, and furthermore, the identity of these names with the corresponding historical or divine person. Thus Mark Thomas need only say, "code 4," for example, in order to communicate that he is "Lord" and "Master." He announced his presence in the emergency room in just this manner: "Code 4!, code 4!"

Mark Thomas's world has changed dramatically since his "identity" was uncovered after the "revelation of the esoteric keys." To the question of what God's experience is like, he replied:

> I've been treated like a dog by the world. They've treated me in the reverse of what I've really deserved to be treated like. Instead of being treated with love and respect, it's been like an ignoramus and a dog. The churches didn't even feed me. I had to beg. I would preach scripture to them. It was like I was a goat or wolf in sheep's clothing.

And when did you feel most like a dog? "When they put me in special education and said I was mentally retarded, thought I wasn't capable of functioning like a normal person." He "felt like he was a lost case and had been forgotten," much in contrast to the discovery that he was "an important being--God!, someone valuable that they could use." He has come to understand "he is an important leader--King, Lord, and Son of Man." His "name has even been put on the Mark IV Lincoln Continental." Now he has "knowledge," and "knowledge is power," he said in a questioning tone. "A lot of people claim to be Jesus Christ, but they can't prove it--that's the difference between them and me."

The emotional ramifications of the "A-B-C-1-2-3" system may be painfully obvious at this point, yet there is a quite specific feature of Mark Thomas's divinity which is yet to be made clear. What is the most important aspect of being God? "The most important part is my classification--my identity, my true identity, so that people can see the light of the world in you, the god that's within the person that you see, since my identity is a universal identity." Are you the only God? "No, there are others, other people that have their classification straight. That's why they're functioning out there in the world--working people! Just trying to get my identity established so that people will know who I am and treat me as that individual so that I can function."

Our conversation ended with my asking whether he was worried about losing "power" from having told so many secrets. No, he would "like to give power to other people so they can use it to get things done and have the power to unlock their identities. " He rambled further, remarking upon the danger of "walking around saying 'I am Jesus Christ,' despite its being true," and glancing toward me with a glazed, knowing expression after noticing his white hospital gown, the very color of Christ's robe in his vision.

Teresa

History

Teresa is a slim, tall, black woman of 24. The psychiatric history is quite complete in that there have been many hospitalizations, most of them clustering around her 16th year, during several of which a careful history was taken. The social history is minimal.

Teresa is the oldest of three sisters. The father's whereabouts "is unknown," and she has had "chronic difficulty in adapting to two stepfathers."

The diagnoses and comments during the 1974 admissions reflect the doctors' impression of the seriousness of Teresa's problems. It was remarked during the first of the series that there had been "a deterioration of her school performance and relationships with other people." "Identity confusion" and "schizoid object-relations" were noted, and despite her "grossly disturbed thinking, with looseness of associations and numerous *non sequiturs*," there was not "clear-cut evidence of delusions." Her "pursuits and goals" were thought to be "masculine," thus echoing the personal history which notes her claim to be "homosexual" and "interested in other girls from a sexual standpoint from age 6 or 7." She is quoted as saying she wants to be a "priest," presumably in the "Baptist-Methodist Church." "Nocturnal and hyponogogic hallucinations" were thought to be present "2 years" prior. "Emotional outbursts" had occurred often in the past, sometimes centered on her feeling that "everyone has it in for her." She impressed one doctor with her "meticulousness," and the mother "put a great deal of emphasis on her being a perfectionist who makes great demands on her school work." Evidence for "obsessiveness or phobic behavior" was absent.

These 1974 admissions, one of which was at the state hospital, led to a variety of diagnostic impressions. The doctors would typically underemphasize the sociopathic features of Teresa's behavior, commenting, for example, "this is more than an adolescent adjustment reaction or a psychopathic personality--she has several of the cardinal features of a nuclear shizophrenia," or giving diagnoses such as these: "adolescent turbulence with diffusion of sexual identity and impending paranoid schizophrenia," "chronic undifferentiated schizophrenia," and "undifferentiated adolescent schizophrenia." Neurological examinations have been normal consistently.

There were two offenses for car theft prior to 1975. One hospitalization occurred after the staff was unable to control her at Juvenile Hall following an arrest. Since then there has been another charge for "grand theft auto" and "hit-and-run." There is a lengthy history of drug abuse involving alcohol and marijuana prior to 1974, and heroin addiction since then.

The most recent admission occurred after the police were called to her home where her grandfather was "physically restraining" her. She had "accused the grandfather of killing her grandmother." In the emergency room, she said "she would like to be dead and had tried to kill herself several times in the past" and that she had "three hearts and feels dead when she breathes." The admitting diagnosis was acute exacerbation of chronic schizophrenia. Over the lifespan, my impression would be pseudopsychopathic schizophrenia in a schizoid personality with an atypical gender identity disorder, this having evolved rapidly to a schizophreniform psychosis during the 16th year and followed by a settled and chronic undifferentiated schizophrenia within the few years preceding the present admission. I would estimate her level of intelligence to be within the dull normal range.

During conversation, Teresa had the wide-eyed, open face of a spooked child. She examined the room carefully, but without the attention and concentration apparent in most other persons' effort to comprehend their surroundings. She seemed ready to jump with fright. Her conversation had the same tentative, staccato air. Her tangentiality made her difficult to follow and perhaps the most difficult to keep focused on a single experience at a time. The variety and number of her experiences of God compounded this problem. As she said, "I seen so many different visions, it's getting hard to distinguish which one's God." Amongst those which she has identified as visions of God have been a "black Jesus, white Jesus, Indian Jesus and Japanese Jesus." Despite the variety and number of such experiences, she identifies readily her two most powerful experiences of God, the outstanding one having occurred 3 years before in 1978, the second most powerful 2 years before in 1979. These two are given in this sequence.

Narrative

In 1978, Teresa was taken to jail for "disturbing and destruction." She had been "walking in the streets when she kicked a garbage can."

The police came and told her "to pick it up." She refused to do so and they "commenced to beating her." She fell asleep in her jail cell that evening, laying on her right side on a jailhouse "bunk hooked to the wall." Later "somebody shook her shoulder" and told her to awaken. "All of a sudden she had a funny feeling and woke up." "He was right there!" Jesus was "hanging on the wall, midair on the wall!" She felt "scared" and recoiled, falling "right off the bottom bunk."

Jesus was a "white, kind of skinny guy" with "brownish looking hair" and "no beard." He wore a "magnificent white robe with bell-bottomed sleeves" and "didn't even have no sandals." The magnificence of the robe was such that she felt "glad he shared it with her." He had never "showed her a white robe before." Jesus "held out his arms to his side." Neither of them spoke.

Jesus' position was unusual and partly the source of her fear. He was "in the wall," not in front of it. He was there where the wall "dead ends." It was "not a picture of him." "He was human and had a body, he wasn't a spirit." And yet he was "against the wall," somewhat analogous to the way a film might be projected on a surface, thus giving the illusion of depth behind. Teresa got "scared because he was standing in the middle of the air on the wall." The wall was apparent except for the space occupied by Jesus and "the black that was all around him." She initially saw Jesus--"he was white"--and then "looked at the black background after I seen him." "This scared her."

Teresa's response upon seeing Jesus was intense. Along with the fear associated with noticing the black mandorla was the "thought" that "he would lay me down and kill me." She "didn't know why he would do that," but "just to see Jesus is a fear." She explained further her fear, saying: "I told myself he would take care of me because this is his world. All this down here belongs to him. That's why I fear him, because he know he made everything. I ain't gonna do nothing to hurt anybody, it's all in God's hand, I know that."

After falling from the bunk, Teresa got up and "ate five pieces of bread and went back to bed, thinking, 'bless me, Jesus,'" and telling herself, "you scared me because I fear you because I love you."

Teresa's second most powerful experience occurred during a psychiatric hospitalization, once again upon awakening. She "set up and looked straight forward" toward the wall opposite the foot of the bed. There she saw "Jesus Christ burning in the fire" like "Hadrash, Mashirash, and Bendigo." The fire was "solid, burning red." He was "standing" and "looked the same as with the white robe." After all, "he never changes" and in both visions "they were the same person." She "felt pretty good when she woke up" and "didn't be scared--it was good to see him, just to know he's alive." "This time he wasn't on the wall; this time he was in front of the wall." As before, neither Jesus nor Teresa spoke. A nurse then entered the room and asked her to come out. Teresa asked if she saw the vision, to which the nurse replied that it was nothing to be afraid of and to come along.

To my question of what she had thought of these experiences since their happening, Teresa answered: "I never even given it a second thought. No way! Once I see something I just don't go back to it, because I know ways have ways of taking care of themselves. God take care of everybody. There's nothing on this that God does not belong to Him because He is the creator. He's the master. I'm frightened of God. Anybody that can take my life I would be scared of." And she has her reasons for knowing this to be so. "He took her life once and He brought her back." She "drank some poison on purpose, trying to give a self-sacrifice." She "just wanted to die." Her "stomach was pumped and she was sick 7 days" before recovering.

Steven

History

Steven is a handsome, 29-year-old Caucasian. There have been five hospitalizations since his first in 1977. The inital presentations have been dramatic and well detailed in admitting notes and psychiatric records. The social history is minimal. He is divorced and has a daughter. He has been jailed for burglary.

Steven was brought to the hospital by the police for his first admission of 1978. "He had threatened a woman with a 2 foot, painted wooden stake, saying he was John the Baptist and he walked the earth in search of blood." At a later admission in 1978, he seemed catatonic. Initially, this was thought to be a "toxic phenothiazine reaction," but the absence of "cogwheel rigidity," the lack of improvement after 2 weeks without medicine, and the failure of intravenous Diphenhydramine to alter his condition cast doubt on this supposition. The question was raised of whether a "post-psychotic depressive syndrome" was present. The first admission of 1980 followed his "jumping off a bridge on the freeway with the idea of killing himself" and sustaining "bilateral fractures of his feet," and a second when he became disturbed after "seeing ferris wheels in the sky" and "hearing auditory hallucinations from buses and trees telling him to kill himself." There were medical hospitalizations in 1981 for "upper G.I. bleeding" and "duodenal ulcer." And the most recent admission, during which our conversation took place, came about after the police found Steven "making bonfires along the highway and claiming he was an apostle." Diagnoses have typically been paranoid schizophrenia. I would concur, and supplement the diagnostic history with an episode of catatonic schizophrenia in 1978.

With rosy cheeks and bright blue eyes, Steven's face was the very image of a boyish cherub. He was tan and clean shaven with neatly combed blond hair and an endearing smile. His appearance contrasted radically with his sarcastic, sotto tone of voice and the utterly emotionless manner in which he recounted in detail such incidents as his molestation of a "14- or 15-month baby girl."

Steven's most powerful experience of God contrasts with those of the other patients because of its being a delusionally based interpretation of certain phenomena which, in themselves, would seem not to involve the seeing or hearing of an object thought to be God at the moment. The narrative describes this most powerful experience of God, followed by a description of the second most powerful, and concludes with yet another experience of God which contrasts with the preceding two. The theme of punishment binds together all three.

Narrative

At several stops along the way to San Francisco, "people were calling Steven 'God'--behind his back, to his face, to his left and right. They would say 'Here comes God' when he walked into a restaurant." He "didn't like the fact these people were calling him 'God,' them making fun of him and smirking, laughing at him, doing all manner of evil against him." He stopped further along the road. "He had been spitting in his hands and rubbing it on his face, and he'd eaten some ice plant, little green pieces of plant. He had put dirt in his mouth and drank from dirty water. He also swallowed a couple of rocks." He was unable to provide an explanation for why he might do this, but once he "puked on the ice plants," he knew. He had been "having all sorts of weird delusions about who's good and bad," and he worried "that people would gain his knowledge of God." Eating the ice plant "would counteract them knowing," he thought. But this was his first error and one of the reasons for God to punish him, since "by throwing up on the ice plant, that's how they got my knowledge of God--when I fertilized the earth with my puke." And besides, "everyone is entitled to their own beliefs." He had no real way "of counteracting the ocean of people having knowledge of God," and God was to "punish him for thinking he could counteract something that had already taken place." Steven continued to San Francisco.

Arriving in downtown San Francisco, Steven "thought it was Judgment Day" and made the error of "trying to make Bible history come true before it was actually suppose to happen." He determined it was Judgment Day by "the way everyone was walking and acting; it was night-time, there were no stars, complete blackness over the city, and people were walking and talking and acting crazy--it was just scary." His precipitous attempt to "make Bible history" came about during a call to his father asking for help. "He thought he was calling up China and rigging an atomic bomb or nuclear holocaust by means of using the telephone." His situation only worsened from this point. He experienced "pain beyond that any human has ever felt" when his "left testicle felt like it was in a clamp, like something on the inside of him was just closing in and squeezing it tighter," and there began a "deformation in his hands and arms" from the elbow down to the "tips of his fingers." He "bit his arm to succomb the pain." He "layed down and began crying and screaming, 'Why, God?! Why, God?!'" He was "led outside." He entered another public building, thinking to "take his vitamins and lotions and lay down." He approached a group of blacks who "proceeded to beat the hell out of him, hitting him on the head with their fists." Finally "the police came" and removed him.

To my question of what accounted for this being an experience of God, Steven replied with more animation and irritation than usual, as if I could really be so dull: "It was all in my body, in my own body." The entire episode "shows you the force of the Almighty, how if you do something wrong, you'll eat something or drink something or take something into your system that will rebel against you later on." After all, much of "learning about God" is a matter of "health foods, of everything you take into your system, everything you eat, take in, ingest."

Steven's second most powerful experience of God resulted from "cursing His Name" and "denying his faith." As a consequence, he was "punished." The punishment consisted of his "being handcuffed with his hands behind his back and his feet strapped" while carried to a hospital in an ambulance. He "cried for release," saying "he had not broken any laws." If only he "had kept his faith and confessed God in front of other people, instead of bull-shitting away, thinking about Mother Goose, fairy tales and Disneyland," this would not have happened.

The final experience of God occurred prior to the two already described. Steven "was asleep and woke up and saw a ball of light--a brilliance, a flash of light in the room." Instantly he "thought it was God." He "felt remorseful," "scared," and "afraid of God's wrath." He knew "God was angry" and that he had "better go tell others." He dressed, and once outside, saw "an Hawaiian or Oriental guy dressed all in white" who he "thought was an angel of God." This convinced him that "he was doing the right thing." He walked to a coffee shop and announced, "God is angry," then went to the streets to announce the same. He began "crying and begging God not to destroy the earth." "Give him time and he would change the people." Afterward he "felt better." And why had all of this come about? "Maybe because he had masturbated." And had he masturbated? Steven did not remember doing so.

Sebastian

History

Sebastian is a 35-year-old, bilingual Mexican American. A thorough psychiatric history is available from the first admission in 1974 to the present. Some social history antedating these years is also available, its having been taken in 1974.

Sebastian is the seventh of 14 children. Two additional siblings died during childhood. The parents moved from Mexico to Texas, where they lived until 1959, then moving to California. Both are in their late 60s. They felt Sebastian's behavior was "normal" until his first "psychotic break" in 1969. He is remembered by the family as always having been "shy and isolated, less social and aggressive than other members." He has always lived at home. He quit school after completing the eighth grade. I would estimate his level of intelligence to be within the borderline range.

The episode of 1969 "followed his having several teeth pulled and losing a great deal of blood." It is unclear just how soon afterwards he became disturbed or just what comprised this episode. The parents mentioned also that Sebastian was involved in a "serious car wreck" and "witnessed a gory accident in which a worker lost his hand in a machine" during the interim between the episode of 1969 and the 1974 admission. The family described Sebastian's "symptoms as appearing and disappearing in a sporadic fashion" during this period, though it is unclear whether these disturbing incidents correlate with the symptomatology.

The incident precipitating the 1974 admission was recalled in some detail. It involved a "work incident in which a fellow worker either accidentally or on purpose fell on Sebastian and knocked out his breath." He then "went wild" and needed to be "physically restrained." Subsequently he "withdrew from family and friends, lost his appetite and slept excessively." He "washed his hands excessively, refused to use his right hand and claimed this was due to paralysis." He "played with his food and ate only the center portion of whatever was served him." He "threatened his siblings." Occasionally he would "become fearful and shake all over."

The admitting diagnosis at the 1974 admission was catatonic schizophrenia. The neurological examination mentioned "somewhat bizarre stance and gait" with

> classical waxy flexibility. The extremities can be placed in bizarre positions with one arm behind his back, one arm in the air, and one foot elevated in the sitting position. He will hold these positions indefinitely, but will place the limbs in a more or less normal position when asked to do so.

Auditory hallucinations, a fear of others hurting him, and disorientation for date were noted also. He had been "threatening his siblings" and upon admission "repeated continuously 'queen, ace, jack, seven.'"

There are five admissions for 1980, each with a schizophrenic diagnosis. He presented similarly for all of them, although the catatonic symptomatology was less evident, or altogether absent, since none of the diagnoses involve catatonia.

The current admission was for December 1981, and once again the catatonic symptomatology was apparent. The treating psychiatrist questioned whether the admission was precipitated by a reduction in his medicine (Fluphenazine with the anti-Parkinson agent Trihexyphenidyl), but he remained essentially the same throughout his 3-week hospitalization with heavy dosages of major tranquilizer. He "drooled continuously," was "unresponsive," and "showed some waxing and waning of flexibility." An injection of the antihistaminic anticholinergic agent Diphenhydramine did not resolve the rigidity, and consequently, the conclusion that his "catatonia" was actually a matter of extra-pyramidal side-effects from the major tranquilizer was not fully substantiated.

Conversation was conducted in a small office with Sebastian seated stiffly, drooling, smelling of perspiration and the vaguely rancid, tallow-like odor common for very old or very sick people who have been bedridden for a long period. His voice was marked with a quiver, the volume always very low. Occasionally he would tremble. His rigidity and dexterity were such that he was unable to wipe away the mucoid saliva from his mouth and face. His rapidly answering "yea" to each statement, and the occasional instances when an echolalic response seemed apparent, prompted the question of how well he understood our conversation. He understood quite well. He corrected himself when he inadvertently changed the place of the experience of God from the hospital to his home. And when he gave inconsistent answers to the same question asked several times, he would eventually correct the ambiguities. A prominent feature of his remembrance of the experience of God involved his sense of time. God spoke only once and did so at an identifiable moment during his hospitalization 16 months prior to conversation, and yet he was uncertain whether God's speaking took place over the course of "1 week," a "day-and-a-half," or "30 minutes." The experience itself is the least complex of the series.

Narrative

Upon his admission in August 1980, Sebastian spoke with the doctor, who asked "What was wrong with him," to which he replied, "Maybe I have a disease." This was in reference to Sebastian's fear that he had contacted a venereal disease from a prostitute. Whether he had actually been with a prostitute is open to question, although Sebastian felt and continues to feel that this is the cause of his problems. The doctor reassured him, "Maybe, no, you don't have a disease." At this point God spoke directly to Sebastian, saying, "Don't be that way." He was certain this was God; the voice sounded different than others he was then hearing or had heard in the past. In contrast to these other voices, God's was "loud," "weird," "strange," and "friendly." Also setting it apart from other voices was Sebastian's emotional reaction. "It made me cry," while none of the other voices had done so. The sequence of his emotional reactions was "sadness" and "crying," followed by his feeling "excited," "frightened," and "happy." The words "excited" and "frightened" seem equivalent to a certain autonomic reaction which Sebastian described as his "beginning to shiver" and feeling "excited inside himself." It is unclear whether he was motorically retarded, if not catatonic, at the time of the experience. It would seem he was. Sebastian's understanding of God's meaning was plain: He meant that Sebastian should not be "mean" to his mother. Conversation revealed this conclusion to be erroneous. It so happened the doctor told Sebastian, "Don't be mean to your mom," shortly after he heard God speak. Consequently, Sebastian concluded that God meant for him not to be "mean." When the sequence of events was clarified, Sebastian acknowledged that he did not know what God meant despite having originally thought that He meant for him not to get "mad" when his mother "says things she doesn't suppose to say to me."

APPENDIX C

TRANSCRIPTION OF CONVERSATION WITH JOHN

D: Let me explain a little bit about the kind of thing I'm really interested in. It's one thing to have an experience of God and it's something else altogether to think about it, or talk about it, or try to figure it out. It's the experience itself I'm interested in.

J: I was afraid when I heard Him talking through the thunder.

D: You were afraid when you heard Him talking through the thunder?

J: Yea. The last thunderstorm that hit Salinas. That was the one when I heard Him.

D: The last thunder storm that hit Salinas you heard Him?

J: Yes, he said, "John, OD." And I said, "What!?"

D: He said, "John, OD." You mean like overdose? I can imagine you were surprised, huh? "John, OD?"

J: Yea, it meant He was an OD creature, an overdose creature.

D: Who?

J: God. That was the way I felt about it; that He meant He was an overdose creature.

D: But all He said was, "John, OD?"

J: Yea. . . [inaudible]

D: Well, how did that have to do with the thunder? You said there was a thunderstorm in Salinas?

J: Ya. I heard His voice crackle in the thunder.

D: You heard the thunder?

J: But it sounded like God's voice, not thunder.

D: O.K., I understand. When you heard that, how did you know that that was like His voice?

J: 'Cause it was loud. I've only heard two voices that loud. His and Satan.

D: I got it. So it was loud enough that. . . Was that the only thing that let you know it was Him?

J: Well, I was doing something sinful at the time.

D: What was that?

J: Waking up from a Soviet Union dream.

D: That was sinful?

J: It was about witch . . . and witch. . . . It was about witch chanting. Going: "Aaaaah." Witch tone and witch chant. That was when I heard the thunder crackle and God said, "John, OD." I got scared.

D: Let me make sure I got it. Now, incidentally, as we talk about these things I need to ask you lots of questions so I'll understand. You know what I mean? Just try to be patient with me if I ask lots of questions. That's only so I can understand better.

J: O.K.

D: You were having a dream in which people were chanting.

J: Ya. The whole country of the Soviet Union.

D: The Soviet Union was chanting a witch chant that went "aaaaah." And then did you wake up?

J: Then I woke up and I heard thunder and God talked to me.

D: What was sinful about your dream?

J: We were practicing witchcraft. My race was.

D: Oh, I see.

J: [inaudible] My race

D: Your what?

J: My race. It was Russian. I'm a quarter Russian.

D: You're a what Russian?

J: Quarter.

D: Quarter? I don't know what that word means.

J: One fourth.

D: Oh, quarter. You're a quarter Russian.

J: And that's why I have so much contact with Satan.

D: O.K., let's go back to when you heard God first. We'll come to

Satan later. You were having a dream, you woke up. Was it night then?

J: Ya, I remember I slept all day, through a whole day.

D: So you woke up. Do you remember about what time it was or did you even check it out?

J: Ya, it was already getting dark.

D: Your room was dark?

J: Everything was dark.

D: And there was a storm going on?

J: Ya.

D: Thunderstorm?

J: To the best of my recollection.

D: And then tell me exactly what happened. You heard--

J: After the witch chant, God started talking to me, 'cause He knew I was going astray from this country's beliefs. You see, this country believes in God, but Russia doesn't.

D: They believe in--

J: Satan.

D: I see. So God was trying to straighten you out, you thought?

J: Ya.

D: Tell me more about how you knew it was His voice when you heard the thunderstorm.

J: 'Cause nobody talks that loud.

D: The loudness.

J: Yea, the strength in His voice. Said, "OD," like a giant, like a giant was screaming out loud.

D: Tell me, was His voice in the thunder or did you hear the thunder and then hear His voice?

J: No, I heard it in the thunder.

D: Was His voice the same as the thunder?

J: Yes, exactly the same as the thunder. He was speaking through the thunder.

D: Speaking through the thunder? So His voice was the thunder but the thunder made words, or did God thunder and then speak? You know, if you can remember back specifically.

J: It was at the same time--the thunder that I heard His voice.

D: O.K. I think I got it. It was loud. Was it a man's or woman's voice?

J: A man's.

D: And what was it He said again?

J: "John, OD."

D: And what did you think that meant again?

J: That He was going to OD me. That He was an OD creature.

D: What is an OD creature?

J: Overdose giant . . . overdose of giant-ness.

D: Of giant-ness? What does that mean?

J: That's how big He is.

D: Oh, He's a giant. Well, I don't understand how He--when He said--let me get it straight. You figure when He said, "John, OD," that meant several things--one, that you should straighten up and not get with the Soviet Union. You also think that it meant He was saying He was an OD creature. An OD creature is someone--

J: Who can OD people, overdose people.

D: Oh. And how did it figure that He was big? What was--

J: The loudness in the thunder. That's what made me think it was big.

D: O.K. I understand now. Thank you. How can He--what did you mean that He's an OD creature, that He could OD other people? What's that like?

J: He's got the power of life and death .

D: Oh.

J: He was going to kill me for going to Satan.

D: He was threatening you?

J: Yea. For going to Satan.

D: Now tell me what are your dealings with Satan?

J: I'm cannibalistic sometimes. My moods will get cannibalistic.

D: What do you mean?

J: My telepathic powers are Satanistic.

D: I don't know what you mean by "cannibalistic."

J: I can drink blood from people's bodies telepathically when they're attacking me. When they're planning an attack, I start drinking their blood out of their body, absorbing it through the air.

D: You take it in through the air. How does it get in your body?

J: Through the pores of my skin, through my mind.

D: Through the pores of your skin.

J: And my mind.

D: And your mind. Tell me, this experience you've just told me, is that the most powerful experience of God you've ever had?

J: That's the best.

D: The best? What made it the best one?

J: The science fiction part of the thunder talking.

D: Oh, you like that, huh?

J: Yea [inaudible].

D: That makes me think, there's a part of this whole experience that we really haven't talked about, and it's important--

J: I remember another experience that I had with God, too.

D: Let's finish this one before we move on, O.K.? Before we go on to the other experience of God, which I do want to come to, there's another question I want to ask about this one. The one in the thunder. And that's how you felt?

J: I felt afraid.

D: At which part? All the time, or at a certain time, or--

J: The instant after He said "OD."

D: You felt afraid?

J: Yea. But I got my strength back later on. After He stopped talking to me. He said those two--that was the first time He ever talked to me.

D: That was the first time?

J: Yea.

D: Now was this other experience we're going to talk about after that one?

J: Yea. It was after.

D: When did this happen, this first one with the thunder?

J: About 3 years ago.

D: About three?

J: If you can remember our last thunderstorm in Salinas, you'll have the date.

D: It rained just a few weeks ago, didn't it?

J: I know, but that wasn't the thunder.

D: Oh, that wasn't the one?

J: I'm talking about thunder and lightning.

D: Oh, a big storm.

J: Yea.

D: O.K. . . . Look, you said you were afraid. Were you afraid when you heard the voice or immediately afterwards?

J: Immediately afterwards.

D: Did you have any feeling during the moment you heard it?

J: I felt like I was living in a science fiction movie.

D: What was that feeling?

J: Like I took part in some kind of miracle.

D: What feeling was that? It was like you were in a miracle. What was the feeling?

J: I felt that a miracle happened .

D: What was the miracle?

J: The miracle was that God showed me there was such a creature.

D: Oh. That He showed you what?

J: That He existed.

D: Oh, that was a miracle?

J: So I decided to try to kill Him.

D: We'll come to that. I'm still interested in your feelings. Right after you heard, you were afraid. Right? When you heard, it was like you were in a miracle? And then the miracle part of it was because it was so unusual that God would talk to you, the first time like that.

J: I didn't believe in Him. I didn't believe there was such a creature.

D: I see. But then when you heard Him, what?

J: Then I was shocked.

D: Shocked. I'm still--Can you say more how you felt right when you heard Him? Afterwards you were afraid, when you heard Him it was like it was a miracle. What was that feeling then?

J: It's hard to explain an emotion. It was an emotion as if--like I took part in a science fiction movie except the science fiction movie turned real. It was a reality that shocked me . . . of there being such a creature . . . the reality of God.

D: I follow. Are there any words for that feeling?

J: Well, I felt as if I was taking part in a science fiction story. That was a form of science fiction story.

D: I'm trying to imagine what that was like. When you really--you didn't believe in God. Then you woke up and you heard the voice of the thunder, and that was something so unusual that you felt a special way right at first. I'm wondering what that way was. Something that you didn't believe, it came true. You heard how big it was, right?

J: Yea.

D: Powerful.

J: Strong.

D: Can take life or death.

J: Yea.

D: I wonder what that feeling was? To discover that. Right--right when it happend. Can you think back? I know it's hard, but can you think back?

J: I don't remember.

D: It's hard.

J: It's hard to describe some emotions.

D: It is. I know it is.

J: There is only one way you can find out about other people's emotions and that's to experience it yourself.

D: It's tough. That's why I've got to ask so many questions, is to try to follow as best I can. Did you hear the voice right after you woke up or had you been awake for a minute or two?

J: I'd been awake for about 15 minutes to a half an hour.

D: Oh. Was the storm going on?

J: Yea.

D: How did you feel in that 15 minutes after you woke up and before you heard the voice?

J: I was proud of my race, the Soviet Union.

D: Oh, you were pleased with the dream?

J: I was pleased with the dream.

D: What were you doing in that dream incidentally when the others were chanting the witch chant. Were you in the dream?

J: I was hiding--I was running from something. From an execution squad or something like that. And I hid in this building and then I heard the chant go "aaah." It searched me out and found me. Then I woke up feeling proud.

D: Proud of what?

J: My religion.

D: Your religion is what?

J: Satan.

D: Oh, the chant was a witch chant of people who were on Satan's side. Is that right?

J: Yea. The whole country of Russia.

D: I see. So you felt that like you were a part of that group that was chanting?

J: Yea.

D: But they searched you out, you said. The chant did.

J: I don't remember why I ran. I just know I was scared.

D: You were scared there in the dream?

J: Yea. 'Cause it was my first Russian dream.

D: Oh.

J: I've had dreams I was in Hell too. The Soviet Union gave me dreams like that. See, I don't sleep on my own, people put me to sleep.

D: Let's get back to that 15 minutes after you woke up before you heard God. Were you just laying in your bed there? Just sort of laying back?

J: Yea. Thinking about my dream.

D: Thinking about your dream. Were you hearing any voices or seeing anything strange or were you just sitting there thinking?

J: Just thinking.

D: No voices, nothing like that? And then you heard the--

J: The thunder.

D: You heard the thunder, it was very loud.

J: The emotion was, was kind of a shock--shocked me through the reality of God. It shocked me into belief. It gave me a belief feeling, a belief emotion.

D: Oh. Was that good, bad, neutral? How was that, that--here's the way I understand it, tell me if I've got it. You've had your dream, and in the dream you've been frightened because you were being chased. You hide and then you're proud to hear the witch chant of the Soviets. You wake up, you're laying quietly in your bed thinking of your dream, meanwhile there's a big storm going on, lightning, electricity and all, lightning and thunder outside, and then after about 15 minutes you hear a crash of thunder and at the very same time hear God's voice.

J: And then I felt reality--

D: And that voice was, did you say one of--the loudest, or one of the loudest that you've ever heard.

J: Almost as loud as the Soviet Union chant. They were both that loud.

D: How did it compare in loudness to other voices you hear?

J: I never heard thunder talk before.

D: So then you heard that and it was like a miracle. It was like science fiction that came true.

J: Yea.

D: And then you felt afraid afterwards.

J: I felt a feeling of believing, like I found something new to believe in.

D: That was before the afraid part?

J: Yea. That was the impact, the shocking impact.

D: I got it. Did that change your life?

J: I still believe in Satan.

D: But did it change your life?

J: Yea. It made me want to go to war with God. Sometimes I feel I'm the anti-Christ.

D: Before we get to that let's really look as close as we can at that experience. After the afraid part, what happened? What happened then? You got to the afraid part after the voice. Then anything?

J: I sent out vibrations throughout eternity for God and every living creature to feel suicidal.

D: You sent out vibrations to every creature about what?

J: Every creature throughout eternity. I sent out vibrations to feel suicidal.

D: That felt what?

J: Suicidal.

D: I don't understand. What do you mean when you sent out vibrations that--

J: I controlled other people's emotions and minds.

D: And what kind of control were you making then?

J: Like God's, I had the power to feel eternity. See, when I look around the room or anything, or up to the sky or on the ground, I always see an OD-ness. I see eternity. I can see forever.

D: So after the afraid part you sent out vibrations of great control, the control--the power of God.

J: I almost won too.

D: What was the purpose of sending out control then?

J: To kill God.

D: O.K. Now we come to that. Why did that experience make you want to kill God?

J: Because He was against Russia. It's kind of a prejudiced racialist belief.

D: What, your position?

J: Yea, my position--

D: Did you say were--you knew something about the anti-Christ?

J: When I sent out that vibration, God felt suicidal and every creature on earth started feeling suicidal, and I saw God slipping into unconsciousness. And they died. God showed me what would happen if He died: everything else would die too.

D: How did you determine--did you figure that out?

J: Because I felt it--when God turned suicidal He started dying. And I felt my body starting to die along with them so I had to resurrect them again.

D: Wait a minute. I'm not sure I understand that part. O.K., so you had the afraid part, then you sent out vibrations that made every creature suicidal. Right? This is all within a few minutes after hearing God, or is this the next day or the next week or when is this?

J: I believe it was the next feeling.

D: Next what?

J: Next emotion I experienced. See, God's for the United States, He's not for Russia.

D: After you sent out the vibrations, tell me again what happened?

J: God started showing me what would happen if He died.

D: And how did He show you that?

J: He started dying.

D: How did you know He was starting to die then?

J: 'Cause I felt everything surrounding me was starting to die.

D: What was that like--the feeling that everything around you was starting to die?

J: The emotion of dying.

D: Can you tell me what that was like there when you were there in your room at night? You know, give me an idea of what that was like to be there and then believe that everything was dying . . . including your own body?

J: It was a physical feeling and emotional.

D: Can you say more about that?

J: Everything started to zap out of existence.

D: What was it like on your body? You say it was a physical feeling. What was your body like? What was it doing?

J: I felt my spirit start not to exist.

D: How did you know that's what was happening?

J: 'Cause I seen it. I experienced it. I have experienced the feeling of dying.

D: What kind of feeling was that? A good one, a bad one? Horrible, happy?

J: Kind of scary.

D: Scary . . . the feeling of dying, of your spirit leaving and dying. Right?

J: Yea.

D: I'm really struggling to try to understand what that was like. Is there any way you can help me?

J: When you go, you'll see. It's like what you imagine death to be like. Everybody imagines it the same way. The spirit leaving the body.

D: You said there was another experience you had of God, but not as powerful as this one?

J: I don't remember now what I was talking about.

D: It was the one you said was more recent. This one was about 3 years ago, is that right--that first one?

J: Yea.

D: And you said you've had one more recently since then?

J: I can't remember what I was talking about.

D: Oh, you don't?

J: I'm trying to remember.

D: Well, give yourself a minute and it will probably come to you.

J: I know it would help if I talk about my religion a little more.

D: If you want to.

J: O.K. I can also turn people into living corpses and eat their flesh telepathically. But my mom telepathically turned my power off so I can't do it no more.

D: Your mom?

J: She was fighting me mentally because I was trying to destroy all of mankind because I believed I was the anti-Christ.

D: How did you determine that you might be the anti-Christ?

J: Because I got the power to control the weather telekinetically.

D: To control what?

J: The weather.

D: The weather telekinetically?

J: Yea. That was my rain that washed away that mountain that killed all those people.

D: Oh.

J: I made it overnight. It took a whole night. Actually it took about 3 days to make that rain, then I kept coming back and coming back worse and worse.

D: How did you send out that power?

J: By yanking out my hair and saying the chant.

D: Oh.

J: And then I look at the ground and I could see colors coming up out of the ground and going into my eyes. Then I look up in the sky, straight up, then I see clouds leaving my eyes and going into the air.

D: I see. That means the power is going out into making rain or whatever.

J: Yea. The reason I turned it off was because people got killed. So I spent the day pulling sunshine out of the ground and putting sunshine into the air. That's why it stopped raining. I don't think I want to mess with the forces of nature any more after those people got killed.

D: It can be dangerous. . . You said you thought you might--Do you think maybe you're the anti-Christ, or do you think you are the anti-Christ? Just what is all that about?

J: Well, after I sent those vibes out of feeling suicidal, I felt--

D: This was back when you heard God?

J: Yea.

D: O.K., go ahead.

J: I heard, I asked telepathically alien beings and creatures how many got killed with my suicidal vibrations?

D: Yea.

J: And they said that--they can see forever--and there's a whole forever-ness of dead things that belong to me. I control them to kill other people and that's what makes me think that I'm anti-Christ 'cause I can kill telepathically.

D: I got it. Now, when you sent that question out to the alien beings, when you did that, how did they answer back?

J: By showing me my dead bodies.

D: How did they show you?

J: They let me get into the minds of them and watch how they feel when they're dead.

D: Is that the same thing or different than the feeling that you were dying? Do you understand what I'm talking about? See, if you sent your message out--what did you send, a thought out, or did you speak out loud? Did you send a thought out?

J: Yea.

D: I don't want to put words in your mouth, so if that's not what happened correct me.

J: I did--I sent not just thoughts but emotions.

D: Sent out thoughts, sent out emotions. And then tell me again what happened? When you sent the thoughts out?

J: I just--

D: Not the suicidal power, but when you sent the question out to the alien beings? Am I with you here? Then what happened?

J: The boy I call Frog Face, he answered and said that I got enough power to destroy earth now.

D: Was that a voice that you heard or was that a thought that entered your mind?

J: It was a voice. It was a spirit that entered my mind.

D: Was it a spirit that came as a thought or a spirit that came as a voice?

J: Came as a voice.

D: O.K.

J: Came as a being.

D: A what?

J: A being.

D: A being?

J: An alien being. I was talking to--

D: Who is Frog Face?

J: I saw him. I saw his face and his hands. They had suction cups and they were like frog's feet. And I saw them. I saw his body talking to me from a distance.

D: Was this something you saw in your mind or something you saw out in space in front of you?

J: I saw it in my mind.

D: You saw Frog Face. And he said you have the power to--

J: He said that one dead being of their kind can get into man's minds, can destroy earth.

D: Very powerful. As I understand, you asked the question--What was the question you asked the alien being?

J: How many dead died?

D: How many dead. Then you saw Frog Face. You heard Frog Face's voice saying that he--that he and others?

J: And others.

D: And others have the power to destroy everything.

J: No. He said that I earned the power--

D: You what?

J: That I earned the power by killing.

D: You had already earned the power?

J: Because it was my kill?

D: Which kill? When you sent out the suicidal thought?

J: Yea. That could kill the whole of eternity.

D: I got it. You showed that you had the power, is that right?

J: He showed me I had the power. Frog Face did.

D: Oh, he showed you--

J: There were other aliens, too.

D: He showed you because he let you know what he knew. And he knew that many people had died. Have I got it?

J: Yea. Not just people, aliens as well.

D: Aliens. O.K. John, if I'm not right on something, correct me, O.K.?

J: O.K. I know you want the truth.

D: Now, how did he let you know that other beings had died?

J: He let me see the dead bodies.

D: And how did he let you see them? Through pictures in your mind?

J: He let me feel the emotion of the dead, of the dead bodies with no spirit at all.

D: I got it. And that's the feeling you described back before--

J: That's my anti-Christ power to kill--is making men get into the minds of the dead. And then they feel somewhat like when God felt suicidal. It kills them, the same when God tried to kill me dead. By showing me the emotion of the dead.

D: That's what you felt, you said. The physical feeling, you said. And it was a feeling of dying and the spirit leaving. Can you tell me any more about what that was like? You said that I would know when my time came. But I'm wondering, beforehand can you tell me a little more what that's like?

J: Well, I have my own beliefs about after life. I believe that--

D: No, I mean your experience. When Frog Face let you know that others were dying, and he let you know that by letting you feel dead. Can you say, that feeling of death for you, what it was like?

J: And then I pulled out of their minds. I stopped using them to destroy life. See, my goal is to destroy everything in sight telepathically. I won't turn real murderer 'cause that's why I'm in here. 'Cause I don't want to turn real.

D: You don't want to use your hands to kill. You want to use telepathic powers.

J: Yea.

D: I wish that there was some way--maybe you can try--I wish there was some way for me to really understand what that feeling of your dying was. Because if I understand right, that's the physical feeing that lets you know that other creatures were dying. And that God was dying too. Am I right there? That's how you knew, isn't it?

J: Yea.

D: When Frog Face showed you that other creatures were dying, it was--he showed you by letting you experience death, is that right?

J: He let me experience the death of the ones that already died.

D: What was that like, that experience?

J: As if they're nothing but--as if human life is nothing but toys.

D: Toys. Go ahead.

J: And then some other aliens started talking and telling me about how many I killed.

D: What others?

J: Well, after Frog Face I talked to the dark sect.

D: The who?

J: The dark sect. That's what they call themselves.

D: What's the name?

J: Dark sect. It's a universe of darkness.

D: Darkness.

J: And there are dark creatures that live there.

D: Are these voices you heard?

J: Yea.

D: Now we're talking about after hearing God's voice in the thunder, right?

J: Yea. And Frog Face, they came after Frog Face. And they showed me the experience of death too, of the dead. And then I talked to the lightning sector with white light creatures. Then I talked to a hole in the universe. The hole in the universe--the reason there is a hole is 'cause this creature lives there and its emotions are so dark that he left a hole in the universe. Its emotions are that dark.

D: So these are names you've given these creatures? Right? You called one Frog Face because he had these funny things on his hands, was it?

J: Yea, his hands looked like frog feet.

D: And you called the other one the hole in the universe because he's--

J: A dark creature too. Except he's a whole universe himself.

D: You personally gave them these names?

J: No, they kind of gave me names themselves. To describe best they can what their race was like.

D: And then you called them by--you listened to what they said, and were all of them voices incidentally?

J: They are mental images.

D: And voices?

J: That's the way I hear voices. I hear mental images.

D: With Frog Face, you saw in your mind an image, and also heard him?

J: Yea.

D: The others, you also heard? Did you see an image in your mind of these other creatures too? Or just had the voice?

J: I kind of seen an image.

D: And voice?

J: And voice. And they said that I killed forever a hole, a hole in the universe forever. And the universes--I believe in more than one universe.

D: Anything significant happen after all of this, to this point now? Where you realized your powers, where you died. Or did things sort of taper off and come to an end then?

J: Well, then I started having experiences about Jesus Christ.

D: When?

J: About a year ago.

D: So, we've finished then on this one most powerful experience of God.

J: Yea.

D: Do you feel that I've asked about the important parts?

J: Yea.

D: Is there something you feel I've missed and should question about?

J: No. I described it the best I could. It was an experience all right.

D: So we covered that?

J: Yea. It was really an experience.

D: Are you making any of this up or reporting what happened?

J: I'm reporting exactly as it happened.

D: Because I--

J: The way I saw it--in my reality. I'm describing my reality.

D: That's fine. Then we've covered that. That was the most powerful one, you said?

J: Yea.

D: Now, we can move on then, if we want to move on, to something else. Just a moment ago you mentioned Jesus Christ and then a few minutes back you had forgotten what the other experience of God was. Did that one come back to you?

J: No.

D: I'm wondering if we should explore another one or not. It's the very powerful ones that I'm interested in. The one's that--

J: That was the best experience I had about God.

D: Is there another?

J: I've got beliefs about God. How I see how He can take existence and everything that you might want to talk about.

D: Can you tell me very briefly?

J: Yea. I believe that in the beginning there was a vacuum of nothingness, and it was compressed nothing that created something like coal turned into a diamond. That compressed-ness of nothingness turned into God. That's my belief.

D: Oh. . . There was something I wanted to ask. Let me see if I can remember. . . Oh, I remember what it was. Have there been other religious experiences of yours that seem related to or similar to this God experience we talked about? In other words, has there been another religious experience that would help me to understand this most powerful one?

J: I remember whenever we talked about the past I was talking about, about the new experience of God. I was talking about it--when I was talking about it, I was talking it, I was talking about us future talking about it, the suicidal God.

D: Go ahead, if you like. I'm not sure I quite caught on yet, but go ahead.

J: The suicidal God was the part that I was trying to tell you about, the other experience.

D: Oh. The suicidal God was part of this one we've already talked about, isn't it?

J: Yea, that's the one I was talking about futuristically.

D: Oh. Let me make sure I get what you mean. The suicidal God, that's the part where you were given the feelings of dying and then you knew that all other creatures including God were dying.

J: Some are dead.

D: Yea. Am I right, that that's the suicidal God part?

J: Yea.

D: The suicidal God experience is part of hearing God's voice in the thunder. One happened soon after another?

J: After I started believing in God, I started wanting to destroy Him.

D: Can you explain a little about that?

J: I believe Satan forgives better than God 'cause Satan allows sin.

D: Satan allows sin.

J: And God doesn't. And I think that I like Satan 'cause Satan forgives sin better than God does.

D: What makes you know that--or how do you know that?

J: 'Cause he lets people act out sin. Satan does.

D: What does God want of you? What do you think God wanted of you when you heard His voice in the thunder?

J: He wanted me to be chicken. He was threatening me.

D: Chicken and what?

J: He was threatening me.

D: Threatening you. Oh, you know something I'm not sure I'm clear about? You said when He said, "John, OD," there was something about that that made you know how big and powerful He was.

J: Yea.

D: Was it the loudness, and was it anything else that made you know that?

J: I knew that it was His lightning storm and not mine. See, my brother has power to make lightning but he never uses his power. See, Soviets got their own religion. Their religion is by skin texture. The whiteness of the skin gives them the powers.

D: Could we go back for just a second to the voice in the thunder?

J: Yea.

D: What I want to try to understand better is the connection between God's voice and thunder. Here's the way I understand it now. You correct me or add something extra if I haven't got it. O.K.?

J: O.K.

D: You had awoke, gotten up from sleep, you were still laying in bed. There was a thunderstorm and there was some very loud thunder. And at the same time you heard God's voice, "John, OD."

J: It came out as if a voice of thunder was speaking.

D: O.K. I understand that. Now, was God--this may be a tough question, it may not even make sense, you can just tell me if it makes any sense. Was God's voice in the thunder; was God's voice the very same as the thunder; or was God's voice in your mind at the same time the thunder made its noise?

J: It came out of the thunder.

D: Was it different than the thunder?

J: No, it was the same.

D: It came out of the thunder though?

J: Yea.

D: It sounded like thunder?

J: [Inaudible] When I say "John, OD," I'm making thunder at the same time. That's what it was like.

D: O.K., that helps me understand. So the voice and the thunder both were coming from God?

J: Yea, at the same time. Same incident. The same way He used to talk to Adam and Eve is the way He talked to me. That's the experience, that's the feeling I got, as if He was talking to Adam and Eve, I was thinking about that. I felt as if I lived a piece of the Bible. As if I was one of God's creatures, could perform miracles. Except later I found that that was a camouflage that Satan gives me to protect his anti-Christ.

D: What is the cover? What's the protection?

J: To make me look as if I'm God's creature. He uses that for camouflage, Satan does.

D: You're really devoted to Satan, aren't you?

J: Yes. I love Satan. I call him Honey Lamb.

D: Honey Lamb.

J: To me that means OD heterosexual.

D: OD heterosexual.

J: Yea. The reason I call him Honey Lamb is 'cause the Soviets call him that because of his horns and his face. He looks like a lamb.

D: What I'm still thinking of is God and thunder. The thunder came from God. The voice came from God. Right?

J: Yea.

D: When you heard the voice, was it coming from outside or was it loud in your mind?

J: It was coming from out--it was coming from the thunder.

D: O.K., I understand. Thanks. Was it coming with the thunder? Or was it the thunder?

J: It was the thunder.

D: Good. O.K., I think I have understood it now. I finally believe I've got it. God's voice was the thunder.

J: With and was the thunder. Both at the same time.

D: Oh.

J: See, my schizophrenic part of me is that I can see more than one thing at once.

D: What do you mean?

J: I change metamorphically. My schizophrenic power. Instead of changing personalities, I change bodies. See, my skin starts turning red, sometimes it turns purple, sometimes it turns green depending upon whatever power is working at the time. If it turns red, that means it's because I'm drinking somebody's blood. If it turns purple, that means 'cause I'm eating somebody's corpse.

D: You said--back to God and thunder for a moment, O.K.? Can we still talk about that part? God's voice was the thunder and was with the thunder.

J: Yea.

D: How was it with the thunder? You understand what I'm asking? You said it was--

J: God used His ventriloquist voice with the thunder. Threw His voice through the thunder.

D: Go ahead.

J: Like a ventriloquist.

D: I haven't got that part yet. You're gonna have to say a little more about the "with." You see, I understood when you said His voice was the thunder, but I lost you when you said "and it was also with the thunder." What's that part mean?

J: God threw His voice and used the thunder to speak with.

D: God what?

J: God used the thunder as his mouth, to talk.

D: Oh, so God could talk other ways too?

J: Yea. I never experienced them, though, but I believe He can.

D: Was this the only direct experience of God you've had?

J: I used to feel the Holy Spirit sometimes, but I never believed it was God.

D: Then that doesn't count. It's the God experience I'm interested in. Was this the only direct experience of God Himself that you've had?

J: Yes.

D: And this was how many years ago, did you say?

J: Three. About 3 years ago.

D: So, His voice was the thunder, but it was something--and came from God.

J: Yea.

D: Was the voice the same thing as God or was it--

J: It was God speaking. And that's what I firmly believe.

D: And you knew that because it was so loud, because you knew how powerful it was when He said "OD."

J: Plus I had that feeling--that shocked feeling. That belief--belief like Adam and Eve had.

D: Like a miracle came true.

J: Yea.

D: Did you feel special?

J: Yea, I felt like, I felt like, I felt like, like, like, I was an OD creature like God 'cause I could see forever and I could emotionalize forever. I got the powers of God Himself.

D: Emotionalize? You mean to send out?

J: Yea.

D: Did that experience--did you have greater power because of that experience than you had before?

J: No.

D: Oh, so you didn't get extra power because of it?

J: No. Well, I always could see forever, but, see, I came from a different dimension than normal human beings.

D: Well, here's what I mean, did you get anything extra from this experience of God that you had not had before? Or, did you lose anything?

J: No.

D: You didn't lose anything?

J: I just gained. I gained some insight.

D: What did you get extra?

J: The power to kill. I learned that if I messed with God, I could kill for eternity.

D: You didn't know that before?

J: No.

D: You didn't have that power before?

J: Until I tried. I was first.

D: What's funny?

J: I hear your voices talking to me. [Laughter]

D: You're hearing--

J: Yea, I see mental images of you thinking, and then they said, "You <u>cabron</u>."

D: You're what?

J: They say, "You <u>cabron</u>."

D: You cob-grown?

J: <u>Cabron</u>. You're cussing at me because I wanted to disturb God.

D: John, I'm not cussing at you. O.K.? I'm trying to understand. And you--

J: You said it teasing though, I heard it.

D: Don't get caught up in your voices now, because the truth is--and this should be clear to you--I'm trying to understand, and I'm taking this seriously enough to do a recording and to think about what you said. I haven't got secret things going on in my head bad about you. That may be something else you're hearing, but it's not a secret going on in my head.

J: It could be Satan playing tricks on me.

D: It could be any number of things, but I'm here trying to understand. It's clear that I'm taking this seriously, I hope, and that I haven't got bad thoughts and secrets that are getting into you.

J: I take voices as if they are real.

D: Yes, that can be dangerous, huh, sometimes? Anything more we need to say?

J: No, that covers the whole subject, everything I said.

D: I want to thank you very much for giving me all the information you have.

J: O.K.

D: O.K., let's get with it here, huh? All right. [Handshake.] Thank you very much.

J: O.K.

Philip Mellen

GERHART HAUPTMANN
Religious Syncretism and Eastern Religions

American University Studies (Germanic Languages and Literature) vol. 24
339 pages paperback $ 30.55

For public consumption Gerhart Hauptmann was Germany's greatest naturalist writer. Another, private existence is however revealed in and by the religious studies he undertook from ca. 1885 to 1945. His quest for that which underlies man's diverse perspectives of the supernatural and binds them into a whole leads him to study Christianity, eastern religions, the writings of Jacob Boehme, etc. Material from Hauptmann's notebooks, diaries, marginalia from his personal library, and a careful examination of the texts he actually read, show the effects of this preoccupation on his thinking and works, as well as explains his intense interest in German mysticism and philosophies of the East.
Contents: Christianity-Alchemy; Buddhism-Schopenhauer; Hinduism; Taoism-Confucianism; Gnosticism; Jacob Boehme; *Michael Kramer-Indipohdi; Der neue Christophorus.*

PETER LANG PUBLISHING, INC.
34 East 39th Street
USA - New York, NY 10016

Robert Hauptman

THE PATHOLOGICAL VISION: JEAN GENET, LOUIS-FERDINAND CELINE, AND TENNESSEE WILLIAMS

American University Studies (Comparative Literature) vol. 5
146 pages paperback $ 15.25

The Pathological Vision is a study of aberrancy in the works of Jean Genet, Louis-Ferdinand Céline, and Tennessee Williams. Concomitantly, it examines the *Weltanschauung* of each of these authors within the axio-ethical sphere: Genet apotheosizes evil; Céline observes it; and Williams transcends it.

Contents: Pathology – Evil – Axiology – Ethics – Comparative literature.

PETER LANG PUBLISHING, INC.
34 East 39th Street
USA – New York, NY 10016

Donald W. Hudson Jr.

ASSERTI-CARE
ASSERTION TRAINING FOR THE ELDERLY CLIENT

American University Studies (Psychology) vol. 1
169 pages paperback $ 17.35

Reports of successful treatment, utilizing assertiveness training, have been established mainly through research efforts coordinated with youthful populations. Lengthy literature reviews reveal only five attempts with the elderly population; only three interventions were empirically based and results have been inconclusive. This book discusses negative stereotypes of the aged and prevailing attitudes found within our profession which influence the psychological diagnosis and treatment of the elderly (i.e. «Why bother with them when there's no need to effect a change so late in life?»). The author reports a study which examines the effect of an assertiveness training program on assertion, self-esteem, locus of control, and health for an elderly population.

PETER LANG PUBLISHING, INC.
34 East 39th Street
USA – New York, NY 10016